9 –
2/6

All that Summer She was Mad

All that Summer She was Mad

Virginia Woolf: Female Victim of Male Medicine

Stephen Trombley

CONTINUUM · NEW YORK

1982

The Continuum Publishing Company
575 Lexington Avenue
New York, N.Y. 10022

Printed in the United States of America

Library of Congress Cataloging in Publication Data

Trombley, Stephen.
  All that summer she was mad.

  Includes index.
  "Select bibliography of works by Virginia Woolf's
doctors": p. 327
  Bibliography: p. 317
  1. Woolf, Virginia, 1882–1941—Biography—Health.
2. Novelists, English—20th century—Biography. I. Title.
PR6045.072Z886 1982   823'.912 [B]   81-19439
ISBN 0-8264-0207-0   AACR2

Contents

For Harland and Betty Taylor, with deep affection

Acknowledgements

I am indebted to the staffs of the following libraries for their assistance in obtaining obscure materials: Arts Library, University of Nottingham; University College Hospital Library, the Thane Library and Senate House Library, University of London; the British Medical Association Library; the Library of the Wellcome Institute for the History of Medicine; and the Library of the Royal College of Physicians. Mr John Burt guided me through the Monk's House Collection of the papers of Leonard and Virginia Woolf at the University of Sussex Library. Mr Andrew Russell of the Queen's Medical Centre Library, University of Nottingham, gave generously of his time and knowledge.

The following people have read sections of this work, and have provided useful comments: Dr Roger Poole, Dr Aaron Esterson, Mary Garvey, Andrew Holt and Dr Tony Delamothe. Michael Mason, Susan Rea and Judy Bette-Bennett have all made useful editorial suggestions. Responsibility for error rests solely with me.

I am grateful to Catherine Oriel and Murray Mindlin for their kind support.

For permission to quote from works by Leonard and Virginia Woolf and Quentin Bell, I am grateful to Quentin Bell, Angelica Garnett and The Hogarth Press. I am grateful to Faber and Faber for permission to quote from T. S. Eliot's *The Family Reunion*. I am also grateful to Messrs. Churchill Livingstone for permission to quote from Sir Maurice Craig's *Psychological Medicine*.

I am grateful to the BBC Hulton Picture Library for permission to reproduce photographs of Leonard and Virginia

Woolf, Sir Leslie Stephen, Vanessa Bell, Vita Sackville-West, George Duckworth and Sir Henry Head. The photograph of Dr T. B. Hyslop is reproduced by courtesy of the Wellcome Trustees. I am indebted to the Royal College of Physicians for permission to reproduce photographs of Sir G. H. Savage and Sir Maurice Craig.

A Note on the Text

While the doctors under consideration in this work, in common with various commentators on Virginia Woolf, use the words 'madness' or 'insanity' in various senses, it should be understood that my use of these terms in the text should be considered as qualified by inverted quotes.

In quoting the *Letters* and *Diary* of Virginia Woolf I have followed her editors in retaining misspellings and idiosyncratic punctuation. These are often inconsistent throughout the *Letters* and *Diary*. The reader may refer to the first volumes of each of these works for a full explanation of editorial method. Textual intrusions by the editors of these autobiographical volumes are contained within parentheses; my intrusions are contained within brackets. I have, on the whole, followed the chronology of the editors, and their method of citing uncertain dates followed by a question mark (25? March 1918, for instance).

'My life is a constant fight against Doctors follies, it seems to me.' Virginia Woolf to Violet Dickinson, 26 November 1904

Introduction

Was Virginia Woolf mad? Many critics, including her biographer, Quentin Bell, and her husband, Leonard, have said that she was. Yet these are lay critics, who have no knowledge of medical science. What did her doctors think: did they diagnose her as insane? What were their views on madness — its causes, definition and treatment? How did Virginia Woolf see herself in this context? What were her views with regard to madness in general, and her own condition in particular? How did these questions figure in her writing, both fictional and autobiographical?

Few modern writers have been the subject of more attention than Virginia Woolf. With the publication of her letters and diaries now almost complete we have perhaps the most fully documented literary life of the twentieth century. Yet, in spite of (or perhaps as a result of) the great mass of primary sources available, Virginia Woolf remains an elusive entity, both as a writer and as a person. One eminent critic can proclaim that Virginia Woolf was a philosophical realist in her fiction, while another confidently asserts that she is a transcendental idealist. Her most eminent biographer claims that she was a genius, yet that she was, periodically, insane; however, another noted critic would agree that she was a genius, but disagrees vehemently that she was insane. Literary controversies will always rage, and no author, no matter how highly esteemed by posterity, will be immune from the disagreements — some petty, some fundamental — of the critics who find their justification in a reading of that author's work. Indeed, this is a healthy phenomenon, indicative of a tolerant society. However, judgements about the

1

life of a writer, when they are made in an extra-literary context, employing criteria other than purely literary-critical ones, are bound (or should be bound) by the same restrictions or considerations which inform us in our published judgements of any other human being.

This book seeks to uncover some of the presuppositions behind the attribution of madness in the case of Virginia Woolf; briefly in relation to the lay persons who have maintained that she was not sane (Leonard Woolf and Quentin Bell in particular), and at length where four of her doctors were concerned. While this book may possess an immediate appeal to literary scholars and those interested in the life of Virginia Woolf, I hope that its importance may lie beyond the highly specialized fields of literary or biographical inquiry. The particular circumstances in which Virginia Woolf found herself in relation to her family and to the medical profession are the occasion for more general reflections on the nature of madness, and the way in which those suspected of harbouring madness have been dealt with, especially if they happened to be women.

In the pages that follow we shall encounter eminent doctors writing of concepts such as 'moral insanity' and 'aesthetic insanity', concepts which cannot be rigorously defined, and which often find a spurious justification in social, political, class or sexual bias. In reading the passages quoted from the works of these doctors, we would do well to remember that they are not writing in the mid-nineteenth century, but at the turn of the century and into the 1930s. Yet, as we shall discover in detail, so-called diagnoses of insanity were often the result of a magical rather than a medical disposition. In many cases, the diagnosis of insanity represents nothing more than an attempt on the part of the medical profession to enforce unwritten social codes as if they were the law of the land.

As I hope to show by the end of this book, the Virginia Woolf of *Three Guineas* was perfectly sane; and, what is more, her comments in that work may be seen, in retrospect, to have been startlingly clear and informed, particularly where the so-called 'objectivity' of science — especially medical science — is concerned. Prior to considering this question at length, we would do well to review the background of Virginia's so-called madness.

The view that Virginia Woolf was mad has gained currency in the public mind largely due to the opinions of five people: Leonard Woolf in his autobiography[1]; Quentin Bell (Virginia's nephew) in his biography of her[2]; Nigel Nicolson and Joanne Trautmann, in their edition of Virginia's letters[3]; and Anne Olivier Bell in her edition of the diary[4]. It is my belief that the attribution of madness is a serious matter, not unlike a judgement of criminal guilt. Before the law, a man is innocent until proved guilty; he is entitled to representation by someone familiar with the law who is retained to defend his rights; and there is always the right of appeal. In the case of judging madness, particularly in Virginia's day, the same safeguards did not exist to protect the rights of the individual. The medical diagnosis of insanity was made under privileged conditions. It was made out of the public gaze. It was made by professionals who claimed the right to be free of any lay intervention or criticism[5].

Even a cursory questioning of the manner in which Virginia's madness is discussed by Leonard Woolf, Quentin Bell or the editors of the *Letters* and *Diary* shows that their use of the term is at best uncritical, and at worst irresponsible. It is not necessary to quote every instance of this in Bell's biography; but this brief example gives the general flavour of his attitude:

> To know that you have had cancer in your body and to know that it may return must be very horrible; but a cancer of the mind, a corruption of the spirit striking one at the age of thirteen and for the rest of one's life always working away somewhere, always in suspense, a Dionysian sword above one's head — this must be almost unendurable. So unendurable that in the end, when the voices of insanity spoke to her in 1941, she took the only remedy that remained, the cure of death.
>
> (Bell, 1, p. 44.)

Bell writes of Virginia that, following the death of her father, 'all that summer she was mad' (Bell, 1, p. 90). Sanity is discussed in the same offhand fashion when Bell writes of

Leslie Stephen's father, 'there was something a little mad in
Stephen's self-mortification'; but, on the other hand, his
wife, Jane Catherine Venn, 'was as sane a woman as ever
breathed' (Bell, 1, p. 6). Clearly, the term 'mad', as Bell
uses it here, can have no medical meaning, no serious significance. The term has been relegated to a popular vernacular.
Of Leslie Stephen, Bell writes that he had 'a view of the
world which was essentially honest and responsible and sane'
(Bell, 1, p. 10). Already, in these early pages of Bell's biography, we can see that the term mad is employed in two very
different ways. When Bell refers to Virginia's madness, he
means that she was mad in some clinical sense. When he
writes of there being something 'a little mad in Stephen's
self-mortification', or that Jane Venn was 'as sane a woman
as ever breathed', he has chosen a vernacular usage for the
purpose of quick characterization. In referring to Leslie
Stephen, sanity is joined with honesty and responsibility —
a moral judgement, not a medical one. If we go back to the
first instance of Bell's use of the term mad quoted above, we
see how the question of morality may be bound up with the
medical one: he speaks of 'a cancer of the mind, a corruption
of the spirit'. In examining the work of Sir George Henry
Savage, one of Virginia's earliest doctors, we will encounter
his use of the diagnosis of 'moral insanity', a dubious concept
which is marked by a similar confusion of morality and
medicine.

We must, at this point, be critical of Bell's moral judge-
ment of his subject. Leslie Stephen is praised for his virtues.
On one occasion, Virginia is condemned for exercising chastity.
Bell writes of her flirtation with his father, Clive Bell,

> In fact I doubt whether the business would have lasted for
> so long or, for a time, have become so important to them
> both, if Virginia had given him what he wanted. But this
> she never did and, in a very crude sense, her conduct may
> be described as virtuous.
>
> (Bell, 1, p. 133.)

Bell only cites the following criteria in support of his
belief that Virginia was mad: she believed that people

laughed at her in the street (paranoia); that she had an undue
fear of being run down in the street; that she would, periodically, refuse to eat; that she behaved unreasonably toward
Leonard, her sister Vanessa and her nurses when ill; and that
she suffered from hallucinations, i.e. following her father's
death she heard birds singing in Greek and King Edward VII
using 'the foulest possible language' (Bell, 1, p. 90). All of
these symptoms can be explained, and all of them have
meaning. That people did laugh at her in the street is substantiated by Leonard Woolf in his autobiography, in passages which we will examine shortly. Virginia's refusal of
food was a symbolic act bound up with her rejection of
Leonard's sexuality and the ban against having children
which was forced on her (the significance of which is discussed in the final chapter of this book). It is true that
Virginia behaved violently toward her family and her nurses
because she felt she was being persecuted. Her own reasons
for this feeling can be reconstructed, and they make sense.
The significance of Virginia's behaviour following her father's
death has been discussed by Roger Poole in his study, *The
Unknown Virginia Woolf*.[6] As for her fear of being run down
in the street, Bell takes this as a serious symptom, and
writes

It seemed to her that the streets had become murderous.
On 25 February she had been in a carriage accident; on
26 March she saw a lady cyclist run over by a cart; on
8 May she had witnessed two accidents in Piccadilly; on
the 12th a cart horse fell down in front of her; on the
13th there was a collision between a runaway carriage
horse and a waggon. Did these accidents really occur? Her
state of health since the wedding and, even more, since
Stella's illness had been deteriorating. On 9 May she was
examined by Dr Seton and lessons were stopped, she was
ordered to have milk, outdoor exercise, and medicine. She
was certainly in a nervous condition and I think that she
imagined or greatly exaggerated some of the accidents;
but one of them – the accident with the lady cyclist,
certainly did happen. It was a particularly agitating business because the lady, who ran straight into a cart in
Gloucester Road, came from the direction and at an hour

which Vanessa would have taken on her way back from her art school. Leslie, who was there, thought for a moment that it was indeed she.

(Bell, 1, p. 55.)

As Poole points out, those who believed Virginia was mad consistently 'disconfirmed' her perceptions.[7] Bell doubts that these accidents really occurred, but admits that one did, and that even Leslie Stephen — an 'honest and responsible and sane' man — thought for a moment that it might indeed have been Vanessa who was involved in the cycle accident. My casual notes on the number of accidents witnessed by Virginia in the first volume of the *Diary* and the first three volumes of the *Letters* list some fourteen occasions. There is little point in presenting a catalogue, but some of the incidents were unnerving, and struck close to home. It is significant too that many of them can be verified. For instance, Virginia writes to Vanessa Bell in 1916, 'Do you see that Aunt Mary has been killed by a motor car? (*Letters*, 2, p. 113). An editorial note confirms Virginia's report: 'Mary Louisa Fisher, the sister of Virginia's mother, was born about 1840. She was killed by a car on 24 August' (*Letters*, 2, p. 113n). On 5 January 1915 Virginia writes in her diary, 'Three bodies were seen yesterday swiftly coursing downstream at Teddington' (*Diary*, 1, p. 7). An editorial note confirms, 'On the morning of 1 January 1915 a local train at Ilford, Essex, was cut in two by an express from Clacton; ten people were killed and over thirty injured' (*Diary*, 1, p. 7n). On 12 April 1924 Virginia writes to Katherine Arnold-Forster, 'we've had the devil of a time — Angelica [Bell, Virginia's niece] being knocked over by a motor' (*Letters*, 3, p. 96). Further letters to Vanessa substantiate this. On 8 April 1925 Virginia writes to Gwen Raverat, 'I went out early this morning to see Nessa's new house (37 Gordon Square), and saw a woman killed by a motor car. This pitches one at once into a region where there is no certainty and one feels somehow, abject and cowed — exalted' (*Letters*, 3, p. 177). The list goes on.

What may appear at first to be the most damaging of the symptoms noted by Bell is the fact that Virginia did, as far

as we know, suffer from hallucinations during the breakdown which followed her father's death in 1904. After making a feeble suicide attempt by throwing herself out of a low window, Virginia convalesced for some months with her friend, Violet Dickinson. It is here, Bell tells us, that 'she lay in bed, listening to the birds singing in Greek and imagining that King Edward VII lurked in the azaleas using the foulest possible language' (Bell, 1, p. 90). This hallucination makes perfect sense when we consider the chain of association in Virginia's mind. Merely by pausing to consider what possible meaning the connection between Greek and foul language could have for Virginia, Roger Poole is able to supply an answer. For the simple fact is, Virginia was, in various ways, molested by her half-brothers, George and Gerald Duckworth, throughout her childhood, adolescence and young adulthood, and one of these scenes took place while Virginia was working at her Greek lessons. In a letter to Vanessa Bell dated 25? July 1911, Virginia wrote of Janet Case, her Greek teacher,

> She has a calm interest in copulation (having got over her dislike of naming it by the need of discussing Emphies symptoms with a male doctor) and this led us to the revelation of all Georges malefactions. To my surprise, she has always had an intense dislike of him; and used to say 'Whew — you nasty creature', when he came in and began fondling me over my Greek. When I got to the bedroom scenes she dropped her lace . . .
> (*Letters*, 1, p. 472, quoted by Poole, p. 32.)

The explanation is simple. George's 'malefactions' were at fever pitch during that time when Sir Leslie Stephen was dying of cancer, and Virginia bore the brunt of nursing him and running the household. The 'foul language' follows naturally enough from this, but why does Edward VII appear? There is a commonsense answer for this too. During Sir Leslie's final days, he was attended by Sir Frederick Treves, and possibly by Herbert William Allingham. Allingham was surgeon to the household of Edward VII, and Treves had operated on Edward VII in June 1902. It is

perfectly understandable that all of these factual components should be mixed in a bizarre way in the mind of an over-wrought young woman.

At this point it is necessary to consider the nature of the sexual interference by George and Gerald Duckworth. In his biography, Quentin Bell noted the interference by Gerald Duckworth, whom he had confused with George[8] (Bell, 1, p. 44). He quotes Virginia's letter to Ethel Smyth in which she writes, 'I still shiver with shame at the memory of my half-brother, standing me on a ledge, aged about 6 or so, exploring my private parts.' Bell's comment on this is, 'Unusual behaviour for a man in his twenties.' Indeed. Then came Jeanne Schulkind's edition of unpublished autobiographical essays by Virginia, *Moments of Being*. These, particularly the essay entitled '22 Hyde Park Gate', made it clear that both half-brothers had molested Virginia.[9] There is no need to quote at length texts which are now widely available. But the fact of the matter is that Virginia was interfered with to such an extent that a normal sexual relationship became impossible for her. Her experiences at the hands of her half-brothers made heterosexual physical love seem abhorrent. This was not simply physical repulsion; it was complicated by the fact that, after Sir Leslie's death, George took it upon himself to introduce Virginia and Vanessa Stephen to society, and while being excessively critical of his half-sisters' attitudes, dress and intellectual precocity, erected himself as an example of social decorum — thereby appearing to them as a hypocrite and humbug of the worst sort.

If we consider that Virginia was aged '6 or so' in 1888, and that the interference continued until 1904, when she was twenty-two years old, that is a period of sixteen years. Gerald Duckworth was born in 1870, and so was eighteen years old when he stood Virginia on a ledge and 'explored' her. In 1895, George Duckworth was twenty-seven years old, and his interference continued until 1904, when he was thirty-six years of age.

If we want to understand the nature of Virginia's illness of 1904, all we need do is try and imagine the impact upon a young girl of the protracted death of her father, and the

traumas imposed by sexual abuse masquerading as brotherly comfort and affection.

Throughout Virginia's life, eminent doctors were called in to examine her.[10] None of them were much help, and some even made her situation more difficult. Virginia's madness was considered to be a medical problem. Yet, in the works of those who maintain that Virginia was mad — the Bells, Leonard Woolf, the editors of the *Letters*, Spater and Parsons[11] — there is no real medical evidence to suggest that this is the case. It is merely a lay assumption. To my knowledge, no one has made a truly scientific medical study of Virginia Woolf. Until concrete evidence is produced, it is irresponsible to speak of her as having been mad.

But that is not to say that there was nothing 'wrong' with Virginia. She was, clearly, at various periods in her life, distressed to such an extent that she could not work, could not concentrate — indeed, on occasion she lost the will to live. But it seems to me futile to attribute these episodes to some inherent madness which cannot be substantiated when a number of very adequate non-medical reasons exist. Breakdowns followed such traumatic events as death in the family; the failure of the sexual side of marriage; a desire to have children which was thwarted by her husband and by medical opinion; guilt over her 'flirtation' with Clive Bell, which was largely a means of retaliating against her sister for marrying when Virginia most needed her; the appearance of her first and subsequent novels; and her uncertainty about herself as a writer and as a person. In this work, Virginia's breakdowns will be considered in the context of the pressures which bore upon her at the time.

Finally, the image of Virginia as a bedridden lunatic is one that ought to be dispelled. She spent more time in bed because of diagnosed physical ailments than she did because she was mad. She suffered incessantly from influenza; she had pneumonia; possibly as a result of both of these, she had a weak heart; she had almost interminable trouble with her teeth; and she suffered from headaches. None of this is madness.

But our need for certainty, our predilection for tidiness makes us ask: What was actually wrong with her? If Virginia were alive today and could be examined by any contemporary doctor, we would be no further along the road to certainty. Some would argue manic depression; various types of schizophrenia would be diagnosed; some would find *anorexia nervosa* during one particular episode; depression would have its supporters; and any number of psychoanalytical diagnoses would be proffered. Perhaps she would not have been better off today than yesterday in that respect. Yet, the question lingers: what was actually wrong with her? No single person or school of thought can provide a categorical answer to this question. It does seem to me, however, that there is a means by which one central factor of all Virginia's breakdowns and illnesses can be profitably illuminated. I refer to a phenomenological analysis at the level of the body: an analysis of embodiment.

Firstly, embodiment. By this I mean the manner in which Virginia experienced her body — what Merleau-Ponty calls *le corps vécu*. During all of Virginia's breakdowns, she had a peculiar relationship to her body. She felt that it was sordid; she found eating repulsive; she felt as if her body was not the centre of her 'self' — that she somehow existed at odds with it, or divorced from it. Not only is a problematical sense of embodiment a central factor in all of her breakdowns, but it is also one of the perennial themes of her novels and, indeed, of her essays, letters and diary. Secondly, phenomenological analysis. What I mean by this is not identical with the programmes of research outlined by Husserl, Heidegger and others. Rather, I mean by it the very practical use to which R. D. Laing put it in his early work, *The Divided Self.*[12] Borrowing from Laing, my programme of phenomenological analysis may be defined briefly: the reconstruction of the other person's experience from his own point of view. This is the means by which the birds singing in Greek come to have a significance of vital import; it is the means by which they (and other signs) speak to us from the realm of meaning, rather than from the abyss of insane babble.

Before discussing Virginia's madness in the context of the periodical and book-length publications of four of the doctors who treated her, I will attempt to outline some of the situations from which her so-called madness stemmed. In

Chapter 1, I examine the problem of embodiment in her first novel, *The Voyage Out*, viewed in the context of her life up until 1915, when the novel appeared. Relevant passages from other novels will also be discussed. In Chapter 2, I single out one aspect of the problem of embodiment — the question of food and eating — and discuss this in the light of statements made by Quentin Bell and Leonard Woolf. Against these are juxtaposed Virginia's own statements on the subject, and readings of passages from *Mrs Dalloway*, *The Waves* and other relevant texts. In Chapter 3, I trace Virginia's early experiences of the medical profession, and consider the manner in which doctors are presented in two novels — *The Voyage Out* and *Mrs Dalloway*. Chapters 4, 5, 6 and 7 consider Virginia's madness in the context of the writings of the following doctors: Sir George Henry Savage; Sir Henry Head; Sir Maurice Craig; and Dr T. B. Hyslop. In Chapter 8 I discuss Virginia's experiences at Burley, the private asylum in Twickenham to which she was sent on four occasions, and consider the relevance of her 'biography' of Elizabeth Barrett Browning's dog, *Flush*, read as autobiography.

1

The Problem of Embodiment

Quentin Bell has maintained that part of Virginia's madness consisted in the fact that she thought that other people laughed at her; that they found her ridiculous. The truth is that people did laugh at her, did find her appearance ridiculous on occasion. Our authority for this is Leonard Woolf. He writes,

> to the crowd in the street there was something in her appearance which struck them as strange and laughable . . . they would stop and stare and nudge one another — 'look at her' . . . they did not merely stop and stare and nudge one another; there was something in Virginia they found ridiculous . . . the crowd would go into fits of laughter at the sight of Virginia.[1]

Virginia's knowledge of unease in the body is evident from the early pages of *The Voyage Out*. As Rachel Vinrace prepares herself for dinner on board the *Euphrosyne*, on the night when she meets the Dalloways, we are told,

> Again, the arrival of strangers made it obvious to Rachel, as the hour of dinner approached, that she must change her dress; and the ringing of the great bell found her sitting on the edge of her berth in such a position that the little glass above the washstand reflected her head and shoulders. In the glass she wore an expression of tense melancholy, for she had come to the depressing conclusion, since the arrival of the Dalloways, that her face was not the face she wanted, and in all probability never would be.[2]

This suggests a problem much deeper than the usual adolescent vanity or lack of confidence. There is an ominous cutting-off of possibilities, an amputation of the future in the words, 'her face was not the face she wanted, and in all probability never would be'. In *The Voyage Out*, Rachel begins life operating from a position which may be called 'ontologically insecure' — she is not certain enough of her own existence to find fulfilment in herself, or in relations with others. At dinner, Rachel is compared unfavourably with her mother, and this continues throughout her stay among the British colony on Santa Marina. Helen's husband, Ridley, exclaims at dinner, ' "Ah! She's not like her mother" ' (*TVO*, p. 11). Rachel's quest for identity is partly thwarted by the dominant image of her mother, of whom she feels herself to be a mere reflection. Helen notices that Rachel 'was like her mother, as the image in a pool on a still summer's day is like the vivid flushed face that hangs over it'[3] (*TVO*, p. 21).

Rachel lacks two primary love relations: a mother, and a romantic, or sexual one. She is at once eager to discover the dead mother, and to move forward in search of romantic attachment. However, the possibility of finding the romantic relationship is, in part, thwarted by the search for and coming to terms with the mother. While Rachel wants to know what her mother was like (Helen supplies her with glowing recollections), she also feels herself to be in competition with her. Her beauty and social accomplishments make Rachel feel insignificant, a failure. This aggravates the ontological insecurity she already feels, and decreases her ability to participate in a successful romantic relationship. Rachel's ontological insecurity thus gains a temporal component, a paralysis which leaves her hovering uncertainly between an irretrievable past and an uncertain future.

When Dalloway brutally kisses Rachel, this experience is similar to Virginia's at the hands of her half-brothers. And the result is the same: Rachel-Virginia divorces herself from the body which is the object of this damaging attention:

'How strange to be a woman! A young and beautiful woman,' he continued sententiously, 'has the whole world at her feet. That's true, Miss Vinrace. You have an inestimable power -- for good or for evil. What couldn't you do --' he broke off.

'What?' asked Rachel.

'You have beauty,' he said. The ship lurched. Rachel fell slightly forward. Richard took her in his arms and kissed her. Holding her tight, he kissed her passionately, so that she felt the hardness of his body and the roughness of his cheek printed upon hers. She fell back in her chair, with tremendous beats of the heart, each of which sent black waves across her eyes. He clasped his forehead in his hands.

'You tempt me,' he said. *The tone of his voice was terrifying*. He seemed choked in fight. They were both trembling. Rachel stood up and went. Her head was cold, her knees shaking, and the physical pain of the emotion was so great that she could only keep herself moving above the great leaps of her heart. She leant upon the rail of the ship, and *gradually ceased to feel, for a chill of body and mind crept over her*. Far out between the waves little black and white sea-birds were riding. Rising and falling with smooth and graceful movements in the hollows of the waves they seemed singularly detached and un-concerned.

(*TVO*, pp. 72-3, my italics.)

Like George Duckworth seen from Virginia's point of view, Dalloway is a great hypocrite. He professes to stand for 'civilization', and a just and orderly society — with all of the philosophical baggage that accompanies social vision with a basis in 'morality'. Yet he is subject to uncontrollable desires which he allows to possess him momentarily, desires which he will later deny, or pretend do not exist. Critics hostile to *The Voyage Out* may complain that Rachel's extreme reaction is little more than evidence that Rachel-Virginia is an oversensitive character whose difficulties may be ascribed to an inability to live in the real world, to accept the minor blows and misfortunes that every adolescent must face. But *The Voyage Out* is best understood in the context of the life of the young woman who wrote it. *The Voyage Out* is an autobiographical novel in which Virginia confronts her situation, yet leaves out the specific details. What remains intact, however, are the reactions to the various situations

in which she found herself. This novel went through numerous drafts, in which specific references to Virginia's own
situation were systematically cut out.[4] The result is that the
reasons for Rachel-Virginia's extreme reactions are concealed
(unsuccessfully), yet the reactions retain their potency and
significance. The code by which these actions are obscured is
the challenge presented by the novel.

Rachel-Virginia's reaction to Dalloway-Duckworth's kiss
is extreme, and has devastating consequences. 'The tone of
his voice was terrifying.' There can be no mistaking this. But
the result is what matters for us here: 'She ... gradually
ceased to feel, for a chill of body and mind crept over her.'
She becomes anaesthetized. Rachel's predicament is the
prototype of one which appears again in Virginia's novels:
Septimus Smith in *Mrs. Dalloway*; Rhoda in *The Waves*.
Certain actions are a violation of the person, and result in a
break between body and self. Rachel suffers a mild form of
disembodiment. She identifies with the waves and the sea-
birds out on the horizon; like them she becomes 'singularly
detached and unconcerned'.

The situation is further complicated by the fact that
Dalloway divorces himself from his action. Throughout the
remainder of his stay on the *Euphrosyne* we are made aware
of the split in his behaviour, of the total divorce between the
public and the private man, between his ideals and his actual
behaviour. Again, we are reminded of George Duckworth.

The kiss is a kind of amputation. It is unhinged, free-
floating, leading to nothing — a moment of passionate,
almost meaningless abuse. Images of amputation are rife in
the novel: flowers with their 'juicy stalks' cut, left to lie on
cold altars in village churches; chickens' heads being sliced
off outside the hotel kitchen; and the image of an old woman
slicing the head off a bust in Rachel's hallucinations as she
lies dying. That Dalloway's kiss was not only traumatic but,
in a sense, fatal, the final blow to a life whose possibilities,
as we have already seen, are severely limited, is given to us as
indisputable fact:

By this new light she saw her life for the first time a
creeping hedged-in thing, driven cautiously between high

walls, here turned aside, there plunged in darkness, made dull and *crippled for ever* -- her life that was the only chance she had -- a thousand words and actions became plain to her.

(*TVO*, p. 79, my italics.)

After the kiss, Rachel has a terrifying nightmare which is directly related to the traumatic experience:

She dreamt that she was walking down a long tunnel, which grew so narrow by degrees that she could touch the damp bricks on either side. At length the tunnel opened and became a vault; she found herself trapped in it, bricks meeting her wherever she turned, alone with a little deformed man who squatted on the floor gibbering, with long nails. His face was pitted and like the face of an animal. The wall behind him oozed with damp, which collected into drops and slid down. Still and cold as death she lay, not daring to move, until she broke the agony by tossing herself across the bed, and woke crying 'Oh!'

Light showed her the familiar things: her clothes, fallen off the chair; the water jug gleaming white; but the horror did not go at once. She felt herself pursued, so that she got up and actually locked her door. A voice moaned for her; eyes desired her. All night long barbarian men harassed the ship; they came scuffling down the passages, and stopped to snuffle at her door. She could not sleep again.

(*TVO*, p. 74.)

After the onset of her illness, Rachel experiences a hallucination which contains many of the elements of this dream:

Rachel again shut her eyes, and found herself walking through a tunnel under the Thames, where there were little deformed women sitting in archways playing cards, while the bricks of which the wall was made oozed with damp, which collected into drops and slid down the wall. But the little old women became Helen and nurse McInnis after a time, standing in the window together whispering, whispering incessantly.

(*TVO*, p. 336.)

Both the dream and the hallucination borrow recognizable elements from the lives of Rachel and Virginia. These passages are at once autobiographical and fictional. For instance, the elements in the first dream are easily recognizable as references to events which have already occurred in the novel. Rachel dreams she is being pursued, as she was by Dalloway. In the hallucination, she finds herself walking through a tunnel beneath the Thames. Since her aunts live in Richmond (and she with them), it is to them that the images unflatteringly refer. The cards symbolize the kind of tyranny that aunts like old Mrs Paley represent. Images of cold and damp are appropriate to Rachel's state of mind. (The hint of conspiracy involving Helen and the nurse cannot be understood until later in the chapter, when we have considered Helen's relationship with Rachel more fully.) These passages are convincing and successful fictions.

But their autobiographical import is more profound, and since they 'work' successfully as fiction, we run no risk of reducing the novel to a neurotic or psychotic case history. I have said that Dalloway has an autobiographical significance in the novel, as a reference to George Duckworth. This is substantiated by the essays in *Moments of Being*. We are already familiar with the nature of George and Gerald's 'attentions'. If we add to this Virginia's general description of George Duckworth, we see just how similar he and Dalloway are; and, more important, that the particular imagery used to describe the deformed man in the tunnel (in the dream) refers us specifically to Duckworth. This passage from *Moments of Being* serves to equate Dalloway and George Duckworth -- they are both characterized by the same passionate hypocrisy:

Stupid he was, and good natured; but such qualities were not simple; they were modified, confused, distorted, exalted, set swimming in a sea of racing emotions until you were completely at a loss to know where you stood. Nature, we may suppose, had supplied him with abundant animal vigour, but she had neglected to set an efficient brain in control of it. The result was that all the impressions which the good priggish boy took in at school and college remained with him when he was a man; they were not extended, but were liable to be expanded into enormous proportions by violent gusts of passion; and (he) proved more and more incapable of containing them. Thus, under the name of unselfishness he allowed himself to commit acts which a cleverer man would have called tyrannical; and, profoundly believing in the purity of his love, he behaved little better than a brute.[5]

Virginia speaks of his 'animal vigour'. In another passage, his 'animal' qualities are made more specific, and here is the source of the little deformed man in the tunnel:

> When Miss Willett of Brighton saw him 'throwing off his ulster' in the middle of her drawing room she was moved to write an Ode Comparing George Duckworth to the Hermes of Praxiteles -- which Ode my mother kept in her writing table drawer, along with a little Italian medal that George had won for saving a peasant from drowning. Miss Willett was reminded of the Hermes; *but if you looked at him closely you noticed that one of his ears was pointed; and the other round; you also noticed that though he had the curls of a God and the ears of a faun he had unmistakably the eyes of a pig.*[6]

Further evidence pointing to Duckworth may be found in the dream. The passage describes how, when Rachel awoke, 'Light showed her the familiar things: her clothes, fallen off the chair; the water jug gleaming white.' We recall immediately the passage which describes George's entrance to Virginia's bedroom following a disastrous evening at Lady Carnarvon's and the French theatre:

> In a confused whirlpool of sensation I stood slipping off my petticoats, withdrew my long white gloves, and hung my white silk stockings over the back of a chair . . . Then, creaking stealthily, the door opened; treading gingerly, someone entered. 'Who?' I cried. 'Don't be frightened,' George whispered.[7]

We have yet to consider the significance of the tunnel for Rachel. At the risk of being accused of employing a crude, ready-made Freudian interpretation, I believe that the long, narrow tunnel leading to a vault suggests a womb. This symbol, however, does not find its meaning in the Freudian catalogue, but in a careful consideration of Virginia's particular circumstances (it is a phenomenological rather than a psychoanalytical interpretation). The tunnel is a reference to the womb of the mother. For in the tunnel, a full knowledge of Virginia's predicament is found. When Rachel awakens from the dream crying 'Oh!', the horror is not so much Rachel's at being pursued as it is Virginia's at realizing fully the incestuous nature of the Duckworths' attentions. She is horrified to discover, in the oneiric journey into the past, in search of her mother, that she and the Duckworths were given birth by the same mother. She is already paralysed temporally because she is unable to come to terms with her mother's ghost, and the presence of the deformed man in the womb in which she is seeking ontological security is horrific. Another option seems to be closed off. The two primary love relations which she is lacking, a mother and a romantic attachment, are both thwarted here.[8]

The brick walls oozing with damp refer to 22 Hyde Park Gate, the family home and scene of the early traumas. That house, following the death of her parents, became for Virginia a symbol of the antithetical qualities of honesty and creative endeavour pitted against social and moral hypocrisy and philistinism. For her, the very structure of the house suggested this split: 'downstairs there was pure convention: upstairs pure intellect. But there was no connection between them.'[9] This split in sensibility, between philistine convention and imaginative achievement, was reinforced at the sexual level: 'George would fling himself on my bed, cuddling and kissing and otherwise embracing me in order, as he told Dr Savage later, to comfort me for the fatal illness of my father — who was dying three or four storeys lower down of cancer' (Bell, 1, p. 96n). In 1922, Virginia realized that her illness of 1895, the year of her mother's death, was 'not unnaturally the result of all these emotions and complications'.[10] In a letter to Phillip Morrell dated 30 June 1919, she refers to George Duckworth's responsibility for

because she cannot consummate her relationship with Hewet
(or with any other partner). However, Poole reduces the
existential significance of her death by arguing that it is
merely a technical device, the only possible ending to the
novel. It is a romantic ending.[12] Certainly the illness from
which Rachel suffers has a meaning beyond this. It is not
a meaning which many medical doctors would credit, and it
is a meaning which could only be accepted provided one sub-
scribed to a certain philosophical position with regard to the
nature of human embodiment. I believe that Maurice Merleau-
Ponty's *Phenomenology of Perception* provides such an
existential view of the body which is coherent, well-
documented with case histories, and as logically argued as
it could be, given the insusceptibility of human subjectivity
to absolutely logical explanation. It places human embodiment at the centre of the subjective world — indeed, it is
only by means of our bodies that we are able to have a world
at all, to have any conception of time or space. Our bodies
connect us with the world and with other people by means
of what Merleau-Ponty calls the 'intentional arc'. For Merleau-
Ponty, sexuality is always part and parcel of embodiment,
and this is one reason why his theory is so applicable to an
explanation of Rachel's illness and death:

> the sexual is not the genital, sexual life is not a mere effect
> of the processes having their seat in the genital organs,
> the libido is not an instinct, that is, an activity naturally
> directed towards definite ends, it is the general power,
> which the psychosomatic subject enjoys, of taking root in
> different settings, of establishing himself through different
> experiences, of gaining structures of conduct. It is what
> causes a man to have a history. *In so far as a man's sexual
> history provides a key to his life, it is because in his
> sexuality is projected his manner of being towards the
> world, that is, towards time and other men.* There are
> sexual symptoms at the root of all neuroses, but these
> symptoms, correctly interpreted, symbolize a whole
> attitude, whether, for example, one of conquest or of
> flight. Into the sexual history, conceived as the elabora-
> tion of a general form of life, all psychological constituents
> can enter, because there is no longer an interaction of two

causalities and because the genital life is geared to the whole life of the subject. So the question is not so much whether human life does or does not rest on sexuality, as of knowing what is to be understood by sexuality.[13]

What must be noted is that Merleau-Ponty does not reduce man to his sexual functions (as classical psychoanalysis too often does), but rather reconstructs the whole of living man from this vital and important aspect of his being. Elaborating on this point (and answering his own question, 'What is to be understood by sexuality?'), Merleau-Ponty goes on to say:

When I move my hand towards a thing, I know implicitly that my arm unbends. When I move my eyes, I take account of their movement, without being expressly conscious of the fact, and am thereby aware that the upheaval caused in my field of vision is only apparent. Similarly sexuality, without being the object of any intended act of consciousness, can underlie and guide specified forms of my experience. Taken in this way, as an ambiguous atmosphere, sexuality is co-extensive with life. In other words, ambiguity is of the essence of human existence, and everything we live or think has always several meanings. A way of life — an attitude of escapism and need of solitude — is perhaps a generalized expression of a certain state of sexuality. In thus becoming transformed into existence, sexuality has taken upon itself so general a significance, the sexual theme has contrived to be for the subject the occasion for so many accurate and true observations in themselves, of so many rationally based decisions, and it has become so loaded with the passage of time that it is an impossible undertaking to seek, within the framework of sexuality, the explanation of the framework of existence. The fact remains that this existence is the act of taking up and making explicit a sexual situation, and that in this way it has always at least a double sense. There is interfusion between sexuality and existence, which means that existence permeates sexuality and *vice versa*, so that it is impossible to determine, in a given decision or action, the proportion of sexual to other motivations, impossible to label a decision or act 'sexual' or 'non-sexual'.[14]

Merleau-Ponty concludes his chapter on 'The Body in its Sexual Being' with this apposite remark:

> There is no explanation of sexuality which reduces it to anything other than itself, for it is already something other than itself, and indeed, if we like, our whole being. Sexuality, it is said, is dramatic *because* we commit our whole personal life to it. But just why do we do this? Why is our body, for us, the mirror of our being, unless because it is a *natural self*, a current of given existence, with the result that we never know whether the forces which bear us on are its or ours — or with the result rather that they are never entirely either its or ours. There is no outstripping of sexuality any more than there is any sexuality enclosed within itself. No one is saved and no one is totally lost.[15]

If we accept this view of sexuality as part and parcel of our existence, then Rachel's illness and death begin to acquire meaning for us. Let us return to the novel and consider those passages which describe Rachel's experience.

Rachel is taken ill quite suddenly, while listening to Hewet read from Milton's *Comus*:

> There is a gentle nymph not far from hence,
> That with moist curb sways the smooth Severn stream.
> Sabrina is her name, a virgin pure;
> Whilom she was the daughter of Locrine,
> That had the sceptre from his father Brute.

and

> Sabrina fair,
>   Listen where thou art sitting
> Under the glassy, cool, translucent wave,
>   In twisted braids of lilies knitting
> The loose train of thy amber dropping hair,
> Listen for dear honour's sake,
>   Goddess of the silver lake,
>   Listen and save!

(TVO, pp. 331-2.)

The song of threatened innocence is appropriate, and soon

after hearing it (we are told that the words 'seemed to be laden with meaning . . . they sounded strange; they meant different things from what they usually meant' (*TVO*, p. 331)), Rachel is plunged into a state where

> all landmarks were obliterated, and the outer world was so far away that the different sounds, such as the sounds of people passing on the stairs, and the sounds of people moving overhead, could only be ascribed to their cause by a great effort of memory. The recollection of what she had felt, or of what she had been doing and thinking three days before, had faded entirely. On the other hand, every object in the room, and the bed itself, and her own body with its various limbs and their different sensations were more and more important each day. She was completely cut off, and unable to communicate with the rest of the world, isolated alone with her body.
>
> (*TVO*, pp. 334-5.)

That Rachel's state of embodiment is out of the ordinary is self-evident. Her ability to organize the world into a coherent whole has failed her. Her sense of time is upset. The temporal paralysis from which she suffered at the beginning of the novel, whereby the past seemed cut off, and the future no longer a possibility, has increased. There is nothing but the immediate present, and a kind of primitive connection with what is immediately to hand — her body, and the objects in her room. She is unable to reflect; she has no memory. She has become merged with the world in a primordial, pre-reflective fashion. Her experience of her body and the radically altered structure of her space are inextricably linked. In cutting herself off from a world which she finds hostile and terrifying, she has pushed subjectivity to an almost impossible limit.

That this withdrawal from the human world has to do with the experiences we have discussed in this chapter is obvious. But what is the nature of this withdrawal? It is no good seeking an empirical explanation; we already know the cause, though this may not be proveable in empirical terms. Merleau-Ponty may help us to understand more fully the process by which Rachel's world changes:

What protects the sane man against delirium or hallucination, is not his critical powers, but the structure of his
space: objects remain before him, keeping their distance
and, as Malebranche said speaking of Adam, touching him
only with respect. *What brings about both hallucinations
and myths is a shrinkage in the space directly experienced,
a rooting of things in our body* . . .[16]

Merleau-Ponty goes on to elaborate hallucinatory experience
by noting its relation to ordinary, everyday experience. The
person suffering from hallucinations experiences a shrinkage
in the space he perceives, a rooting of things in his own
body, and 'the overwhelming proximity of the object, the
oneness of man and world, which is, not indeed abolished,
but repressed by everyday perception or by objective thought,
and which philosophical consciousness rediscovers'.[17] Rather
than dismissing hallucinations as 'crazy', alien experiences
which have no meaning, Merleau-Ponty argues that they may
be understood, at least in part, as pre-reflective experience;
and by discussing the concept of myth in this context, he
gives the phenomenon of hallucination a broad anthropo-
logical meaning instead of reducing it to a medical or psychiatric category. He goes on to prescribe a method of
sympathetic reconstruction which, no doubt, influenced the
Laing of *The Divided Self*:

It is true that if I reflect on the consciousness of positions
and directions in myths, dreams and in perception, if I
posit and establish them in accordance with the methods
of objective thinking, I bring to light in them once more
the relationships of geometrical space. The conclusion
from this is not that they were there already, but on the
contrary that genuine reflection is not of this kind. In
order to realize what is the meaning of mythical or schizo-
phrenic space, we have no means other than that of
resuscitating in ourselves, in our present perception, the
relationship of the subject and his world which analytical
reflection does away with.[18]

Applying the phenomenological method in this case, and
keeping in mind the significance of Dalloway-Duckworth's

kiss and Rachel-Virginia's reaction to it — her anaesthesia and detachment, her profound sense of shame where anything to do with the body is concerned — it is not surprising to find that Rachel finally experiences herself as disembodied. In *The Divided Self*, Laing describes how the embodied self

> has a sense of being flesh and blood and bones, of being biologically alive and real: he knows himself to be substantial. To the extent that he is thoroughly 'in' his body, he is likely to have a sense of personal continuity in time. He will experience himself as subject to the dangers that threaten his body, the dangers of attack, mutilation, disease, decay, and death. He is implicated in bodily desire, and the gratifications and frustrations of the body. The individual thus has as his starting-point an experience of his body as a base from which he can be a person with other human beings.[19]

However, the self can become, to use Laing's phrase, 'unembodied':

> In this position the individual experiences his self as being more or less divorced from his body. *The body is felt more as one object among other objects in the world than as the core of the individual's own being.* Instead of being the core of his true self, the body is felt as the core of a *false self*, which a detached, disembodied, 'inner', 'true' self looks on at with tenderness, amusement, or hatred as the case may be.
>
> Such a divorce of self from body deprives the unembodied self from direct participation in any aspect of the life of the world, which is mediated exclusively through the body's perceptions, feelings and movements (expressions, gestures, words, actions, etc.). The unembodied self, as onlooker at all the body does, engages in nothing directly. Its functions come to be observation, control, and criticism *vis-à-vis* what the body is experiencing and doing, and those operations which are usually spoken of as purely 'mental'.[20]

Indeed, this is what has happened to Rachel as a result of her experience:

She [the nurse] put down the candle and began to arrange the bedclothes. It struck Rachel that a woman who sat playing cards in a cavern all night long would have very cold hands, and she shrunk from the touch of them.

'Why, there's a toe all the way down there!' the woman said, proceeding to tuck in the bedclothes. Rachel did not realise that the toe was hers.

(*TVO*, pp. 335-6.)

Rachel has disowned her body. Her 'true' self is located somewhere else, while her body, which she now considers to be her 'false' self, has passed into the hands of others.[21]

From now on, Rachel's hallucinations become more frightening. The horrible old women now wield knives:

'You see, there they go, rolling off the edge of the hill,' she said suddenly.

'Rolling, Rachel? What do you see rolling? There's nothing rolling.'

'The old woman with the knife,' she replied, not speaking to Terence in particular, and looking past him. As she appeared to be looking at a vase on the shelf opposite, he rose and took it down.

'Now they can't roll anymore,' he said cheerfully.

(*TVO*, p. 338.)

Merleau-Ponty has made it clear that when settled in 'the realm of death', we 'make use of the structures of being in the world, and borrow from it an element of being indispensable to its denial'. This is not a mere contradiction, but an accurate description of what Rachel does. She borrows elements from her everyday world in order to refute it, in order to turn her back on it. The horrifying sight of the old woman with the knife in the passage above has its origins in Rachel's early experiences in the novel: Mr Pepper cutting up roots with his penknife; the old women whom Rachel watches with horror as they slice the heads off chickens; and Dalloway peeling an apple while relating how his Skye terrier was run over by a cyclist. The old woman with the knife has an explicit source in Virginia's life, and the autobiographical meaning, once again, refers to the Duckworths:

There were 'winter evenings when the fire-wood could be cut into shape. "The others" [George, Gerald, and Stella Duckworth] were not brothers and sister, but *beings possessed of knives.*'[22] In Virginia's novels, the knife is usually a symbol of male aggressiveness and destructiveness (Peter Walsh opening and closing his pocket knife; Sara Pargiter's mimicking of Sir Digby 'pirouetting up and down with his sword between his legs')[23] which contrast sharply with her female characters' use of needle and thread. In *The Voyage Out*, however, the oppressive old women do not possess the kind of intuitive female consciousness which Virginia so much admired, and so they are 'beings possessed of knives', or they employ their scissors in a destructive fashion rather than to create beauty: 'in thousands of small gardens, millions of dark red flowers were blooming, until the old ladies who had tended them so carefully came down the paths with their scissors, snipped through their juicy stalks, and laid them upon cold stone ledges in the village church' (*TVO*, p. 27). Caught between the oppressive attitude of a Victorian matriarchy and the hypocrisy of Dalloway and his kind, Rachel's sexual identity does not manage to establish itself, and so when Hewet kisses her as she lies in a semi-conscious state, all she can see is 'an old woman slicing a man's head off with a knife':

> Terence sat down by the bedside. Rachel's face was changed. She looked as though she were entirely concentrated upon the effort of keeping alive. Her lips were drawn, and her cheeks were sunken and flushed, though without colour. Her eyes were not entirely shut, the lower half of the white part showing, not as if she saw, but as if they remained open because she was too much exhausted to close them. She opened them completely when he kissed her. But she only saw an old woman slicing a man's head off with a knife.
>
> (*TVO*, p. 344.)

As she approaches death, Rachel is completely unable to assign meaning to the external world:

> For six days indeed she had been oblivious of the world

outside, because it needed all her attention to follow the hot, red, quick sights which passed incessantly before her eyes. She knew that it was of enormous importance that she should attend to these sights and grasp their meaning, but she was always being just too late to hear or see something which would explain it all. For this reason, the faces — Helen's face, the nurse's, Terence's, the doctor's — which occasionally forced themselves very close to her, were worrying because they distracted her attention and she might miss the clue. However, on the fourth afternoon she was suddenly unable to keep Helen's face distinct from the sights themselves; her lips widened as she bent down over the bed, and she began to gabble unintelligibly like the rest. The sights were all concerned in some plot, some adventure, some escape. The nature of what they were doing changed incessantly, although there was always a reason behind it, which she must endeavour to grasp. Now they were among trees and savages, now they were on the sea, now they were on the tops of high towers; now they jumped; now they flew. But just as the crisis was about to happen, something invariably slipped in her brain, so that the whole effort had to begin over again. The heat was suffocating. At last the faces went further away; she fell into a deep pool of sticky water, which eventually closed over her head. She saw nothing and heard nothing but a faint booming sound, which was the sound of the sea rolling over her head. While all her tormentors thought that she was dead, she was not dead, but curled up at the bottom of the sea. There she lay, sometimes seeing darkness, sometimes light, while every now and then someone turned her over at the bottom of the sea.

(*TVO*, pp. 345-6.)

Rachel's illness has no empirical aetiology. Her decline is of the nature of a lapse of *being*. Merleau-Ponty tells us that: 'Beneath the intelligence as an anonymous function or as a categorial process, a personal core has to be recognized, which is the patient's being, his power of existing. It is here that the illness has its seat.'[24] Since our power to exist resides in intentionality, it is the failure of intentionality that drains all meaning from Rachel's world, which leaves her unable to organize the world into a coherent whole, the centre of which is her body:

> the life of consciousness –- cognitive life, the life of desire
> or perceptual life –- is subtended by an 'intentional arc'
> which projects round about us our past, our future, our
> human setting, our physical, ideological and moral situa-
> tion, or rather which results in our being situated in all
> these respects. It is this intentional arc which brings about
> the unity of the senses, of intelligence, of sensibility and
> motility. And it is this which 'goes limp' in illness.[25]

Finally, the intentional arc does go limp, and Rachel slips
into non-being:

> She had come to the surface of the dark, sticky pool, and
> a wave seemed to bear her up and down with it; she had
> ceased to have any will of her own; she lay on top of the
> wave conscious of some pain, but chiefly of weakness.
> The wave was replaced by the side of a mountain. Her
> body became a drift of melting snow, above which her
> knees rose in huge peaked mountains of bare bone. It was
> true that she saw Helen and saw her room, but everything
> had become very pale and semi-transparent. Sometimes
> she could see through the wall in front of her. Sometimes
> when Helen went away she seemed to go so far that
> Rachel's eyes could hardly follow her. The room also
> had an odd power of expanding, and though she pushed
> her voice out as far as possible until sometimes it became a
> bird and flew away, she thought it doubtful whether it ever
> reached the person she was talking to. There were immense
> intervals or chasms, for things still had the power to appear
> visibly before her, between one moment and the next; it
> sometimes took an hour for Helen to raise her arm, paus-
> ing long between each jerky movement, and pour out
> medicine. Helen's form stooping to raise her in bed
> appeared of gigantic size, and came down upon her like the
> ceiling falling. But for long spaces of time she would
> merely lie conscious of her body floating on the top of the
> bed and her mind driven to some remote corner of her
> body, or escaped and gone flitting round the room. All
> sights were something of an effort, but the sight of
> Terence was the greatest effort, because he forced her to
> join mind to body in the desire to remember something.

She did not wish to remember; it troubled her when people tried to disturb her loneliness; she wished to be alone. She wished for nothing else in the world.

(*TVO*, pp. 351-2.)

The dominant image in this passage and the previous passage quoted is water. It signifies fluidity, softness, comfort, and absence of hardness or resistance. It is the antidote for the hardness of male abstraction, for the relentlessly analytical attitude, the opposite of the hard kitchen table which Mr Ramsay's philosophy calls to mind in *To The Lighthouse*, or the 'beak of brass' which Poole singles out as the archetype of male aggression in the work of Virginia Woolf.[26] In the end, Rachel's attitude is one of flight. She seeks refuge, as Virginia would ultimately do, in the female element. Curling up at the bttom of the sea, Rachel has completed a malignant form of rebirth.

In the above passage, Rachel's body emerges as an object which is alien to her, and is described in terms of masculine images which are diametrically opposed to the female ones of water. At this nearly final moment, the wave upon which she feels herself to be borne (once again, referring us back to the scene with Dalloway, and the waves with which she longed to identify) becomes the side of a mountain.[27] As her body becomes a drift of melting snow, her knees appear as 'huge peaked mountains of bare bone': hard, naked images of death. The bones will endure, but the snow (water in another form) must decompose and lose itself in formlessness. Rachel has no sense of personal continuity in time, to use Laing's phrase, and this, perhaps more than any other symptom, tells us that Rachel is totally disembodied. At this point, the destruction worked upon her is complete.

Virginia's preoccupation with embodiment is not confined only to problematical states. She is also concerned with what might be called normal states, observations on the body as our means of insertion into the world, the means by which we can have a world.[28] We may detect three general forms of embodiment in her work. The first, which may be called normal, is the detailed phenomenological description of experience available to all embodied subjects. It is this fundamental ontological fact which Virginia is always seeking to clarify. It pervades each of her novels (we recall how *The Voyage Out* begins with a description of the 'body life' of the perfectly normal Helen Ridley). Even a light exercise like *Orlando* confronts the question of embodiment. The book abounds with exquisite examples of what Orlando's existence is like, and most of them operate at the level of the body.

The essays are full of observations on the body. For instance,

> Humour, after all, is closely bound up with a sense of the body. When we laugh at the humour of Wycherly, we are laughing with the body of that burly rustic who was our common ancestor on the village green.[29]

What makes Spenser a great poet, in Virginia's estimation, is that he does not exclude body experience from his work, and so achieves a more complete conception of character and life:

> the poet's body seems all alive. A fearlessness, a simplicity that is like the movement of a naked savage possesses him. He is not merely a thinking brain; he is a feeling body, a sensitive heart. He has hands and feet, and, as he says himself, a natural chastity, so that some things are judged unfit for the pen. 'My chaster muse for shame doth blush to write.' In short, when we read *The Faery Queen*, we feel that the whole being is drawn upon, not merely a separate part.[30]

And so on. There is hardly an essay, chapter in a novel, or short story which does not contain one of these phenomenological accounts. As her conception of the novel progressed, so her preoccupation with body life became more central. The most damning criticism she can make of Edward John Trelawny's *Letters* (writing to Clive Bell in 1910), is that 'The imagination is often very watery, and the strength the strength of a man of action, whose brain is a simple machine divorced from his body' (*Letters*, 1, p. 445). This becomes a neatly ironical point (the man of action, whose mind is divorced from his body) when juxtaposed against one made twelve years later, in a letter to Roger Fry. She has just read the first volume of Proust (emphatically not a 'man of action'):

> I am in a state of amazement; as if a miracle were being done before my eyes. How, at last, has someone solidified what has always escaped -- and made it too into this beautiful and perfectly enduring substance? One has to put the book down and gasp. The pleasure becomes physical — like sun and wine and grapes and perfect serenity and intense vitality combined.
>
> (*Letters*, 2, p. 566.)

In a letter to Vita Sackville-West dated 29 December 1928, she writes,

> But its true that the image of ones loves forever changes: and gradually (you know how I like noticing physical symptoms) from being a sight, becomes a sense — a heaviness betwixt the 3rd and 4th rib; a physical oppression: These are the signs writers should watch for. Love is so physical; and so's reading — the exercise of the wits.
>
> (*Letters*, 3, p. 570.)

The second mode of embodiment which Virginia describes is a borderland between the normal and pathological. This state is not 'abnormal', but it is out of the ordinary. It is perhaps best described as problematical. Many of her characters experience it momentarily, and it is safe to say that we all experience it at one time or another. It may be described as a kind of 'epiphany', often self-critical; or, it may be the result of fatigue, or slight illness. A good example may be found in *Mrs Dalloway*. Throughout the novel, Clarrissa's and Septimus's lives are contrasted. Septimus is mad, and represents an extreme pole, while Clarissa is (perhaps tediously) sane. As we shall see later in this chapter, one of the symptoms of Septimus's disorder is a highly pathological state of disembodiment, in which he not only feels that he is cut off from the world, but that he is cut off from his own body: he cannot feel. But the eminently sane Clarissa can feel that

> she had a narrow pea-stick figure; a ridiculous little face, beaked like a bird's. That she held herself well was true; and had nice hands and feet; and dressed well, considering that she spent little. But often now this body she wore (she stopped to look at a Dutch picture), this body, with all its capacities, seemed nothing — nothing at all. She had the oddest sense of being herself invisible; unseen; unknown; there being no more marrying, no more having of children now, but only this astonishing and rather solemn progress with the rest of them, up Bond Street, this being Mrs Dalloway; not even Clarissa any more; this being Mrs Richard Dalloway.[31]

It is clear what is at the bottom of this peculiar feeling. She is no longer 'Clarissa' — her identity is merged with that of her husband, whose main roles and interests are more social and political than familial. The 'no more having of children now' is to be regretted because having children and accepting the role of mother gives an identity. Richard Dalloway is either working, or involved with one of his committees, or dining with his colleagues (a life from which, for the most part, Clarissa is excluded), while Clarissa is left with time on her hands, and no clear and useful role to play. Dalloway is lunching that day with Lady Broughton, and it is the thought of Lady Bexborough, another of Dalloway's friends, which gives rise to this self-criticism. Clarissa thinks,

> Oh if she could have had her life over again! she thought, stepping on to the pavement, could have looked even differently!
> She would have been, in the first place, dark like Lady Bexborough, with a skin of crumpled leather and beautiful eyes. She would have been, like Lady Bexborough, slow and stately; rather large; interested in politics like a man; with a country house; very dignified, very sincere.

> (*MD*, p. 13.)

This is not mere vanity. Clarissa does not want to be like Lady Bexborough because she thinks Lady Bexborough instrinsically better than she; but because she knows Lady Bexborough appeals to her husband, that her husband admires her.

Finally, there are occasions on which Virginia deals with states of embodiment which are best described as dissociated, or disembodied. The best example of this is Septimus Smith in *Mrs Dalloway*. Rhoda, in *The Waves*, is another example.

Unlike *The Voyage Out*, *Night and Day* does not describe states of dissociation. Its preoccupation is with phenomenological descriptions of the normal embodiment of its characters, particularly Katherine Hilbery, and her two suitors, Ralph Denham and William Rodney. The novel's main theme is a consideration of the difficulty of knowing (and perhaps loving) another person; it is an examination of the way in which we idealize the other person, the way in which we create fantasies around him. The problem, for Ralph Denham and Katherine Hilbery, is to find the 'real' other behind the fantasy, and finally to accept that our perceptions of other people are often a mixture of the two.

The novel is concerned primarily with normal states of embodiment, but there are important passages which consider the problematical forms. For instance, at the beginning of the novel, Rodney reads a paper to a private society. The man is profoundly conscious of the awkwardness of his appearance, and realizes that it does not go unnoticed by the audience. We are told that when he enters the room, 'even the faces that were most exposed to view, and therefore most tautly under control, disclosed a sudden impulsive tremor which, unless directly checked, would have developed into an outburst of laughter'.[32] The audience, though supposedly friendly, possesses a collective streak of cruelty. Virginia describes Rodney's 'horrible discomfort under the stare of so many eyes'. She claims that the audience's desire to laugh is 'entirely lacking in malice', but that Rodney's 'impulsive stammering manner, which seemed to indicate a torrent of ideas intermittently pressing for utterance and always checked in their course by a clutch of nervousness, drew no pity' (*ND*, p. 47).

Mr Rodney was evidently so painfully conscious of the oddity of his appearance, and his very redness and the starts to which his body was liable gave such proof of his own discomfort, that there was something endearing in this ridiculous susceptibility, although most people would probably have echoed Denham's private exclamation, 'Fancy marrying a creature like that!'

(*ND*, p. 47.)

Denham, who is much more sure of himself than Rodney (his physical presence is much more imposing), is liable to experience a problematical state of embodiment. When he discovers that Katherine is engaged to Rodney his world becomes insubstantial. Katherine has come to represent an ideal for him, and the fact of her engagement to Rodney removes her from the centre of his world, a world in which she has become a unifying presence, providing purpose and cohesion. Now,

Rodney and Katherine herself seemed disembodied ghosts. He could scarcely remember the look of them. His mind plunged lower and lower. Their marriage seemed of no importance to him. All things had turned to ghosts; the whole mass of the world was insubstantial vapour, surrounding the solitary spark in his mind, whose burning point he could remember, for it burnt no more. He had once cherished a belief, and Katherine had embodied this belief, and she did so no longer. He did not blame her; he blamed nothing, nobody; he saw the truth. He saw the dun-coloured race of waters and the blank shore. But life is vigorous; the body lives, and the body, no doubt, dictated the reflection, which now urged him to movement, that one may cast away the forms of human beings, and yet retain the passion which seemed inseparable from their existence in the flesh. Now this passion burnt on his horizon, as the winter sun makes a greenish pane in the west through thinning clouds.

(*ND*, p. 146.)

Katherine too, who usually maintains a cool equanimity, is subject to the experience of her body as problematical. Depressed by the conditions in which Mary Datchet (who loves Denham) has to live, and by the apparent insolubility of her own situation, Katherine

> determined to lunch at a shop in the Strand, so as to set that other piece of mechanism, her body, into action. With a brain working and a body working one could keep step with the crowd and never be found out for the hollow machine, lacking the essential thing, that one was conscious of being.
>
> (*ND*, p. 240.)

It is clear from one of the earliest phenomenological descriptions in the novel that the problem of knowing the other is often a sexual one. Following Rodney's lecture, Katherine meets Mary Datchet. As they stand together, Katherine 'was conscious of Mary's body beside her, but, at the same time, the consciousness of being both of them women made it unnecessary to speak to her' (*ND*, p. 51). With Denham, however, things are different. Denham feels that 'the bulk of Katherine was not represented in his dreams at all, so that when he met her he was bewildered by the fact that she had nothing to do with his dream of her' (*ND*, p. 84). Virginia accentuates Katherine's inaccessibility to Denham by frequently portraying her in motion, usually walking quickly: 'She walked very fast, and the effect of people passing in the opposite direction was to produce a queer dizziness both in her head and in Ralph's, which set their bodies far apart' (*ND*, pp. 84-5). After walking together for a while, they decide to take a bus. The manner in which she leaves the bus, when they reach her stop, has a profound effect upon Denham. Katherine

> said good-bye with her usual air of decision, and left him with a quickness which Ralph connected now with all her movements. He looked down and saw her standing on the pavement edge, an alert, commanding figure, which waited its season to cross, and then walked boldly and swiftly to the other side. That gesture and action would be added to the picture he had of her, but at present the real woman completely routed the phantom one.
>
> (*ND*, pp. 86-7.)

Later, Denham is walking along the Strand on his way to a business engagement. Katherine walks quickly past, not noticing him, but the effect upon Denham is remarkable. Before he sees her, he is looking in shop windows:

> None of these different objects was seen separately by Denham, but from all of them he drew an impression of stir and cheerfulness. Thus it came about that he saw Katherine Hilbery coming towards him, and looked straight at her, as if she were only an illustration of the argument that was going forward in his mind. In this spirit he noticed the rather set expression in her eyes, and the slight, half-conscious movement of her lips, which, together with her height and the distinction of her dress, made her look as if the scurrying crowd impeded her, and her direction were different from theirs. He noticed this calmly; but suddenly, as he passed her, his hands and knees began to tremble, and his heart beat painfully. She did not see him, and went on repeating to herself some lines which had stuck to her memory: 'It's life that matters, nothing but life — the process of discovering — the everlasting and perpetual process, not the discovery itself at all.' Thus occupied, she did not see Denham, and he had not the courage to stop her. But immediately the whole scene in the Strand wore that curious look of order and purpose which is imparted to the most heterogeneous things when music sounds . . .
>
> (ND, pp. 119-20.)

This extraordinary final sentence points to the nature of the relationship between Katherine and Denham. It is true that each individual consciousness, through the act of perception, imposes order and unity upon the 'heterogeneous things' of the external world. But that ability to order the world can cause a fundamental cleavage between individuals. Each individual's world is uniquely his own (despite our mutually agreed points of reference), and his point of view is the result of his own unique embodiment, and the perceptual powers and personal history which he brings to each act of perception. Yet the sympathy between Denham and Katherine is potentially so great that her mere presence can order his world. This is the basis of intersubjectivity.

But while Denham has his fantasies and his occasional glimpses of the real Katherine, she herself inhabits a different, private world to which Denham has not access. In her spare time she studies mathematics for pleasure. She likes the impersonality and order of the subject, which contrasts so sharply with the difficulties and seeming disorder of her personal life. The effect of her studies, however, is not wholly positive, for it underlines a split in her being, and suggests that she is refusing to confront the questions and situations which complicate her life. As they walk along the embankment, Katherine thinks she

> was feeling happier than she had felt in her life. If Denham could have seen how visibly books of algebraic symbols, pages all speckled with dots and dashes and twisted bars, came before her eyes as they trod the Embankment, his secret joy in her attention might have been dispersed.
>
> (*ND*, pp. 278-9.)

She carries on a conversation with Denham, but

> all the time she was in fancy looking up through a telescope at white shadow-cleft discs which were other worlds, until she felt herself possessed of two bodies, one walking by the river with Denham, the other concentrated to a silver globe aloft in the fine blue space above the scum of vapours that was covering the visible world.
>
> (*ND*, p. 279.)

Here, the possibilities for a genuine shared existence that were hinted when Denham observed Katherine walking in the Strand are threatened. While Katherine is dreaming of algebraic symbols and stars, Denham experiences her as a fusion of dream and reality:

> Since they had stopped talking, she had become to him not so much a real person, as the very woman he dreamt of; but his solitary dreams had never produced any such keenness of sensation as that which he felt in her presence. He himself was also strangely transfigured. He had complete mastery of all his faculties. For the first time he

was in possession of his full powers.

(*ND*, pp. 279-80.)

For Denham, Katherine cannot exist purely as a dream, or purely as a real presence. Paradoxically, she becomes the woman he dreams of when she is present. Both Katherine and Denham experience these feelings as they walk along in silence. When they finally speak, the mood is broken, and there is a crisis:

> He was now conscious of the loss that follows any revela-
> tion; he had lost something in speaking to Katherine, for,
> after all, was the Katherine whom he loved the same as the
> real Katherine? She had transcended her entirely at
> moments; her skirt had blown, her feather waved, her
> voice spoken; yes, but how terrible sometimes the pause
> between the voice of one's dreams and the voice that
> comes from the object of one's dreams!
>
> (*ND*, p. 281.)

Against the exultation experienced by Denham as he sees Katherine in the Strand must be juxtaposed this paradoxical truth that, when they are together, they can seem further apart than when each considers the other in solitude. Denham feels, 'one's voyage must be made absolutely without companions through ice and black water' (*ND*, p. 305).

In the end, Katherine succumbs to Denham's love. She tells him the secret of her passion for mathematics, but his fantasy remains. They accept that their alliance must be based on this, half real, half dream. 'She had now to get used to the fact that some one shared her loneliness' (*ND*, p. 457). Touching his arm, she thinks, 'What a fire! ... She thought of him blazing splendidly in the night, yet so obscure that to hold his arm, as she held it, was only to touch the opaque substance surrounding the flame that roared upwards' (*ND*, p. 467). The conclusion is not ideal, but it is not a retreat into solipsism. 'Together they groped in this difficult region, where the unfinished, the unfulfilled, the unwritten, the un-returned, came together in their ghostly way and wore the semblance of the complete and the satisfactory' (*ND*, p. 470).

In *Mrs Dalloway*, Virginia presents one of the most sustained and convincing accounts of disembodiment in literature. Septimus Warren Smith, who has come back from the Great War a broken man, is introduced to us walking with his wife, Lucrezia. His strange behaviour causes her to think she 'must take him away into some park' (*MD*, p. 19). As they cross the street, the fact of Septimus's disembodiment is made perfectly clear: 'She had a right to his arm, though it was without feeling. He would give her, who was so simple, so impulsive, only twenty-four, without friends in England, who had left Italy for his sake, a piece of bone' (*MD*, p. 19). Septimus's body, like Rachel's during the final stage of her illness, has passed into the realm of objects. It has for him the quality of 'otherness'. It is not his, he does not live in it. He is incapable of feeling. This is the meaning of disembodiment.

Septimus's personality is dis-integrated. His body is not the firm centre of consciousness. His self, instead of being concentrated in and identified with his body, is diffused throughout the external world:

> leaves were alive: trees were alive. And the leaves being connected by millions of fibres with his own body, there on the seat, fanned it up and down; when the branch stretched he, too, made that statement. The sparrows fluttering, rising, and falling in jagged fountains were part of the pattern; the white and blue, barred with black branches. Sounds made harmonies with premeditation; the spaces between them were as significant as the sounds. A child cried. Rightly far away a horn sounded. All taken together meant the birth of a new religion —
>
> (*MD*, p. 26.)

We are told that, for Septimus, 'Scientifically speaking, the flesh was melted off the world. His body was macerated until only the nerve fibres were left. It was spread like a veil upon a rock' (*MD*, p. 76). Septimus experiences the world as if from behind a pane of glass. And while his condition allows for some extraordinary perceptions, Septimus remains at a distance from them. He regards his own experience as one looks at a film, or hears a description of another's experience:

The earth thrilled beneath him. Red flowers grew through his flesh; their stiff leaves rustled by his head. Music began clanging against the rocks up here. It is a motor horn down in the street, he muttered; but up here it cannoned from rock to rock, divided, met in shocks of sound which rose in smooth columns (that music should be visible was a discovery) and became an anthem, an anthem twined round now by a shepherd boy's piping. (That's an old man playing a penny whistle by the public-house, he muttered) which, as the boy stood still, came bubbling from his pipe, and then, as he climbed higher, made its exquisite plaint while the traffic passed beneath. This boy's elegy is played among the traffic, though Septimus. Now he withdraws up into the snows, and roses hang about him ‐ ‐ the thick red roses which grow on my bedroom wall, he reminded himself. The music stopped. He has his penny, he reasoned it out, and has gone on to the next public-house.

But he himself remained high on his rock, like a drowned sailor on a rock.

(MD, pp. 76-7.)

Unlike the previous description, in which experience seemed to be taking place outside of Septimus's body, in the world of objects, it is now internalized: 'The red flowers grew through his flesh.' But Septimus does not have access to this, for he remains, as William Golding's Pincher Martin does, 'like a drowned sailor on a rock'.

Clarissa and Septimus are presented as a complementary pair of characters. Septimus is clearly meant to be severely disturbed, and Clarissa is the epitome of the upper-middle-class, middle-aged housewife, of normality. Yet, as we saw in her judgement of herself as she thought about Lady Bexborough while walking in Bond Street, she is subject to experiences of her body which are problematical. When she returns home after shopping,

she thought, feeling herself suddenly shrivelled, aged, breast-less, the grinding, blowing, flowering of the day, out of doors, out of the window, out of her body and brain which now failed, since Lady Bruton, whose lunch parties were said to be extraordinarily amusing, had not asked her.

(MD, p. 35.)

Underlying this critical and detached attitude toward her self and her body is a vague sexual insecurity. This is brought to the fore as Peter Walsh, an old suitor, returns from India to visit her. And at the back of her mind, her husband's neglect of her is compared with the serene intimacy she felt in her relationship with Sally Seton when she was a young woman. As she contemplates her situation (feeling 'shrivelled, aged, breastless'), Clarissa comes close to some understanding, and the moment reaches a climax of great physical intensity, in which her thoughts assume a tangible presence:

Lovely in girlhood, suddenly there came a moment — for example on the river beneath the woods at Clieveden — when, through some contraction of this cold spirit, she had failed him. And then at Constantinople, and again and again. She could see what she lacked. It was not beauty; it was not mind. It was something central which permeated; something warm which broke up surfaces and rippled the cold contact of man and woman, or of women together. For *that* she could dimly perceive. She resented it, had a scruple picked up Heaven knows where, or, as she felt, sent by Nature (who is invariably wise); yet she còuld not resist sometimes yielding to the charm of a woman, not a girl, of a woman confessing, as to her they often did, some scrape, some folly. And whether it was pity, or their beauty, or that she was older, or some accident — like a faint scent, or a violin next door (so strange is the power of sounds at certain moments), she did undoubtedly then feel what men felt. Only for a moment; but it was enough. It was a sudden revelation, a tinge like a blush which one tried to check and then, as it spread, one yielded to its expansion, and rushed to the farthest verge and there quivered and felt the world come closer, swollen with some astonishing significance, some pressure of rapture, which split its thin skin and gushed and poured with an extraordinary alleviation over the cracks and sores. Then, for that moment, she had seen an illumination; a match burning in a crocus; an inner meaning almost expressed. But the close withdrew; the hard softened. It was over — the moment.

(*MD*, p. 36.)

These reflections of her sexual insecurity (or ambivalence), and the abrasive manner in which her relationship with Sally Seton was cut short by Peter Walsh ('It was like running one's face against a granite wall in the darkness! It was shocking; it was horrible!' (*MD*, p. 41), give way to a calm feeling as she sews her dress. Clarissa's needle and thread become a symbol of female constructiveness (which is contrasted throughout the novel by the aggressive Peter Walsh, who constantly fingers his pocket knife), and peace is restored to the body:

> Quiet descended on her, calm, content, as her needle, drawing the silk smoothly to its gentle pause, collected the green folds together and attached them, very lightly, to the belt. So on a summer's day waves collect, over-balance, and fall; collect and fall; and the whole world seems to be saying 'that is all' more and more ponderously, until even the heart in the body which lies in the sun on the beach says too, that is all. Fear no more, says the heart. Fear no more, says the heart, committing its burden to some sea, which sighs collectively for all sorrows, and renews, begins, collects, lets fall. And the body alone listens to the passing bee; the wave breaking; the dog barking, far away barking and barking.
>
> (*MD*, pp. 44-5.)

In *The Waves*, descriptions of embodiment comprise one of the main vehicles for characterization. Minute attention is paid to the peculiar experiences that each of the six characters has of his or her body. Bernard and Susan represent poles of normality. Louis and Neville have problematical experiences of their bodies, while Rhoda feels herself to be disembodied. Jinny, the seductive one, the one who is successful in the great world of ballrooms and restaurants, poses something of a dilemma. It is true that she, being beautiful, does not suffer from the looks of others as, say, Rhoda does. Rather, she suffers if the others *don't* look. But there is no question of Jinny's body not being accepted. On her way home from school, for the summer holidays, she is sitting in a train going north:

The gentleman pulls up the window. I see reflections on the shining glass which lines the tunnel. I see him lower his paper. He smiles at my reflection in the tunnel. My body instantly of its own accord puts forth a frill under his gaze. My body lives a life of its own. Now the black window glass is green again. We are out of the tunnel. He reads his paper. But we have exchanged the approval of our bodies. There is then a great society of bodies, and mine is introduced; mine has come into the room where the gilt chairs are.[33]

She is always in complete control of her body: 'I meet the eyes of a sour woman, who suspects me of rapture. My body shuts in her face, impertinently, like a parasol. I open my body, I shut my body at will' (TW, p. 54). Yet, throughout her life, Jinny can never for a moment forget this superiority, this place among the elect. She is always considering herself, how she looks, how she will impress others. She is always self-conscious. While her experience is the inverse of Rhoda's (and, to some extent, of Louis's and Neville's), it is also dissimilar to that of Susan and Bernard, and does not fall neatly into one of our three categories.

It is Rhoda whose experience of her body is so painful as to be an impediment to any form of personal security or social competence. Not sure of her own self, she is ontologically insecure in the way that Rachel is. As a child, she tries to assume the identities of others, but fails:

'As I fold up my frock and my chemise,' said Rhoda, 'so I put off my hopeless desire to be Susan, to be Jinny. But I will stretch my toes so that they touch the rail at the end of the bed; I will assure myself, touching the rail, of something hard. Now I cannot sink . . .'[34]

(TW, p. 22.)

By touching the bedrail with her toes, Rhoda tries to focus her experience of herself within her body; she tries to call herself back to it. She thinks, 'Now I cannot sink; cannot altogether fall through the thin sheet now' (TW, p. 22). But it is no use. As she spreads herself out on her bed, trying to stay together, she fails. She experiences her self as divorced from her body:

> Now I spread my body on this frail mattress and hang
> suspended. I am above the earth now. I am no longer up-
> right, to be knocked against and damaged. All is soft,
> and bending. Walls and cupboards whiten and bend their
> yellow squares on top of which a pale glass gleams. *Out of
> me now my mind can pour. I can think of my Armadas
> sailing on the high waves. I am relieved of hard contacts
> and collisions. I sail on alone under white cliffs. Oh, but
> I sink, I fall!*
>
> (TW, p. 22, my italics.)

The core of what Rhoda feels to be her true self is located
outside her body. Like Rachel, she puts herself out to sea,
identifying physically with waves in an effort to avoid the
unpleasant interpersonal collisions for which she is not
prepared, because she lacks a secure sense of her body as
the vehicle by means of which her true self may be inserted
into the world. As she falls asleep, her experience is described
in terms virtually identical to those used to describe Rachel's
dreams and hallucinations:

> Let me pull myself out of these waters. But they heap
> themselves on me; they sweep me between their great
> shoulders; I am turned; I am tumbled; I am stretched,
> among these long lights, these long waves, these endless
> paths, with people pursuing, pursuing.
>
> (TW, p. 23.)

Her existence is negated. Looking over Susan's shoulder into
a mirror, Rhoda thinks, 'that face is my face. But I will
duck behind her to hide it, for I am not here. I have no face'
(*TW*, p. 35). She thinks, other people 'know what to say if
spoken to. They laugh really; they get angry really; while
I have to look first and do what other people do when they
have done it' (*TW*, p. 36). Rhoda suffers from what Laing
(following Sartre) calls an alterated personality. She doesn't
experience the negation that gives us identity, the understanding that I am what I am not (that is, other people),
and I am not what I am (that is, the other's necessarily

limited perception of me). She is what others decide her to be, or she is what she thinks they would like her to be. She says, 'I leap high to excite their admiration. At night, in bed, I excite their complete wonder. I often die pierced with arrows to win their tears' (*TW*, p. 36). All of Rhoda's successes are short-lived, existing only for the brief moment in which she is experienced by someone else. 'Alone, I often fall down into nothingness', she thinks. She is disembodied: 'I have to bang my head against some hard door to call myself back to the body' (*TW*, p. 37).

The presentation of Neville's embodiment begins with his traumatic experience as a child of overhearing the cook say that a man had been found in the gutter with his throat cut:

> He was found with his throat cut. The apple-tree leaves became fixed in the sky; the moon glared; I was unable to lift my foot up the stair. He was found in the gutter. His blood gurgled down the gutter. His jowl was white as a dead codfish. I shall call this stricture, this rigidity, 'death among the apple trees' for ever.
>
> (*TW*, p. 20.)

This experience is significant for Neville because it seems to bar him from further experience. Time, which is experienced via the body, ceases for Neville: he cannot pass.[35] He suffers a temporal paralysis similar to that experienced by Rachel in *The Voyage Out*, when she considers her body in the context of her relation to her mother and her wakening sexuality. Neville thinks, 'the ripple of my life was unavailing. I was unable to pass by' (*TW*, p. 20). There is a sense of horror which is compounded by the fact that this is not an experience which impedes because it is buried in the unconscious; rather, it is brash, remaining in full view at all times, doing its work defiantly. Neville's consciousness of it does nothing to dispel it or to prevent its effect on him. And Neville suggests that this is not a pathological condition, but one shared, in some form, by all of us, that we all have our own apple tree: 'But we are all doomed, all of us, by the apple trees, by the immitigable tree which we cannot pass' (*TW*, p. 20).

Neville does not have an unproblematical sense of his body as do Susan and Bernard, nor does he belong to the aristocracy of bodies as Jinny does. Still less does he experience the profound sense of disembodiment that Rhoda does. Neville's body and self are firmly intact, yet the unity is, for him, an occasion for pain. When Bernard is going through his Byronic phase — greasy handkerchief, yellow gloves, cloak and cane — Neville pays him a visit. Neville thinks, ' "I am one person — myself. I do not impersonate Catullus, whom I adore" ' (*TW*, p. 74). Yet that one person whom Neville knows himself to be is intolerable to him:

> while you gesticulate, with your cloak, your cane, I am trying to expose a secret told to nobody yet; I am asking you (as I stand with my back to you) to take my life in your hands and tell me whether I am doomed always to cause repulsion in those I love.
>
> (*TW*, p. 75.)

Having arrived early at the farewell dinner so he can sit next to Percival, whom he loves, Neville thinks, after watching Jinny's grand entrance, her body demanding and getting attention and admiration,

> I shall have riches, I shall have fame. But I shall never have what I want, for I lack bodily grace and the courage that comes with it. The swiftness of my mind is too strong for my body. I fail before I reach the end and fall in a heap, damp, perhaps disgusting. I excite pity in the crises of life, not love. Therefore I suffer horribly.
>
> (*TW*, p. 110.)

Neville's body (he is hoplessly in love, for it is unlikely that Percival would ever notice, much less return, Neville's love for him) is not merely a symbol of failure, it *is* that failure. The awkward, pathetic, damp heap that is his body is inescapably what it is — and that is a constant source of pain for Neville. By admiring the classical form (which Percival embodies for him), Neville tries to relieve, for a moment, his damp, disgusting existence. Considering himself repulsive in body, Neville is intent upon enforcing order and beauty around him by way of compensation. 'Everything must be done to rebuke the horror of deformity', he declares (*TW*, p. 154). 'One must slip paper-knives, even, exactly through the pages of novels, and tie up packets of letters neatly with green silk, and brush up the cinders with a hearth broom' (*TW*, p. 154). Neville possesses extraordinary courage, for in spite of the fact that he is the antithesis of beauty (or that he sees himself in this way), he neither shuns nor covets beauty. He is not jealous, he merely accepts. He is not blind to his own body, repulsive as he feels it to be, and he remains open to the bodies of others, particularly Percival's. And perhaps it is Neville's suffering that enables him to read with precision the body of Percival, who is so different from himself. Neville's place is in the library, Percival's on the playing field. Neville can admit these two antithetical types (which are perhaps akin to the Apollonian and Dionysian) in his universe, and let them rest side by side. It is Neville's openness to Percival's body that can recognize that Percival is 'removed from us all in a pagan universe':

> But look — he flicks his hand to the back of his neck. For such gestures one falls hopelessly in love for a life-time. Dalton, Jones, Edgar and Bateman flick their hands to the backs of their necks likewise. But they do not succeed.
>
> (*TW*, p. 30.)

It is by recognizing the entire person unfolded in the slightest gesture that Jacob learned to love Florinda in *Jacob's Room*.[36] And Neville realizes, as Jacob did in his way, 'it is Percival I need: for it is Percival who inspires poetry' (*TW*, p. 33).

But of all the characters in *The Waves*, it is Louis who formulates precisely the nature of the difficulty of self and other, consciousness and object, as experienced via the body. In Louis, the imaginary and the real are well mixed: ' "I begin to wish," said Louis, "for night to come. As I stand here with my hand on the grained oak panel of Mr Wickham's door" ' — in other words, confronting hard, solid reality. He says, in the same sentence, ' "I think myself the friend of Richelieu, or the Duke of St Simon holding out a snuff-box to the king himself. It is my privilege" ' (*TW*, p. 44). Confronting the great oak door, Louis fantasizes, and his fantasy and the door complement one another, each keeping the other in check (as in the economy of Denham's perception of Katherine Hilbery in *Night and Day*). Yet, for a moment, the imaginary almost succeeds in obliterating the real entirely. Louis is transported from the world of his school to that of Louis XIII:

> My witticisms 'run like wildfire through the court'. Duchesses tear emeralds from their ear-rings out of admiration — but these rockets rise best in darkness, in my cubicle at night. I am now a boy only with a colonial accent holding my knuckles against Mr Wickham's grained oak door. The day has been full of ignominies and triumphs concealed from fear of laughter. I am the best scholar in the school. But when darkness comes, I put off this unenviable body — my large nose, my thin lips, my colonial accent — and inhabit space. I am then Virgil's companion, and Plato's.
>
> (*TW*, p. 44.)

This 'putting off' of an unenviable body is not pathological — it cannot be compared to Rhoda's disembodiment. Rather, it is a yearning for pure, spiritual knowledge. This ideal yearning is expressed in *Jacob's Room*:

> 'Ja-cob! Ja-cob!' shouted Archer, lagging on after a second.
> The voice had an extraordinary sadness. Pure from all body, pure from all passion, going out into the world, solitary, unanswered, breaking against rocks — so it sounded.
>
> (*JR*, p. 7.)

In *Night and Day*, when Denham visits Mary Datchet in Lincolnshire, he reflects,

> Never are voices so beautiful as on a winter's evening, when dusk almost hides the body, and they seem to issue

from nothingness with a note of intimacy seldom heard by day. Such an edge was there in Mary's voice when she greeted him.

(ND, p. 171.)

Conrad assigns this almost mystical quality to the voice of Kurtz in *Heart of Darkness*.

Yet this is only a dream. 'I exist only in the soles of my feet and in the tired muscles of my thighs', says Bernard (*TW*, p. 202). Louis thinks,

> But my body passes vagrant as a bird's shadow. I should be transient as the shadow on the meadow, soon fading, soon darkening and dying there where it meets the wood, *were it not that I coerce my brain to form in my fore-head*; I force myself to state, if only in one line of un-written poetry, this moment; to mark this inch in the long-long history that began in Egypt, in the time of the Pharoahs, when woman carried red pitchers to the Nile. I seem already to have lived many thousand years. But if I now shut my eyes, *if I fail to realise the meeting-place of past and present, that I sit in a third-class railway carriage full of boys going home for the holidays, human history is defrauded of a moment's vision.* Its eye, that would see through me, shuts — if I sleep now, through slovenliness or cowardice, burying myself in the past, in the dark . . .

(TW, p. 56, my italics.)

Louis's life is a quest for a balance between the imaginary and the spiritual on the one hand, and the physical on the other. In his imagination, Louis thinks,

> I am then Virgil's companion, and Plato's. I am then the last scion of one of the great houses of France. But I am also one who will force himself to desert these windy and moonlit territories, these midnight wanderings, and con-front grained oak doors. I will achieve in my life — Heaven grant that it be not long — some gigantic amalgamation between the two discrepancies so hideously apparent to me. Out of my suffering I will do it. I will knock. I will enter.

(TW, p. 44.)

Such an amalgamation can only be effected through the body: for it is the body which is 'the meeting place between past and present'.

Later in the novel, Louis views life in terms of orality: 'Life has been a terrible affair for me. I am like some vast sucker, some glutinous, some adhesive, some insatiable mouth. I have tried to draw from the living flesh the stone lodged at the centre' (*TW*, p. 173). In the next chapter, I will examine the significance of food and eating in Virginia's treatment of the problem of embodiment.

2
The Problem of Food

A fundamental part of the problem of embodiment, both in Virginia's novels and in her life, is the significance which she attached to food and eating. All readers of the novels are aware that some of the most outstanding passages in them are concerned with this subject, and that they play an important structural and thematic role. One thinks immediately of the dinner scene in *To The Lighthouse*, during which Mrs Ramsay brings together her disparate group of guests. That dinner is one of the means by which Mrs Ramsay exercises her extraordinary talent for creating unity, and it is significant that Lily Briscoe discovers the secret of her painting during it. One also thinks of the dinner scenes in *The Waves*, one to mark Percival's leaving, and the other a reunion of old friends after his death. Almost every novel contains an important section to do with food or eating.

But the real importance of the food theme is to be found in the life of Virginia. It is inextricably bound up with her sense of her body, and an understanding of its significance for her helps the reader to understand aspects of her behaviour that have caused some observers to label her mad.

Food is an important sub-theme of the Bell biography, Leonard's autobiography and of Virginia's letters and diary. Bell tells us that during Virginia's 1904 illness (during which she was nursed by Violet Dickinson), 'she heard voices urging her to acts of folly; she believed that they came from overeating and that she must starve herself' (Bell, 1, p. 89). During the 1913-14 illness, Bell tells us, Virginia again refused to eat. 'She became convinced that her body was in some way monstrous, the sordid mouth and sordid belly demanding food — repulsive matter which must then be excreted in a disgusting fashion; the only course was to refuse to eat' (Bell, 2, p. 15). Clive Bell wrote to Molly MacCarthy that Virginia was 'intractable about food — the key to the situation so they say' (Bell, 2, p. 17). In relating this information, Quentin Bell poses a serious problem, but neglects to point up its essential nature, or to attempt an explanation. Towards the end of his biography he takes up the food problem for the last time, and so dismisses it:

> Virginia was always critical of her friends' behaviour at table. Her sensitivity on this point was perhaps connected with her own phobias about eating, phobias which, when she was ill, could make her starve herself and, at ordinary times, made her always very reluctant to take a second helping of anything. George Duckworth, Julian Bell, Kingsley Martin were all, at various times, severely condemned for eating with too little grace and too much enthusiasm. From this we may perhaps conclude that Virginia's condemnation of Ethel [Smyth] was not wholly rational.
>
> (Bell, 2, p. 170.)

Reducing Virginia's complicated situation with regard to this subject to a question of table manners is to trivialize the question. Bell reduces what is fundamentally an ontological question, first to a social one, and then to a psychiatric one. But what do we mean when we say that it is an ontological question? To answer this we must solicit the views of Leonard Woolf. Leonard has written that 'Virginia had a great love of ordinary things, of eating.'[1] But he has also said that

> one of the most troublesome symptoms of her breakdowns was a refusal to eat. In the worst period of the depressive stage, for weeks almost at every meal one had to sit, often for an hour or more, trying to induce her to eat a few mouthfuls. What made one despair was that by not eating and weakening herself she was doing precisely the thing calculated to prolong the breakdown, for it was only by building up her bodily strength and by resting

that she could regain mental equilibrium. Deep down
this refusal to eat was connected with some strange feeling
of guilt: she would maintain that she was not ill, that her
mental condition was due to her own fault — laziness,
inanition, gluttony. This was her attitude to food when she
was in the depths of the depressive stage of her insanity.
But something of this attitude remained with her always,
even when she appeared to have completely recovered.
It was always extremely difficult to induce her to eat
enough food to keep her well. Every doctor whom we
consulted told her that to eat well and drink two or
three glasses of milk every day was essential if she was to
remain well and keep off the initial symptoms which were
the danger signals of an approaching breakdown. Everything which I observed between 1912 and 1941 confirmed
their diagnosis. But I do not think that she ever accepted
it. Left to herself, she ate extraordinarily little and it was
with the greatest difficulty that she could be induced to
drink a glass of milk regularly every day. It was a perpetual,
and only partially successful, struggle; *our quarrels and
arguments were rare and almost always about eating or
resting*. And if the argument became heated, even when
she was apparently quite well, in a mild, vague form the
delusions seemed to rise again to the surface of her mind.
Her hostility to the doctors and nurses which was very
marked during the breakdowns would reappear. She
would argue as if she had never been ill — that the whole
treatment had been wrong, that she ate too much and lived
a life too lethargic and quiet. Below the surface of her
mind and of her argument there was, I felt, some strange
irrational sense of guilt.[2]

Clearly, something is very wrong here. Yet, the trouble with
eating seems to be very much related to Leonard Woolf and
the doctors — to their presences as stern disciplinarians who,
like Elizabeth Barrett's father (as he is portrayed in *Flush*)
would intrude into his daughter's bedroom demanding to
see what was left on her plate; had she eaten all of it? Food
begins to lose its taste, and assume a symbolic meaning
which is associated with male aggression and a blind enforcing of 'empirical method'.[3] When food is mentioned
in a context other than its being administered by Leonard,

we see a completely different Virginia. In a letter to Jacques Raverat, Virginia tells him that Clive Bell's mistress, Mary Hutchinson,

> has a ship's steward to serve at table, and whether for this reason or another provides the most spicy liquors, foods, cocktails and so on — for example an enormous earthenware dish, last time I was there, garnished with every vegetable, in January — peas, greens, mushrooms, potatoes; and in the middle the tenderest cutlets, all brewed in a sweet stinging aphrodisiac sauce. I tell you, I could hardly waddle home . . .
>
> (Letters, 3, p. 164.)

In 1925 she wrote to Lytton Strachey, 'I have been spending 10 days there [with the Keynes's], blasted by dissipation and headache. When I was at my worst, Leonard made me eat an entire cold duck, and, for the first and only time in my life, I was sick! What a hideous and awful experience!' (*Letters*, 3, p. 206). It will become clear that the food problem has an important sexual component. To understand this we need to turn to the events of 1913 from 23 August to 8 September.

During this time, Leonard and Virginia were on holiday at the Plough Inn, Holford. Leonard says in his autobiography that he knew the innkeeper well, as 'I had stayed there before.'[4] What Leonard neglects to mention is that this previous occasion was in 1912, at the beginning of their honeymoon. Leonard writes little of the honeymoon. Sexually, they were incompatible from the beginning.[5] Virginia's letters from Holford in 1912 refer to her marriage in a mannered way which contains nothing of the excitement of a honeymoon: 'we are both as happy as we can be — at least I am — I suppose one oughtn't to say that of ones husband — but I think we do get an enormous amount of pleasure out of being together' (*Letters*, 2, p. 3). The hyperbole is qualified and reluctant. The letter is a mere formality.[6]

Virginia's health declined steadily throughout the first year of her marriage. The event which triggered her suicide attempt of 1913 was their return to the Plough Inn a year and ten days after the honeymoon.

During the last week of July and the first week of August 1913, Virginia was a patient at Burley, the Twickenham nursing home run by Jean Thomas. Virginia found the home loathsome. The letters which survive this period are among the few she ever wrote to Leonard, and are evidence of the misery and hopelessness to which she was reduced during the first year of their marriage.[7] She was considered all the more mad because she would not 'behave': 'I've not been very good I'm afraid — ', she writes, 'but I do think it will be better when we're together' (*Letters*, 2, p. 33). She is reduced to childlike apology to ensure that her stay at Burley will be as short as possible.

Having endured a fortnight there, Virginia was then taken to Holford, a place saturated with unpleasant associations. It is significant that, in describing their return visit to Holford, Leonard's most vivid memories are of the food to be had there. Instead of reminiscing on the joys of the first days of marriage, Leonard talks of

> the most English of English food which could hold its own with the best cuisine in the world, but which people who for the past 150 years have despised all English cooking have never heard of. Nothing could be better than the bread, butter, cream and eggs and bacon of the Somersetshire breakfast with which you began your morning. The beef, mutton, and lamb were always magnificent and perfectly cooked; enormous hams, cured by themselves and hanging from the rafters in the kitchen, were so perfect that for years we used to have them sent to us from time to time and find them as good or better than the peachfed Virginian hams which one used to buy for vast sums from Fortnum and Mason. As for the drink that they offered you, I do not say that you could compare it with, say, Ch. Margaux or La Romanée-Conti or Deidesheimer Kieselberg Riesling Trockenbeerenauslese, but they gave you beer and cider which only a narrow minded, finicky drinker would fail to find delicious.[8]

When the innkeeper and his wife 'saw what state Virginia was in ... they behaved with the greatest kindness, sensitivity, and consideration.'[9] This 'special treatment' no doubt increased

Virginia's anxiety and contributed to her feeling that there
was a conspiracy afoot, a feeling which continued to grow
after her suicide attempt of 1913.

Among Leonard's unpublished papers at Sussex University
Library are a series of letters to and from Dr Miyeko Kamiya,
a Japanese psychiatrist who planned to write a psychological
study of Virginia.[10] In his first letter to Dr Kamiya, Leonard
singles out food as an important factor in such a study. He
makes his point by drawing a parallel between Jane Austen
and Virginia. He mentions that in *Pride and Prejudice* and in
Emma, the heroine is completely mistaken about some
important personal question, though in the end she sees her
mistake and finds happiness. Leonard believes that these
characters are Jane Austen herself — that she unconsciously
worked out her own problems through writing. According to
Leonard, the ultimate successes of Jane Austen's heroines
are compensations for the writer's failure in real life. Leonard
finds a parallel in Virginia's life and work with regard to
food. When she was insane, he says, she refused to eat. But
when she was well, she still had a curious complex about
food. Leonard says that he always found it difficult to get
her to eat enough to keep well, and he notes that food
plays an important role in her books, particularly *To The
Lighthouse*, and *A Room of One's Own*. He maintains that
the admission of a fondness for food (and a recognition of
its importance) in the fiction is by way of compensation
for the irrational rejection of food in real life. Dr Kamiya
replied that Virginia was probably suffering from *anorexia
nervosa*.[11] But to accept this diagnosis would be to confuse
the issue. In Virginia's case, the significance of the problem
is existential, sexual, ontological. This by no means reduces
its seriousness from the medical point of view, but the prevailing medical definition of *anorexia* is not sufficient to
include the real issues behind Virginia's refusal to eat.
According to a current definition,

> the sufferer, usually a young woman, sleeps little, eats
> almost nothing, but is constantly exerting energy upon
> some favourite pursuit; this condition is very liable to end
> in total nervous breakdown. Many of these young women

have developed a phobia about putting on weight, and a severe psychological disorder underlies the physical condition. Treatment is difficult, and usually consists of psychotherapy combined with a tranquilizer such as chlorpromazine.[12]

Peter Lomas, a psychotherapist and author of the excellent study, *True and False Experience*, writes that *anorexia* is 'a condition in which the patient suffers complete loss of appetite and, if female (which is typical of the disease) ceases to menstruate'.[13] Evidence cited by Spater and Parsons might seem to support the diagnosis of *anorexia*. They write, 'in 1913 there was a 98 day interval between periods (from August 6 to November 12) when Virginia's weight fell to its lowest recorded level. Virginia was then extremely ill and under the care of four nurses. There is no indication that she was pregnant.'[14] Spater and Parsons do not introduce the diagnosis of *anorexia nervosa*, but they write, 'Today it is well recognised that there is a direct relationship between weight and menstruation, and that rejection of food may be a sign of sexual conflict — i.e. a rejection of femininity.'[15] Without doubt, there is evidence of a sexual conflict. But this does not involve a rejection of her own femininity —although within strict qualifications this might be argued. We must remember that, even in her flirtations with various women, and in her affair with Vita Sackville-West, Virginia did not reject her 'femininity'. Her letters to Vita are often concerned with buying clothes, new ways of doing her hair, ways in which she can make herself more feminine and attractive. What is more probable is that she is rejecting *male* sexuality, or its effect on her.[16] Lomas notes that: 'Eating comes into the area of sexuality once it is linked, in a woman's mind, with the attempt to mould her figure into a desirable shape. If one recognises the over-simplification, anorexia nervosa can be thought of as a malignant form of dieting.'[17] What Lomas is speaking of is the appropriation of the body by others, and the making of a false self from which the true self feels divorced. The concern to adopt a body which is socially acceptable (in a woman's case, slim, or even skinny) is a widespread one in contemporary Western society. It is a fashion, just as the fashion for plumper women marked an earlier age in art and fashion. But the explanation for Virginia's condition is not to be found in a broad social perspective, but in a unique personal one. Virginia's refusal to eat must be understood by a methodology similar to that employed by Merleau-Ponty in the following brief case history:

> A girl whose mother has forbidden her to see again the young man with whom she is in love, cannot sleep, loses her appetite and finally the use of speech. An initial mani- festation of this loss of speech is found to have occurred during her childhood, after an earthquake, and subse- quently again after a severe fright. A strictly Freudian interpretation of this would introduce a reference to the oral phase of sexual development. But what is 'fixated' on the mouth is not merely sexual existence, but, more generally, those relations with others having the spoken word as their vehicle. In so far as the emotion elects to find its expression in loss of speech, this is because of all bodily functions speech is the most intimately linked with communal existence, or, as we shall put it, with co- existence. Loss of speech, then, stands for the refusal of co-existence, just as, in other subjects, a fit of hysterics is the means of escaping from the situation. The patient breaks with relational life within the family circle. More generally, she tends to break with life itself: *her inability to swallow food arises from the fact that swallowing symbolizes the movement of existence which carries events and assimilates them; the patient is unable, literally, to 'swallow' the prohibition which has been imposed upon her.*[18]

Merleau-Ponty continues, 'Loss of voice does not merely represent a refusal of speech, or anorexia a refusal of life; *they are that refusal* of others or refusal of the future, torn from the transitive nature of 'inner phenomena', generalized, consummated, transformed into *de facto* situations.'[19] What is Virginia rejecting when she refuses food? Roger Poole maintains that Virginia's refusal of food is a result of her belief that 'full bellies' mean 'dull minds'. She was worried 'about the possibility of becoming fat, obese, gross and therefore . . . stupid.'[20] This may be so, but the analysis seems general rather than specific. In his autobiography, Roland Barthes includes a photograph of himself, with a caption which begins, 'Sudden mutation of the body (after leaving the sanatorium): changing (or appearing to change) from slender to plump. Ever since, perpetual struggle with this body to return it to its essential slenderness . . .' Barthes concludes this reflection with the parenthetical aside, '(part of the intellectual's mythology: to become thin is the naive act of the will-to-intelligence)'.[21] It may well be that Virginia shared this naive intellectual myth. But it seems to me that there is a significance to be attached to her refusal of food which is *specific to her*. In part, it is a rejection of male sexuality. Virginia rejected Leonard's first advances during his leave from the Colonial Service early in 1912. But on 1 May, Virginia wrote a letter which, according to the editors, 'decided Leonard. He resigned from the Colonial Service' (*Letters*, 1, p. 497n). Never was there a more discouraging prospect for a suitor. Virginia writes, 'I feel angry sometimes at the strength of your desire. Possibly, your being a Jew comes in also at this point. You seem so foreign.' She continues,

> I sometimes feel that no one ever has or ever can share something — Its the thing that makes you call me like a hill, or a rock. Again, *I want everything — love, children*, adventure, intimacy, work. (Can you make any sense out of this ramble? I am putting down one thing after another). So I go from being half in love with you, and wanting you to be with me always, and know everything about me, to the extreme of wildness and aloofness. I sometimes think that if I married you, I could have everything — and then — is it the sexual side of it that comes between us? As I told you brutally the other day, I feel no physical attraction in you. There are moments — when you kissed me the other day was one — when I feel no more than a rock.
>
> (*Letters*, 1, p. 496, my italics.)

Despite these hurdles, Leonard proposed, and they were married three months later. Certainly, Leonard, being a

passionate man, thought that he could overcome Virginia's
sexual aloofness. But this was not to be the case.

But Virginia's refusal to eat during the honeymoon *déjà vu*
in 1913 is not the only symptom she exhibits. Following the
suicide attempt, she ceases to menstruate from 6 August to
12 November. In her letter to Leonard, she rejects his sexual
advances, but she does want, first of all, love; and, secondly,
children. Children come before adventure and work. But we
know, from Quentin Bell's biography, that Leonard sought
the opinions of a number of specialists as to whether or not
Virginia should have children. He did this before they were
married.[22] When Savage said that, yes, they would be a good
thing for her, Leonard sought contradictory opinions. The
desire for children is expressed repeatedly in her early letters,
and the later ones are full of regret. The intensity with which
she attempted vicariously to experience her sister Vanessa's
motherhood — and her jealousy of it — are reliable indicators
of the strength of this feeling. It is highly probable that
allied with the refusal of food (rejection of sexual relations)
was a reaction against the ban on childbearing, and that this
rejection took the form of a cessation of menstruation. In
Mrs Dalloway, Virginia writes that Sir William Bradshaw, the
Harley Street psychiatrist, 'forbade childbirth, penalized
despair' (*MD*, p. 110).

It is important to remember that there is no mention anywhere of Virginia refusing to eat prior to her marriage. In
later life this ceased to be a problem. In *Flush*, Elizabeth
Barrett's dog refuses to eat the biscuits which the rival for
his mistress's affection, Robert Browning, brings for him.
When the situation is resolved, Flush eats the cakes, even
though they are 'mouldy and fly-blown'. They are symbols
of hatred turned to love.

A New School of Writing

Virginia's interest in food as an essential part of her writing
marked her career from beginning to end. In 1907, eight
years before the appearance of her first novel, she wrote
(in a letter to Lady Cecil), 'Why is there nothing written

about food — only so much thought? I think a new school might arise, with new adjectives and new epithets, and a strange beautiful sensation, all new to print' (*Letters*, 1, p. 278). Is it mere coincidence that the last entry in *A Writer's Diary* reads, 'and now with some pleasure I find that its seven; and must cook dinner. Haddock and sausage meat. I think it is true that one gains a certain hold on sausage and haddock by writing them down.'[23]

Virginia's first sustained use of the food theme occurs in *Mrs Dalloway*, in the remarkable passage in which Doris Kilman takes tea with Elizabeth Dalloway. In 1915 and 1918, there are diary entries which show that this theme was presenting itself with some insistence, and these misanthropic reflections pave the way for the unlovable character of Doris Kilman. In 1915 she writes, 'I begin to loathe my kind, principally from looking at their faces in the tube. Really, raw red beef & silver herrings give me more pleasure to look upon' (*Diary*, 1, p. 5). In the 1918 entry she writes, with a similar irritability, this time under the strain of wartime,

We lunched at Valcheras, & there looked into the lowest pit of human nature; saw flesh still unmoulded to the shape of humanity — Whether it is the act of eating & drinking that degrades, or whether people who lunch at restaurants are naturally degraded, certainly one can hardly face one's own humanity afterwards.

(*Diary*, 1, p. 199.)

Doris Kilman is unique among Virginia's characters in that she is one of the few for whom she had no sympathy whatsoever. If (as Blanch Gelfant argues) love and conversion are the two antithetical forces at work in *Mrs Dalloway*, then Doris Kilman belongs to the converters.[24] She is frustrated, dowdy, a religious maniac and, notably, German. Though she loved to hear Wagner at Bayreuth, Virginia despised the Germans who represented, for her, what was most base and masculine in human nature. German chauvinism as she observed it during both wars seemed to her absolutely to sum up all that conspired to prohibit the free, subjective life.

Elizabeth Dalloway, a mysterious, insubstantial girl who has only her dog, her Bible and Doris Kilman for company, is someone whom the rejected Miss Kilman thinks she might possibly control. Frustrated at having been denied a proper education and profession, at being laughed at by Clarissa Dalloway and the world, she takes her revenge upon Elizabeth. Embodiment and sexuality are clearly linked to food as Doris Kilman considers her experience of

> her unlovable body which people could not bear to see. Do her hair as she might, her forehead remained like an egg, bald, white. No clothes suited her. She might buy anything. And for a woman, of course, that meant never meeting the opposite sex. Never would she come first with anyone. Sometimes lately it had seemed to her that, except for Elizabeth, her food was all that she lived for . . .
>
> (*MD*, p. 143.)

Elizabeth Dalloway guides Miss Kilman through a department store where 'she chose, in her abstraction,' a petticoat. The shop assistant thinks her mad. 'They must have their tea, said Miss Kilman, rousing, collecting herself':

> Elizabeth rather wondered whether Miss Kilman could be hungry. It was her way of eating, eating with intensity, then looking, again and again, at a plate of sugared cakes on the table next to them; then, when a lady and a child sat down and the child took the cake, could Miss Kilman really mind it? Yes, Miss Kilman did mind it. She had wanted that cake — the pink one. The pleasure of eating was almost the only pleasure left her, and then to be baffled even in that!
>
> (*MD*, p. 144.)

There is nothing enlightened about this greediness.[25] Elizabeth becomes uncomfortable: 'Miss Kilman was quite different from anyone she knew; she made one feel so small' (*MD*, p. 145). Elizabeth clearly wants to leave, but

> Miss Kilman took another cup of tea. Elizabeth, with her oriental bearing, her inscrutable mystery, sat perfectly

upright; no, she did not want anything more. She looked
for her gloves — her white gloves. They were under the
table. Ah, but she must not go! Miss Kilman could not
let her go! This youth, that was so beautiful, this girl,
whom she genuinely loved! Her large hand opened and
shut on the table.

(MD, p. 145.)

The irony of the penultimate line is apparent after the final
one, if not before. Miss Kilman is intent upon dominating
Elizabeth completely. It is peculiar, the way in which Miss
Kilman makes Elizabeth feel small; for there is nothing in
the few words they exchange to really do that. It is something else, something that Elizabeth senses. Though there
are no words to express it, an intolerable tension is mount-
ing, and Elizabeth instinctively tries to get away, to preserve
herself. From what? The danger becomes clearer when Miss
Kilman warns Elizabeth against going to parties. 'She must
not let parties absorb her, Miss Kilman said, fingering the last
two inches of a chocolate eclair.'

She did not much like parties, Elizabeth said. Miss Kilman
opened her mouth, slightly projected her chin, and swal-
lowed down the last inches of the chocolate éclair, then
wiped her fingers, and washed the tea round in her cup.
   She was about to split asunder, she felt. The agony was
so terrific. If she could grasp her, if she could clasp her,
if she could make her hers absolutely and for ever and then
die; that was all she wanted. But to sit here, unable to
think of anything to say, to see Elizabeth turning against
her; to be felt repulsive even by her — it was too much;
she could not stand it. The thick fingers curled inwards.

(MD, p. 146.)

Miss Kilman is trying to secure Elizabeth's love once and for
all by metaphorically *consuming* her — for that is what the
tea represents: the total appropriation of Elizabeth so that
she can be remade in the mould desired by Miss Kilman.
Elizabeth has finally understood. She is likened to 'some dumb
creature who has been brought up to a gate for an unknown
purpose, and stands there longing to gallop away' (*MD*,

p. 146). Elizabeth now acts decisively:

> Right away to the end of the field the dumb creature
> galloped in terror.
>   The great hand opened and shut.
>   Elizabeth turned her head. The waitress came. One had
> to pay at the desk, Elizabeth said, *and went off, drawing out,*
> *so Miss Kilman felt, the very entrails in her body, stretching*
> *them as she crossed the room, and then, with a final twist,*
> *bowing her head very politely, she went.*
>
> (MD, p. 147, my italics.)

These final lines show to what extent Miss Kilman has, at
least in fantasy, 'absorbed' Elizabeth. The relationship
between them, as conceived by Miss Kilman, is a malignant
inversion of the one between Sally Seton and Clarissa
Dalloway.

During the first dinner scene in *The Waves*, Virginia tells us
that the room and its contents are on the verge of being, that
'things quiver as if not yet in being' (*TW*, p. 101). As it took
Mrs Ramsay to create unity in *To The Lighthouse*, so it takes
Percival to do the same here. Neville, who has come early so
as to be assured of a place next to Percival, thinks,

> This is the place to which he is coming. This is the table
> at which he will sit. Here, incredible as it seems, will be
> his actual body. This table, these chairs, this metal vase
> with its three red flowers, are about to undergo an extra-
> ordinary transformation.
>
> (TW, p. 101.)

Percival is required to introduce the element of the personal.
He will not only be the central power which assigns meaning
to objects, but will also unite the disparate personalities
gathered round the table.[26] Without this sense of the personal,
we cannot be 'nourished':

> The hospitality, the indifference of other people dining
> here is oppressive. We look at each other; see that we do

not know each other, stare, and go off. Such looks are
lashes. I feel the whole cruelty and indifference of the
world in them. If he should not come I could not bear it.

(TW, p. 101.)

So thinks Neville. The ironical linking of hospitality and
indifference is apt. For one who is truly 'hungry', the mask
of the former never hides the presence of the latter.

The first dinner scene marks the end of youth — of school
and college and relatively carefree days. The trials of childhood are exchanged for those of adulthood, and the love,
hatred and jealousy that were present in the relationships
of the six in childhood are still present, though in a matured
form. Susan, who was reduced to tears as a child when she
saw Jinny kiss Louis, has gained in strength and confidence.
Now, 'To be loved by Susan would be to be impaled by a
bird's sharp beak, to be nailed to a barnyard door,' thinks
Louis (*TW*, p. 102). He sees that Rhoda, though she despises
all of them, still 'comes cringing to our sides because for all
our cruelty there is always some name, some face, which
sheds a radiance which lights up her pavements and makes it
possible for her to replenish her dreams' (*TW*, p. 102-3).
Jinny demonstrates the synthetic power of individual consciousness, its ability to order the world and create meaning. Her existence is in stark contrast to Rhoda's. Rhoda
approaches the table by 'a tortuous course, taking cover
now behind a waiter, now behind some ornamental pillar'
(*TW*, p. 102). Rather than actively intending her environment, Rhoda takes advantage of the opportunities provided
by objects to keep herself 'invisible'. In Jinny's case, it is
the objects and, indeed, the other people in the room which
must bow to her dominant presence:

'There is Jinny,' said Susan. 'She stands in the door.
Everything seems stayed. The waiter stops. The diners
at the table by the door look. She seems to centre everything; round her tables, lines of doors, windows, ceilings,
ray themselves, like rays round the star in the middle of a
smashed window-pane. She brings things to a point, to
order.

(TW, p. 103.)

In *Mrs Dalloway* Septimus, who is much like Rhoda, experiences life as if from behind a pane of glass. Virginia's choice of imagery in the above passage shows a deliberate contrast between two modes of embodiment, the normal and the pathological. In Jinny's case, where mind and body are one, the pane of glass is smashed, signifying the power of consciousness to actively intend its world. Septimus and Rhoda remain behind the pane of glass, not sufficiently rooted in their bodies to constitute a real social world. But, at the same time, Jinny's self-conscious superiority alienates her from the others. Louis, Neville, Rhoda and Susan are all made to feel the extent of their imperfections, and buttress themselves against her accusing beauty by straightening a tie, moving a fork, or hiding a pair of rough hands beneath the table.

Percival succeeds where Jinny does not. Jinny's presence is powerful, but ultimately alienating. Percival's less self-conscious presence is uncanny in its unifying power: ' "Now," said Neville, "my tree flowers. My heart rises. All impediment is removed. The reign of chaos is over. He has imposed order. Knives cut again" ' (*TW*, p. 104).

Throughout the dinner there is a recapitulation of themes developed so far in the novel: Susan's ferocity, and her insecurity; Neville's courageous loneliness, and his unrequited love for Percival; Rhoda's facelessness, her altered identity. The temporal implications of Rhoda's disembodiment are now made clearer:

> I cannot make one moment merge in the next. To me they are all violent, all separate; and if I fall under the shock of the leap of the moment you will be on me, tearing me to pieces. I have no end in view. I do not know how to run minute to minute and hour to hour, solving them by some natural force until they make the whole and indivisible mass that you call life. . . . But there is no single scent, no single body for me to follow. And I have no face.[27]
>
> (*TW*, p. 111.)

There is Bernard's still birth as a writer. His over-concern for the multiplicity of facts and observations available to him determines that he will never be able to see a unity in them, that he will always write phrases in a notebook, but never produce a sustained work. Appropriately, Neville thinks of Bernard, 'He half knows everybody; he knows nobody' (*TW*, p. 104). And there is Louis's sense of insecurity, his compensatory dreams of superiority: the Egyptians, Louis XIII.

In *The Waves* the dinner scenes become, among other things, symbols of the lack of fulfilment in each of the six lives; they are emblematic of the 'existential hunger' they all feel. Louis speaks for all of them when he says, 'I am like some vast sucker, some glutinous, some adhesive, some insatiable mouth. I have tried to draw from the living flesh the stone lodged at the centre' (*TW*, p. 173). Allied to this hunger is the sense of nausea and emptiness that Sartre described in *La Nausée*.

In *The Waves*, Virginia's use of the food metaphor transcends the merely personal or autobiographical (though it does not negate them). Food has occupied a prominent place in the rituals, myths and taboos of many societies from time immemorial, and the manner in which Virginia deals with the subject here reflects its perennial meaning.[28] The dinner scenes in *The Waves* are moments in which, temporarily, individual egos are given over to a communal, almost prepersonal one. As the first dinner draws to an end, the extent of the communion is made clear:

'The circle is destroyed. We are thrown asunder.'
'But, soon, too soon,' said Bernard, 'this egotistic exultation fails. Too soon the moment of ravenous identity is over, and the appetite for happiness, and happiness, and still more happiness is glutted. The stone is sunk; the moment is over. Round me there spreads a wide margin of indifference.'

(*TW*, p. 122-3.)

'Egotistic exultation' is thematic for Bernard during the second dinner as well. He says, 'We have dined well. The fish, the veal cutlets, the wine have blunted the sharp tooth of egotism. Anxiety is at rest' (*TW*, p. 192). This is not the competition of separate and individual egos bent on 'devouring' one another; it is a form of social communion, hence the 'moment of ravenous identity'. This moment is in direct contrast to the tea scene in *Mrs Dalloway*. In *The Waves* the six diners momentarily identify with one another. In *Mrs Dalloway*, Miss Kilman wants to devour, to internalize Elizabeth, to make her part of herself and to rob her of her individual identity.

Virginia suggests that this theme of existential hunger is buried deep in the recesses of each individual consciousness, in that realm where language does not exist, or is, at best, insufficient. Susan remarks (as Flush reflects), 'our hatred is almost indistinguishable from our love.'[29] Neville continues,

> 'Yet these roaring waters . . . upon which we build our crazy platforms are more stable than the wild, the weak and inconsequent cries that we utter when, trying to speak, we rise; when we reason and jerk out these false sayings, "I am this; I am that!" Speech is false. . . .'
>
> (*TW*, p. 118.)

This is the cry of the age in which the novel was written, the age of relativity, of loss of faith in old certainties. Personal identity is threatened. We no longer know who we are. Neville is unflinching in his survey of his own life (his unlovable body, destined to excite pity but never love), and of the predicament of his friends, his generation. But as the dinner progresses, there is a momentary cure:

> 'But I eat. I gradually lose all knowledge of particulars as I eat. I am becoming weighed down with food. These delicious mouthfuls of roast duck, fitly piled with vegetables, following each other in exquisite rotation of warmth, weight, sweet and bitter, past my palate, down my gullet, into my stomach, have stabilized my body. I feel quiet, gravity, control. All is solid now. Instinctively my palate now requires and anticipates sweetness and lightness, something sugared and evanescent; and cool wine, fitting glove-like over those finer nerves that seem to tremble from the roof of my mouth and make it spread (as I drink) into a domed cavern, green with vine leaves,

musk-scented, purple with grapes. Now I can look steadily into the mill-race that foams beneath. . . .'

(*TW*, p. 118.)

Is this the writing of a woman who had an insane hatred of food and the 'disgusting' body?

3

The Doctors: Real and Fictional

They enjoyed about equally the mysterious privilege of medical reputation, and concealed with much etiquette their contempt for each other's skill. Regarding themselves as Middlemarch institutions, they were ready to combine against all innovators, and against non-professionals given to interference.[1]

There is a clever German doctor who has recently divided melancholia into several types. One he calls natural. By which he means, one is born with a temperament. Another he calls occasional, by which he means, springing from occasion. This, you understand, we all suffer from at times. The third class he calls obscure melancholia. By which he really means, poor man, that he doesn't know what the devil it is that causes it.[2]

Anyone familiar with the life of Virginia Woolf is struck by the great number of medical tragedies which occurred in her immediate family. It is suggested, in *Moments of Being*, that the deaths of Julia Stephen and Stella Duckworth need not have occurred when they did. Thoby Stephen, as we shall see, died as a result of medical incompetence. Angelica Bell, Virginia's niece, was knocked down by a car as a child, and 'A doctor at the Middlesex hospital had told Vanessa and Duncan [Grant] that Angelica was very badly hurt and her case was hopeless' (*Letters*, 3, p. 96n). In fact, she had sustained only minor injuries. In 1925, 'during an operation on Karin Stephen [wife of Virginia's brother Adrian] to relieve her deafness, the surgeon cut a nerve in her face, which half-paralysed it and rendered her temporarily speechless'

(*Letters*, 3, p. 216n).

Another incident, involving Ottoline Morrell, served to fuel Virginia's distrust of doctors. In a footnote to the third volume of Virignia's *Letters*, Nigel Nicolson relates that Ottoline had been 'undergoing a cure at Chirk Castle, North Wales (since 1595 the property of the Myddelton family). Dr Marten had given her a fluid with which to inject herself. She passed some of it on to Siegfried Sassoon, who had it analysed. It turned out to be pure milk' (*Letters*, 3, p. 234n).

Despite their many differences in character and outlook, the early experiences of Sir Leslie Stephen and his daughter at the hands of the medical profession were remarkably similar. In his biography of Stephen, Frederick Maitland describes how Sir Leslie possessed, as a child, an exceedingly frail constitution.[3] He very often suffered, as Virginia did, from headaches, fatigue and a general lack of physical strength. Indeed, at one point, doctors advised the child's parents that there was not much chance of his surviving past childhood. During this period, and for the remainder of his life, Leslie Stephen was a voracious reader. He possessed extraordinary powers of recall, and would tirelessly recite lengthy passages of verse. This the doctors discouraged. It did not seem to them a healthy sign; its consequences could not be beneficial. Leslie Stephen survived his childhood and his doctors. He grew up to be a highly regarded rowing coach at Cambridge, an accomplished Alpine climber, and was eventually elected president of the Alpine Club. His biographer tells us that, even towards the end of his life, Stephen could walk the legs off most men one third his age, walking up to fifty miles in one day, for pleasure.

Virginia's account of her experience of the medical profession begins with Leslie Stephen's final days, as he lay dying of cancer at 22 Hyde Park Gate.

Virginia's earliest surviving observations on the medical profession are a series of letters written to her confidante, Violet Dickinson, between May 1897 and the closing months of 1903. During this time, the Stephen's family doctor was David Elphinstone Seton.[4]

One of the very earliest letters included in Virginia's

published correspondence is to Thoby Stephen. On 14 May 1897 she writes, 'My Dear Dr Seton says I must not do *any* lessons this term' (*Letters*, 1, p. 7). An editorial note adds, 'Virginia had been suffering from a slight nervousness which caused her family to fear a repetition of her mental break- down after her mother's death in 1895.' The restrictions which Virginia was to endure (and detest) all her life began at the age of fifteen: no reading, no writing. Virginia also mentions Dr Seton, in this letter to Thoby, with reference to their half-sister Stella Hills (née Duckworth), who had married the lawyer Jack Hills on 10 April 1897. By the end of the month, Stella had contracted peritonitis,[5] and Virginia writes,

> Today Stella went out for the first time in a bath chair — she is much better I think — and really looks fairly well and plump. Dr Seton only comes every other day, and he is quite comfortable about her — one of her nurses has gone, and I think the other goes tomorrow or the day after.
>
> (*Letters*, 1, p. 7.)

On 11 July 1897, Virginia is, according to Quentin Bell, 'feverish and ill' (Bell, 1, p. 191). On 19 July, Stella dies.

Dr Seton reappears in 1902, during Leslie Stephen's final illness. Virginia is now twenty years old, and is critical of Seton: 'Father sees (Dr) Seton tomorrow, and something more may be settled, but Seton is such a woolgatherer' (*Letters*, 1, p. 57). She writes to Thoby that their father is to see Sir Frederick Treves, who had operated on Edward VII in June 1902. He had been Surgeon Extraordinary to Queen Victoria, and was later Serjeant-Surgeon to Edward VII and George V. 'Father has probably told you that he is going to see Treves on Thursday. Seton says he had better, just to quiet his mind. Seton still is certain that he is better if anything' (*Letters*, 1, p. 59). Here, for the first time, Virginia learns that, in matters of life and death, doctors can have radically different opinions. Knowing how she reacted to her mother's death, and knowing that her father's death will upset her equally, Virginia's state of mind is in a delicate balance. Her anxiety is aggravated by the fact that two eminent doctors disagree over what is to them a medical problem, while that 'problem' is, to Virginia, the central concern around which her life, at this time, revolves. She writes to Violet Dickinson in October/November 1902,

> Treves is rather worrying. He thinks father not so well, and says he will probably have to have the operation in about six weeks.
> But Seton says just the opposite: he thinks Treves has forgotten how bad father was in the summer, and doesn't see that he is better now than he was then. Seton still is certain that father *is* better. But Seton cant say this to Treves, apparently. . . . I hope we shall get Allingham to see him first anyhow, but then great doctors are so queer, and Seton wont say anything decided.
>
> (*Letters*, 1, p. 61.)

As time goes on, Sir Leslie's health deteriorates further, and Virginia's anxiety increases. On 28 April 1903 she writes to Violet Dickinson,

> the nurse has told us that she thinks Father weaker. Seton said so in London and wrote to Georgie [Duckworth] and Jack [Hills]. They know very little — only that the thing is getting worse — has got much worse quite lately. Seton expects some other complication, but they can tell nothing for certain. It may be 6 months or a year or even longer.
>
> (*Letters*, 1, p. 74.)

A few weeks later, after she has learned that Sir Leslie is not expected to live much longer, the debate between Seton and Treves assumes a character which, from Virginia's point of view, can only seem muddled and incompetent.[6] Resigned, Virginia writes to Violet on 19 May? 1903,

> Treves came suddenly today. He says that six months is the longest it can last. There are complications which *may* happen before that; he cannot say definitely whether they will happen, but he thinks it more likely than not.

He told us that when he saw Father last he did not expect him to live six weeks. He thinks that at this moment he is better than he was then. I cant understand what he means by this. I think he must have forgotten. . . . the nurse says that Seton absolutely forgot to tell him some of father's symptoms, and made out that he was able to go for long walks. However I dont suppose it matters. Treves said there was nothing to be done. So now we seem to know everything there is to be known.

(*Letters*, 1, pp. 77-8.)

Throughout the summer of 1903, Seton is in charge of the case. Virginia writes to Violet on 22 July, 'Father is about the same. The nurse says he is rather more comfortable just now. (Dr) Seton hasn't been for a month' (*Letters*, 1, p. 86). By the autumn, Leslie Stephen has reached a critical stage, and Hugh Rigby, the surgeon, is called in:

Father has some inflammation — it came on 2 days ago, and Nurse says tonight she thinks it is more serious than they thought and he may become unconscious at any moment. It may spread to the kidneys. Seton said at first that he thought it would go away, but it is no better, and they think that means that it is spreading. Rigby is coming tomorrow. We may know more then, and of course it is still quite possible that it will go down, but we have written to tell Adrian to come (from Cambridge), as it is not safe to wait.

(*Letters*, 1, p. 105.)

Later in the autumn of 1903, Virginia again writes to Violet Dickinson,

Rigby just gone. He says there's no immediate danger, but there may be a change at any moment. He thinks it more likely that he will live till Christmas, and get gradually weaker. He examined him, and found that the growth has increased very fast. He is to keep in bed as much as possible, and not to go downstairs again. We are to have a dr. every day, if not oftener, as he will have to be carefully watched. He cant come himself, so he is getting a friend (Dr Wilson) who lives in Kensington to come. He himself comes every 3 days. He is indignant with Seton, who ought to have been every day.

(*Letters*, 1, p. 106.)

Sir Leslie died on 22 February 1904 at 7 a.m.

To Virginia, Dr Seton must have seemed a harbinger of death, for he had been in attendance at her mother's death. One of the most vivid passages in her diary recalls Seton leaving the house after she had died:

> This is the 29th anniversary of mothers death. I think it happened early on a Sunday morning, & I looked out of the nursery window & saw old Dr Seton walking away with his hands behind his back, as if to say It is finished, & then the doves descending, to peck in the road, I suppose, with a fall & descent of infinite peace. I was 13.
>
> (*Diary*, 2, p. 300.)

The ban against reading and writing — the only activities which made life meaningful for Virginia — began in 1897 with Dr Seton. They begin to re-emerge in a manner which breeds resentment in 1904. At this time, Sir George Henry Savage is the doctor who is most involved with Virginia. Savage already had experience of madness in the Stephen family. In an autobiographical essay, Virginia relates how James Stephen, second son of Fitzjames Stephen, brother of Leslie,

> was in love with Stella. He was mad then. He was in the exalted stage of his madness. He would dash up in a hansom; leave my father to pay it. The hansom had been driving him about London all day. . . . He was a great painter for a time. I suppose madness made him believe he was all powerful. Once he came in at breakfast, 'Savage has just told me I'm in danger of dying or going mad', he laughed. And soon, he ran naked through Cambridge; was taken to an asylum; and died.[7]

In 1904, Savage has banished Virginia from London, and

she is staying in Cambridge with her aunt Caroline Emelia (known to the Stephen children as 'The Quaker', or 'Nun'). She writes to Violet Dickinson,

> London means my own home, and books, and pictures, and music, from all of which I have been parted since February now, — and I have never spent such a wretched 8 months in my life. And yet that tyrannical, and as I think, shortsighted Savage insists upon another two. I told him when I saw him that the only place I can be quiet and free is in my home, with Nessa: she understands my moods, and lets me alone in them, whereas with strangers like Nun I have to explain every random word — and it *is* so exhausting. I long for a large room to myself, with books and nothing else, where I can shut myself up, and see no one, and read myself into peace. This would be possible at Gordon Sq: and nowhere else. I wonder why Savage doesn't see this. As a matter of fact my sleep hasn't improved a scrap since I have been here, and his sleeping draught gives me a headache, and nothing else.
>
> (*Letters*, 1, p. 147.)

A week later, Savage permits Virginia to return to London, and the change in her attitude is marked:

> I am feeling really quiet and happy and able to stretch my legs out on a sofa for the first time for 7 months. If only that pigheaded man Savage will see that this is sober truth and no excuse! — I know I shall sleep tonight as I haven't for a month. The house is a dream of loveliness after the Quaker brown paper.
>
> (*Letters*, 1, p. 153.)

In early 1905, Savage declares Virginia 'cured', and attempts to make their relationship a social one as well as a professional one:

> I am discharged cured! Aint it a joke! Savage was quite satisfied, and said he wanted me to go back to my ordinary life in everything and to go out and see people, and work, and to forget my illness. He asked me to go and dine with

him! He thinks me quite normally well now, and there
need be no special care, which is such a mercy.

(Letters, 1, p. 175.)

After dining with Savage, she writes to Violet Dickinson in
mid-February 1905,

At (Dr) Savages dinner, which was more heavy and
dreary than you can conceive, every person I talked to
spoke almost with tears of the greatness and beauty of
Watts — and wouldn't admit the possibility of criticism,
and this, I suppose, is the sample British Public. Savage
lives with an odd lot of people; a daughter who is not up
to his level, and strange fossils.

(Letters, 1, p. 179.)

Here, for the first time, we note in Virginia's own reflections an important aspect of the nature of the essential
differences which exist between herself and her doctors.
Their discourse is rooted in another age, and can't admit of
the new movements and attitudes which define themselves
negatively against what preceded them. Not 'to admit the
possibility of criticism' of Watts implies a criticism of what is
in the process of becoming. In terms of pictorial art, this
meant post-impressionism (which would make its presence
felt in London in 1910), and the work of the Bloomsbury
painters like Vanessa Bell, Roger Fry and Duncan Grant.
However, Virginia was sufficiently curious to accept another
invitation to dine with Savage in July 1905. She writes to
Violet Dickinson, 'I am dining with Savage tomorrow night,
and I think I shall ask him what bee gets in my bonnet
when I write to you. Sympathetic insanity, I expect it is'
(Letters, 1, p. 198).
Savage played an important role in what is one of the
central dramas of Virginia's life: her trip to Greece with
Thoby, Vanessa, Adrian and Violet Dickinson, and Thoby's
ensuing death. On 8 September 1906, Virginia, Vanessa and
Violet left London for Greece, meeting Thoby and Adrian
at Olympia. At Corinth, Vanessa fell ill, and her illness continued through the first two weeks of October. On 21 October,

Thoby returned to England, and at the end of October, Vanessa was again ill. By November, all of the party had returned to London, and Thoby and Vanessa were confined to their beds. On 20 November, Thoby died of typhoid.[8]

The deaths of Julia and Leslie Stephen were traumas which led to immediate and drastic consequences for Virginia. Thoby's death, on the other hand, plunged Virginia into a state of mourning from which, it may be argued, she never completely emerged. *Jacob's Room* was an attempt to exorcise his ghost in the way that *To The Lighthouse* is an attempt to lay the parents' ghosts to rest. But the matter did not end with *Jacob's Room*. Thoby is the central presence (even by virtue of his conspicuous and meaningful absence at the end of the novel) behind Percival in *The Waves*. One important fact to remember when examining this period of Virginia's life is that, instead of being the patient, the one who is dependent on others, she was in complete control of the family. It was up to her to see to the comings and goings of the doctors, to engage nursing staff, to spend as much time as possible bolstering the spirits of her brother and, significantly, her sister Vanessa, who was also confined to her bed, and displaying 'nervous' symptoms. Here, the full weight of responsibility lay on Virginia's shoulders, and only a short time after the death of her father. Correspondence shows that Virginia was capable of handling the multitude of demands on her resources. Yet, this is the woman who had to be sheltered against her own sensitivity, to be put to bed with warm milk in a darkened room.

Once again faced with daily visits from the doctors, Virginia was confronted with a drama similar to that surrounding her father's death. The uncertainties bred by conflicting medical opinions were relatively fresh in her mind. She did not have Vanessa to turn to for support. Her only support, and virtually her only correspondent at this time, was the sympathetic and faithful Violet Dickinson. The story of Thoby's death and Virginia's second prolonged encounter with the medical profession is told in the letters they exchange.

In her first letter, Virginia relates that 'Thoby has a temp. of 103 and is a great deal bothered with his inside but (Dr)

Thompson is satisifed. Thoby thinks him very slow and
Savage will be a blessing' (*Letters*, 1, p. 239). The next day
(or very soon after — 8? November 1906),

> Savage came at 2. rather hurried and determined that a
> home was necessary before he saw Nessa. She couldn't
> explain — he talked so hard and was so vague — thought
> she couldn't eat and had diarhhoea. Then he dashed off —
> saying that today was a bright day, but you were not an
> alarmist and therefore she must be very weak. So I felt
> rather in despair. Then (Dr) Thompson came — I had a
> long talk, and explained Vs views — he was very nice, and
> said that if she really minded fearfully he would consult
> Savage and tell me. Now he has just been again and had a
> talk with V herself. He says they will certainly allow her
> to be here; with (Nurse) Fardell, in her own room. Savage
> says it is *not* a case of nervous breakdown but merely
> general tiredness, and therefore the treatment need not be
> so strict. He says it will certainly not take 6 weeks, and he
> thinks we can perfectly well manage here, if she prefers it.
> So I am going to London (Hospital) to get Fardell, and
> we shall start probably middle of next week.
> Both Savage and Thompson think it will be a quick
> case, and say there is nothing serious the matter.
> Nessa is very much cheered up, and says she can stand
> this quite well, and it makes all the difference being here.
> Thompson was very nice, and very glad to discuss the
> whole thing, and to hear about her.
> Thoby has taken a sudden turn for the better and his
> temp. is only 100. They think this is really the final
> drop now — so we go to bed cheerful.
> Perhaps I may come round tomorrow morning.
>
> (*Letters*, 1, p. 240.)

Dissatisfied with Dr Thompson (unidentified), Virginia
looks forward to seeing Savage. But she can't have been more
disappointed by his insistence that Vanessa required treatment
in a home, a measure determined 'before he saw Nessa'.[10]
However, the doctors finally decide that Vanessa can be
treated at home (and we must assume that Virginia receives
some comfort and strength from the mere fact of her sister's
presence, even if she is ill), and it is said that Thoby is

improving. But the cause for optimism is only momentary. Virginia writes to Violet Dickinson on 9? November 1906,

> Thoby is kept back by the diarrhoea which is still severe and keeps his temp. up. I am asking Thompson to get a specialist, as the nurse has rather alarmed Nessa, and is alarmed herself. Thompson says it is quite unnecessary; that it is irritation caused by grape pips which he passes in great quantities. But the pain is bad, and I think it will be best to know everything that can be known. . . . It is such a mercy about Nessa. Savage and Thompson both say it is not a severe case, and they expect a quick recovery, as it is more physical exhaustion than nervous. Nessa says she feels she can get perfectly right here.
>
> (*Letters*, 1, pp. 240-1.)

By now the situation has acquired an aspect frighteningly reminiscent (for Virginia) of her father's death. In both cases, it is the nurse who harbours suspicions about the manner in which the doctors are conducting the case. In the case of Leslie Stephen, we recall that the nurse pointed out that 'Seton absolutely forgot to tell him [Treves] some of father's symptoms' (*Letters*, 1, p. 78). But the nurse's uncertainty about Thoby is offset to some extent by Vanessa's progress. Virginia feels she ought to call in a specialist, but is persuaded not to. But the uncertainty mounts, and is expressed in a letter of 10? November:

> Thoby's temp. is still up, and his inside is rather painful, but the dr. declares it is all accounted for; and says it wd. be waste to have another man. But we are prepared to have one at any moment. — I feel complete trust in Thompson. He is now alive to our anxiety.
>
> (*Letters*, 1, p. 241.)

In the same breath she says that she has 'complete trust in Thompson' but that she is prepared to 'have another man'. The last line is of the utmost importance: the doctor must be 'alive to our anxiety'.

It is unusual to see Virginia nursing Vanessa. As Quentin Bell shows in his biography, the reverse was usually the case.

The doctor says Nessa is decidedly better; she weighs nine stones naked, which is very little less than she ought to weigh — and I should like to know what you weigh — the weight of bones, I should th'nk. I have got Mackechnie the nice Scotch nurse to come, and we are going to start massage and food tomorrow. But both Savage and Thompson agree that it is not necessary to isolate her, so she is going to see us as usual though no one else. Then we can get stricter if necessary; but they are very much pleased with her improvement. Thoby is just the same today, which is as they hoped. There are no complications, and he is doing as well as possible.

(*Letters*, 1, p. 242.)

The correspondence from now until 20 November, when Thoby dies, makes unhappy reading. An uneasy optimism prevails, but is soon replaced by the terrible truth discovered by Thoby's nurse. On 13 November, Virginia writes to Clive Bell, one of Thoby's closest friends,

Thoby had a good sleep this evening and the dr says he has had a better day altogether than yesterday. He is asleep now — Everything so far is satisfactory. The dr disapproves of reading — says talk is better.

(*Letters*, 1, p. 242.)

The news that Thoby has typhoid is broken in a letter to Madge Vaughan the next day:

I meant to write before. The doctors are now certain that Thoby has Typhoid. The pneumonia was only part of it and is now almost gone. They hope he is through the worst of it, — he is certainly going on as well as possible. They think him better tonight. Of course it is a very long business, and the next week must be anxious, but his pulse is wonderfully good, and there are no complications.

The doctor is very anxious the Nessa should get completely strong after appendicitis, — advises keeping her in bed for the next week or two, with rubbing and feeding up. She is decidedly better, and they say that she will get perfectly right with rest and care in a short time. She has been rushing about ever since she had it. I will send a card to say how T. gets on.

(Letters, 1, p. 243.)

With her brother severely afflicted with typhoid and her sister suffering from exhaustion, and then appendicitis, Virginia still has time to keep Thoby's friend, and Vanessa's husband-to-be, Clive Bell, informed of his condition. She writes on 14 November, 'The doctor says that Thoby has had a really satisfactory day, and thinks him better in every way' (Letters, 1, p. 243). Virginia's stamina is further evidenced in her stoical and understated humour in a letter to Violet Dickinson:

> Visitors come and use their handkerchiefs a great deal; I begin now by saying my brother has typhoid and my sister appendicitis — don't laugh. Thoby has had an excellent day and the doctor says we can be quite happy, his temp. is going down, and everything is satisfactory.
>
> (Letters, 1, p. 243.)

On 17 November, the situation has become very grave. Virginia writes to Clive Bell,

> Thoby is worse this morning, and the dr. thinks that there is some perforation. They advise an operation at once — at 12 this morning — and will then sew up the ulcer in order to prevent the poison from leaking. It is a serious risk, but they give us hope as his pulse is good.
>
> (Letters, 1, p. 246.)

On 20 November, Thoby died.

The extent of the immediate shock of Thoby's death is touchingly revealed in three letters to Violet Dickinson, written between 23? and 30? November. In them, Virginia adheres to a fantasy in which Thoby is still alive, his condition improving. On 23? November she writes,

> There isn't much change. His temp. is up to 104 again this afternoon, but otherwise his pulse is good, and he takes milk well. The nurse is nice and quiet. The dr. hasn't been yet, but I write.to catch the post. I dont think he will

say anything.

(Letters, 1, p. 249.)

On 25 November she writes,

> Thoby is going on splendidly. He is very cross with his nurses, because they wont give him mutton chops and beer; and asks why he cant go for a ride with Bell, and look for wild geese. Then nurse says 'wont tame ones do' at which we laugh.

(Letters, 1, p. 250.)

In the final letter of this series, Virginia writes,

> Nessa flourishes, and still sits by her fire. Savage came today, and says she has a splendid constitution and we need never feel any anguish about her health. He says she was quite right: and no rest cure was really necessary.
>
> Thoby slept better. He still isn't allowed to move, but next week the feeding stage will begin.

(Letters 1, p. 254.)

It would be wrong to interpret these fantasies as evidence of an unhinged mind. What they do represent is the unwillingness — not the inability — of a sensitive person to come to terms with the death of a loved one. It did not take Virginia very long to come to terms with the empirical reality of her brother's death, and in time she came to view it in such a manner as to be able to deal with it 'objectively' in *Jacob's Room* and *The Waves*. The living must be indulged in their inability to match nature's indifference.

The fictional character of the doctor first appears in *The Voyage Out* towards the end of the novel when Hughling Elliot falls ill. Mrs Thornbury remarks

> 'You know what men are like when they're ill! And of course there are none of the proper appliances, and, though he seems very willing and anxious to help' (here she lowered her voice mysteriously), 'one can't feel that

Dr Rodriguez is the same as a proper doctor.'

(*TVO*, pp. 322-3.)

Mrs Thornbury 'told them that for some days Hughling Elliot had been ill, and the only doctor available was the brother of the proprietor, or so the proprietor said, whose right to the title of doctor was not above suspicion' (*TVO*, p. 323). When Rachel falls ill, it is Rodriguez who is called in. Rachel sees him as 'a little dark man who had — it was the chief thing she noticed about him — very hairy hands' (*TVO*, p. 334). When it becomes clear that Rachel's illness is serious, Rodriguez assumes a role of central importance:

> By Friday it could not be denied that the illness was no longer an attack that would pass off in a day or two; it was a real illness that required a good deal of organization, and engrossed the attention of at least five people, but there was no reason to be anxious. Instead of lasting five days it was going to last ten days. Rodriguez was understood to say that there were well-known varieties of this illness. Rodriguez appeared to think that they were treating the illness with undue anxiety. His visits were always marked by the same show of confidence, and in his interviews with Terence he always waved aside his anxious and minute questions with a kind of flourish which seemed to indicate that they were all taking it much too seriously. He seemed curiously unwilling to sit down.
>
> 'A high temperature,' he said, looking furtively about the room, and appearing to be more interested in the furniture and in Helen's embroidery than in anything else. 'In this climate you must expect a high temperature. You need not be alarmed by that. It is the pulse we go by' (he tapped his own hairy wrist), 'and the pulse continues excellent.'
>
> Thereupon he bowed and slipped out. *The interview was conducted laboriously upon both sides in French, and this, together with the fact that he was optimistic, and that Terence respected the medical profession from hearsay, made him less critical than he would have been had he encountered the doctor in any other capacity. Unconsciously he took Rodriguez side against Helen, who seemed to have taken an unreasonable prejudice against him.*
>
> (*TVO*, pp. 338-9, my italics.)

It is clear that Rodriguez has no idea what ails his patient. He consoles the concerned friends and relatives with the assurance that there are 'many well-known varieties of this illness', though he declines to put a name to them. In lieu of treatment, Rodriguez offers a manner — an assortment of phrases and gestures which exude a false confidence. It is significant that the interview is conducted in a foreign language. Terence, being a good Englishman of his class, respects scientific knowledge, and will not argue against one who possesses a title signifying his initiation into this world. He is also unsure of himself, and will not risk ridicule or rebuff. Because the interview is conducted in a foreign language, there is a fundamental lack of communication, of shared premises, and it is this that Virginia seeks to convey. The fact that the language is French rather than English serves to underline the fact that the doctor's discourse is mystifying. It seeks to conceal what it does not know, and at the same time to convince that it is knowledgeable.

We have discussed the nature of Rachel's illness, and it is clearly too much to expect that Rodriguez or any other member of the party should conceive of Rachel's situation in that manner. Yet the final line of this passage shows the nature of the conflict which exists between subjectivity and the 'scientific' attitude. Helen has taken an intuitive though, it seems to Hewet, irrational, dislike to Rodriguez. She suspects that what is wrong with Rachel is not one of the 'well-known varieties' of illness which he diagnoses. Of course, Helen cannot say why it is that she distrusts Rodriguez. But it is important to note that Hewet, though he himself lacks a sound justification for having faith in Rodriguez, automatically sides with him against Helen. In the face of 'medical knowledge', the otherwise critical Hewet remains silent. We are reminded here of Leonard Woolf who, in his autobiography, more than once states his belief that the doctors who treated Virginia had very little idea of what was the matter with her. Yet, like Terence, he retained a kind of tenuous faith in them, if only for his own peace of mind. If the doctors did not know, then who did? The prospect of such uncertainty where human life is involved is too terrible to endure.

The idea that causes the most horror to a rationalist like Hewet is that of a world in which no apparent logical order exists. Problems and their solutions must be clearly defined, preferably in terms of cause-and-effect, so that a rapid solution may be found, and a return to equilibrium effected. But this sense of security may be purchased at a very high cost. Terence, for instance, is not prepared to endure Helen's criticism of the doctor. In fact, his concern for order even takes precedence over his concern for Rachel's health. But, after considering the matter further, Helen becomes insistent:

> 'We can't go on like this, Terence. Either you've got to find another doctor, or you must tell Rodriguez to stop coming, and I'll manage for myself. It's no use for him to say that Rachel's better; she's not better; she's worse.'
> Terence suffered a terrific shock, like that which he had suffered when Rachel said, 'My head aches.' He stilled it by reflecting that Helen was overwrought, and he was upheld in this opinion by his obstinate sense that she was opposed to him in the argument.
>
> (*TVO*, p. 342.)

There is no concern for Rachel here. What Terence experiences is the unease that contradiction of an insecure position causes. It emerges in this passage that Hewet's first reaction to Rachel's complaint of illness was the same: fear in the face of a situation other than one totally and rationally ordered. But Hewet quickly recovers. He consoles himself, and attempts to defend his insecure position, by disconfirming Helen's view of the situation.

But there have been more muscular rationalists than Hewet, and Helen has succeeded in sowing doubt in his mind:

> 'Do you think she's in danger?' he asked.
> 'No one can go on being as ill as that day after day—' Helen replied. She looked at him, and spoke as if she felt some indignation with somebody.
> 'Very well, I'll talk to Rodriguez this afternoon,' he replied.

Helen went upstairs at once.

(TVO, p. 342.)

His position challenged from without and from within, Hewet feels he must seek recourse to a third party who will confirm him in his original belief, to which he desperately tries to adhere. A man of greater intellectual capability than Helen, he is yet incapable of turning the tools of rational criticism against errant rationalism itself.

Hewet decides to see Rodriguez:

> Directly Rodriguez came down he demanded, 'Well, how is she? Do you think her worse?'
>
> 'There's no reason for anxiety, I tell you — none,' Rodriguez replied in his execrable French, smiling uneasily, and making little movements all the time as if to get away.
>
> Hewet stood firmly between him and the door. He was determined to see for himself what kind of man he was.
>
> (TVO, p. 342.)

Having decided that he will attempt a more objective assessment of Rodriguez, Hewet regains some of his boldness and self-assurance. His 'confidence in the man vanished as he looked at him and saw his insignificance, his dirty appearance, his shiftiness, and his unintelligent, hairy face. It was strange that he had never seen this before' (TVO, p. 343). Until now, Hewet's uncritical acceptance of the medical qualification has blinded him to the reality of Rodriguez. Having chanced a criticism of him, and bolstered by the prospect of success, Hewet regains his composure and asks a perfectly reasonable question:

> 'You won't object of course, if we ask you to consult another doctor?' he continued.
>
> At this the little man became openly incensed.
>
> 'Ah!' he cried, 'you have not confidence in me? You object to my treatment? You wish me to give up the case?'
>
> 'Not at all,' Terence replied, 'but in serious illness of this kind—'

Rodriguez shrugged his shoulders.

'It is not serious, I assure you. You are over-anxious. The young lady is not seriously ill, and I am a doctor. The lady of course is frightened,' he sneered. 'I understand that perfectly.'

'The name and address of the doctor is — ?' Terence continued.

'There is no other doctor,' Rodriguez replied sullenly. 'Everyone has confidence in me. Look! I will show you.'

He took out a packet of old letters and began turning them over as if in search of one that would confute Terence's suspicions. As he searched, he began to tell a story about an English lord who had trusted him — a great English lord, whose name he had, unfortunately, forgotten.

'There is no other doctor in the place,' he concluded, still turning over the letters.

'Never mind,' said Terence shortly. 'I will make enquiries for myself.' Rodriguez put the letters back in his pocket.

'Very well,' he remarked. 'I have no objection.'

He lifted his eyebrows, shrugged his shoulders, as if to repeat that they took the illness much too seriously and that there was no other doctor, and slipped out, leaving behind him an impression that he was conscious that he was distrusted, and that his malice was aroused.

(*TVO*, p. 343.)

Having dared to doubt Rodriguez, Hewet becomes incensed, and has quite forgotten that, only an hour ago, he had taken Rodriguez's side against Helen:

In less than ten minutes St John was riding to the town in the scorching heat in search of a doctor, his orders being to find one and bring him back if he had to be fetched in a special train.

'We ought to have done it days ago,' Hewet repeated angrily.

(*TVO*, pp. 344-5.)

St John Hirst finds a doctor a hundred miles away, and brings him back in a horse-drawn carriage: he 'eventually forced the unwilling man to leave his young wife and return forthwith. They reached the villa at midday on Tuesday' (*TVO*, p. 347).

> Terence came out to receive them, and St John was struck by the fact that he had grown perceptibly thinner in the interval; he was white too; his eyes looked strange. But the curt speech and the sulky masterful manner of Dr Lesage impressed them both favourably, although at the same time it was obvious that he was very much annoyed at the whole affair. Coming downstairs he gave his directions emphatically, but it never occured to him to give an opinion either because of the presence of Rodriguez who was now obsequious as well as malicious, or because he took it for granted that they knew already what was to be known.
> 'Of course,' he said with a shrug of his shoulders, when Terence asked him, 'Is she very ill?'
>
> (*TVO*, p. 347.)

The situation becomes more mystifying for Hewet when he questions the nurse one evening:

> 'Now, Nurse,' he whispered, 'please tell me your opinion. Do you consider that she is very seriously ill? Is she in any danger?'
> 'The doctor has said—' she began.
> 'Yes, but I want your opinion. You have had experience of many cases like this?'
> 'I could not tell you more than Dr Lesage, Mr Hewet,' she replied cautiously, as though her words might be used against her.
>
> (*TVO*, p. 349.)

Again, we are reminded of the role played by the nurse in the exchanges between the doctors as Leslie Stephen lay dying, and the nurse recognizing the undiagnosed typhoid too late in the case of Thoby Stephen. This passage also gives us an important insight into Hewet's nature: 'He looked at her but he could not answer her; like all the others, when one looked at her she seemed to shrivel beneath one's eyes and become worthless, malicious, and untrustworthy' (*TVO*, p. 349). Lesage does nothing to supply the comforting certainties which Hewet craves.

> Dr Lesage confined himself to talking about details, save once when he volunteered the information that he had just been called in to ascertain, by severing a vein in the wrist, that an old lady of eighty-five was really dead. She had a horror of being buried alive.
>
> (*TVO*, p. 355.)

It is strange to reflect that Virginia was writing *The Voyage Out* prior to and just after her marriage to Leonard. In the suicide note she left for him, Virginia wrote, 'You have given me the greatest possible happiness. . . . I don't think two people could have been happier than we have been' (Bell, 2, p. 226). When Rachel dies, we are told of Hewet, 'Unconscious whether he thought the words or spoke them aloud, he said, "No two people have ever been so happy as we have been. No one has ever loved as we have loved." ' (*TVO*, p. 359.)

In *Mrs Dalloway* Virginia presents a sustained attack on psychiatry as she experienced it. The two doctors — Holmes and Sir William Bradshaw — are modelled on the four doctors whose work I will examine in subsequent chapters. In one sense, Holmes and Bradshaw are composite figures whose attitudes and beliefs are culled from each of the four real-life personalities. But, on the other hand, specific references to the four doctors who treated her may be found. For instance, Dr Holmes has much in common with T. B. Hyslop, one of the doctors whom Leonard called in when seeking an opinion as to whether or not his wife should have children:

> Dr Holmes examined him. There was nothing whatever the matter, said Dr Holmes. Oh, what a relief! What a kind man, what a good man! thought Rezia. When he felt like that he went to the Music Hall, said Dr Holmes. He took a day off with his wife and played golf.
>
> (*MD*, pp. 100-1.)

Hyslop was a musician and amateur composer, and wrote

essays on art. He also wrote a little book entitled *Mental Handicaps in Golf*[11], and was a keen sportsman. Like Rodriguez in *The Voyage Out*, Holmes possesses a breezy and somewhat distracted manner. He focuses his attention on external objects rather than on the patient: 'These old Bloomsbury houses, said Dr Holmes, tapping the wall, are often full of very fine panelling, which the landlords have the folly to paper over' (*MD*, p. 101).

We recall that in Bell's biography, there is a great confusion as to whether madness should be assigned a moral or a medical meaning. The choice is very much an either/or: a crude mechanical empiricism; or an uncompromising Christian ethic. Added to the confusion is the fact that the patient (who may be suffering from an acute form of distress which stems from his perception of what seems to him an intolerable personal situation) may experience guilt because he feels he is a burden on his family, that he causes unnecessary expense, and that, if the doctor can find nothing physically wrong with him, then he must be either mad or bad. But if the definition of madness is so arbitrary as to be almost useless, the idea of moral corruption is one with a long tradition, and one which fills the gap left by a non-diagnosis. In Septimus's case, regardless of whether or not he has anything to feel guilty about, Holmes's judgement that there 'is nothing whatever the matter' leaves him convinced that he is corrupt:

> So there was no excuse; nothing whatever the matter, except the sin for which human nature had condemned him to death; that he did not feel. He had not cared when Evans was killed; that was worst; but all the other crimes raised their heads and shook their fingers and jeered and sneered over the rail of the bed in the early hours of the morning at the prostrate body which lay realizing its degradation; how he had married his wife without loving her; had lied to her; seduced her; outraged Miss Isabel Pole, and was so pocked and marked with vice that women shuddered when they saw him in the street. The verdict of human nature on such a wretch was death.
>
> (*MD*, p. 101.)

We cannot discount the possibility that Septimus might have something to feel guilty about. Nor can we discount the possibility that Virginia herself suffered from a form of guilt which occasionally manifested itself in her work. The guilt which Septimus refers to is primarily sexual; and we may ask (though I do not think that we can arrive at a satisfactory answer), might Virginia have suffered from guilt over the extent to which she might have been in collusion with the half-brothers who molested her? But the crux of the matter is, the situation cannot be dealt with adequately by means of the two narrow concepts of an undefined madness on the one hand, or moral corruption on the other. Certainly, there may be guilt which is not a direct result of Holmes's ruling out madness. Genuine moral guilt is, in its way, a positive phenomenon, a point from which to proceed. It can be an authentic position, and provide an opportunity for reassessment. It may be that Septimus suffers from such a form of guilt. But it is certain that the entire issue is confused by Holmes's insistence on two narrow categories which are incapable of embracing the varied complexities of human experience. In the work of Savage, Craig and Hyslop we find that the concepts of madness and badness work hand in hand.

When Holmes visits Septimus for the second time, he assumes some of the characteristics of Maurice Craig, whom Virginia saw prior to her suicide attempt of 1913, and who treated her for many years after that. Craig took great care over his appearance and wardrobe; his obituary tells us that: 'His students enjoyed his distinguished appearance and the tasteful neatness of his dress — he looked so much the part.'[12] His primary method of treating Virginia in the years following her suicide attempt was to get her to eat as much as possible. It is Craig who emerges during Holmes's second visit:

> Dr Holmes came again. Large, fresh-coloured, handsome, flicking his boots, looking in the glass, he brushed it all aside — headaches, sleeplessness, fears, dreams — nerve symptoms and nothing more, he said. If Dr Holmes found himself even half a pound below eleven stone six, he asked

his wife for another plate of porridge at breakfast.[13]
(*MD*, p. 101.)

Throughout his work, Craig expresses scepticism with regard
to the 'arts' side of education. Holmes advises Septimus,
'Throw yourself into outside interests; take up some hobby.
He opened Shakespeare — *Antony and Cleopatra*; pushed
Shakespeare aside' (*MD*, p. 101).

When Holmes comes a third time, Septimus tells his
wife he doesn't want to see him. Holmes's charming manner
gives way to a firmer attitude: 'When the damned fool came
again, Septimus refused to see him. Did he indeed? said Dr
Holmes, smiling agreeably. Really he had to give that charming little lady, Mrs Smith, a friendly push before he could
get past her into her husband's bedroom' (*MD*, p. 102).
Once inside, Holmes adopts the 'moral' approach. He tries
to make Septimus feel guilty for all the trouble he is causing,
hoping thereby to teach him a sense of duty towards others
which will induce him to give up his folly:

> 'So you're in a funk,' he said agreeably, sitting down by
> his patient's side. He had actually talked of killing him-
> self to his wife, quite a girl, a foreigner, wasn't she? Didn't
> that give her a very odd idea of English husbands? Didn't
> one owe perhaps a duty to one's wife? Wouldn't it be
> better to do something instead of lying in bed? For he had
> had forty years' experience behind him; and Septimus
> could take Dr Holmes's word for it — there was nothing
> whatever the matter with him. And next time Dr Holmes
> came he hoped to find Smith out of bed and not making
> that charming little lady his wife anxious about him.
> (*MD*, p. 102.)

The result of this visit is that Septimus feels that 'Human
nature, in short, was on him — the repulsive brute, with the
blood-red nostrils. Holmes was on him' (*MD*, p. 102). Holmes
comes to represent 'human nature' — a concept which, for
Septimus, means an uncompromising view of what constitutes 'normality', and a firm commitment to the repression of 'otherness'.[14]

At this point, the doctor has caused battle lines to be

drawn between husband and wife. The long-suffering Lucrezia thinks that a man so agreeable and so successful as Holmes can only be right: Septimus must be wrong. 'Dr Holmes was such a kind man. . . . He only wanted to help them, he said. He had four little children and he had asked her to tea, she told Septimus' (*MD*, p. 102). This simple woman only wants, as Hewet only wanted, peace and order, cannot understand the nature of the conflict between Septimus and Holmes. Septimus, whether he is mad or not, has a point of view, and in this Holmes is not interested. Holmes is dedicated to the propagation of normalcy, and to the suppression of any deviation from it. When his wife takes Holmes's side, Septimus feels completely abandoned:

> So he was deserted. The whole world was clamouring: Kill yourself, kill yourself, for our sakes. But why should he kill himself for their sakes? Food was pleasant; the sun hot; and this killing oneself, how does one set about it, with a table knife, uglily, with flows of blood, — by sucking a gaspipe? He was too weak; he could scarcely raise his hand. Besides, now that he was quite alone, condemned, deserted, as those who are about to die are alone, there was a luxury in it, an isolation full of sublimity; a freedom which the attached can never know. Holmes had won of course; the brute with the red nostrils had won. But even Holmes himself could not touch this last relic straying on the edge of the world, this outcast, who gazed back at the inhabited regions, who lay, like a drowned sailor, on the shore of the world.
>
> (*MD*, pp. 102-3.)

When Septimus hears the voice of his friend Evans speaking in the room, Lucrezia goes running for the doctor:

> 'You brute! You brute!' cried Septimus, seeing human nature, that is Dr Holmes, enter the room.
> 'Now what's this all about,' said Dr Holmes in the most amiable way in the world. 'Talking nonsense to frighten your wife?' But he would give him something to make him sleep. And if they were rich people, said Dr Holmes, looking ironically round the room, by all means let them go to Harley Street; if they had no confidence in him, said Dr

Holmes, looking not quite so kind.

(MD, p. 104.)

And to Harley Street they go. Sir William Bradshaw has the 'reputation (of the utmost importance in dealing with nerve cases) not merely of lightning skill and almost infallible accuracy in diagnosis, but of sympathy; tact; understanding of the human soul' *(MD,* pp. 105-6). Bradshaw sees right away that Septimus's case is grave. 'It was a case of complete breakdown — complete physical and nervous breakdown, with every symptom in an advanced stage' *(MD,* p. 106). There is then the inevitable conflict of medical opinion:

> How long had Dr Holmes been attending him?
> Six weeks.
> Prescribed a little bromide? Said there was nothing the matter? Ah yes (those general practitioners! thought Sir William. It took half his time to undo their blunders. Some were irreparable.)
>
> *(MD,* p. 106.)

Bradshaw examines his patient. He remarks that Septimus served in the war. 'The patient repeated the word "war" interrogatively. He was attaching meanings to words of a symbolical kind. A serious symptom to be noted on the card' *(MD,* p. 106).[15] When Septimus begins to speak of his own accord, he is ignored. He begins, ' "I have— I have," he began, "committed a crime—" ' *(MD,* p. 107). Bradshaw takes Lucrezia into the next room and explains that Septimus must be sent to a home:

> It was merely a question of rest, said Sir William; of rest, rest, rest; a long rest in bed. There was a delightful home down in the country where her husband would be perfectly looked after. Away from her? she asked. Unfortunately, yes; the people we care for most are not good for us when we are ill. But he was not mad, was he? Sir William said he never spoke of 'madness'; he called it not having a sense of proportion. But her husband did not like doctors. He would refuse to go there. Shortly and kindly Sir William explained to her the state of the case.

He had threatened to kill himself. There was no alternative. It was a question of law. He would lie in bed in a beautiful house in the country.

(*MD*, p. 107.)

Septimus finds himself in the same position as Virginia who was sent, by Savage, to Burley (the Twickenham nursing home run by Jean Thomas) as an alternative to certification. Where suicide, or the possibility of it, is a factor, the doctor must protect himself.[16]

The diagnosis of insanity (or 'lack of proportion') has, in this case, a distinctly legal-punitive flavour. After the private consultation with Bradshaw, Lucrezia returns to her husband, 'the most exalted of mankind; the criminal who faced his judges' (*MD*, p. 107). Like Savage, Bradshaw has his own 'home'.[17]

We will note in the work of the four doctors considered in the following chapters (with the exception of Head) a distrust of education — an irrational feeling that over-education, or that education offered in a democratic fashion, may be a primary cause of madness. There is an irrational fear of knowledge, of other than 'objective' or 'scientific' knowledge. Holmes advises Septimus to seek some therapeutic pastime, but dismisses Shakespeare. Bradshaw suffers from insecure feelings with regard to the knowledge of his profession when faced with those who possess a knowledge different from his own:

'We have been arranging that you should go into a home,' said Sir William.

'One of Holmes's homes?' sneered Septimus.

The fellow made a distasteful impression. For there was in Sir William, whose father had been a tradesman, a natural respect for breeding and clothing, which shabbiness nettled; again, more profoundly, there was in Sir William, who had never had time for reading, a grudge, deeply buried, against cultivated people who came into his room and intimated that doctors, whose profession is a constant strain upon all the highest faculties, are not educated men.

'One of *my* homes, Mr Warren Smith,' he said, 'where

we will teach you to rest.'

(MD, p. 108.)

Bradshaw, like Holmes, applies the 'moral' method of treatment. 'He was quite certain that when Mr Warren Smith was well he was the last man in the world to frighten his wife. But he had talked of killing himself' (*MD*, p. 108). Again Septimus tries to speak, but is ignored:

> 'I— I—' he stammered.
> But what was his crime? He could not remember it.
> 'Yes?' Sir William encouraged him. (But it was growing late.)
> Love, trees, there is no crime — what was his message?
> He could not remember it.
> 'I— I—' Septimus stammered.
> 'Try to think as little about yourself as possible,' said Sir William kindly. Really, he was not fit to be about.
>
> (MD, p. 109.)

As they leave, Sir William whispers to Lucrezia that he will arrange the home and ring her early that evening. But even the simple Lucrezia is not fooled by Bradshaw: 'Never, never had Rezia felt such agony in her life! She had asked for help and been deserted! He had failed them! Sir William Bradshaw was not a nice man' (*MD*, p. 109).

In the analysis of Bradshaw's character which follows, Virginia tells us exactly what she thought about the way in which she was treated by the doctors of psychological medicine. Her criticism, however, is not the tetchy *ad hominem* of a neurotic patient. It is an objective analysis which exposes Bradshaw's service to *power*:

> Worshipping proportion, Sir William not only prospered himself but made England prosper, secluded her lunatics, forbade childbirth, penalized despair, made it impossible for the unfit to propagate their views until they, too, shared his sense of proportion — his, if they were men, Lady Bradshaw's if they were women (she embroidered, knitted, spent four nights out of seven at home with her son), so that not only did his colleagues respect him, his

subordinates fear him, but the friends and relations of his patients felt for him the keenest gratitude for insisting that these prophetic Christs and Christesses, who prophesied the end of the world, or the advent of God, should drink milk in bed, as Sir William ordered; Sir William with his thirty years' experience of these kinds of cases, and his infallible instinct, this is madness, this sense; his sense of proportion.

(MD, p. 110.)

Ironically, it is the eminently sane Peter Walsh who feels, as much as Septimus does, that he has a mission. We recall him sitting atop his mountain, reading the books he had sent out from London, plotting the salvation of the race. Dalloway, too, views his mission as one of salvation. And there can be no doubt that, among all of the men in the novels, it is Bradshaw whose sense of mission is most pronounced. Virginia quite rightly sees his use of psychiatry as an instrument of power as being almost identical to the kind of coercion or conversion practised by Doris Kilman and other religious fanatics. She sees Bradshaw's science as nothing more than a metaphysical-political creed which he invokes regardless of the wishes of others, and irrespective of their rights as individual human beings:

But Proportion has a sister, less smiling, more formidable, a Goddess even now engaged — in the heat and sands of India, the mud and swamp of Africa, the purlieus of London, wherever, in short, the climate or the devil tempts men to fall from the true belief which is her own — is even now engaged in dashing down shrines, smashing idols, and setting up in their place her own stern countenance. Conversion is her name and she feasts on the wills of the weakly, loving to impress, to impose, adoring her own features stamped on the face of the populace. At Hyde Park Corner on a tub she stands preaching; shrouds herself in white and walks penitentially disguised as brotherly love through factories and parliaments; *offers help, but desires power; smites out of her way roughly the dissentient, or dissatisfied; bestows her blessing on those who, looking upward, catch submissively from her eyes the light of their own. This lady too (Rezia Warren Smith divined*

it) had her dwelling in Sir William's heart, though concealed, as she mostly is, under some plausible disguise;
some venerable name; love, duty, self sacrifice.

(MD, pp. 110-11, my italics.)

'But conversion,' Virginia argues, 'fastidious Goddess, loves
blood better than brick, and feasts most subtly on the human
will. For example, Lady Bradshaw':

> Fifteen years ago she had gone under. It was nothing you
> could put your finger on; there had been no scene, no
> snap; only the slow sinking, water-logged, of her will into
> his. Sweet was her smile, swift her submission; dinner in
> Harley Street, numbering eight or nine courses, feeding
> ten or fifteen guests of the professional classes, was
> smooth and urbane. Only as the evening wore on a very
> slight dullness, or uneasiness perhaps, a nervous twitch,
> fumble, stumble and confusion indicated, what it was
> really painful to believe — that the poor lady lied. Once,
> long ago, she had caught salmon freely: now, quick to
> minister to the craving which lit her husband's eye so
> oilily for dominion, for power, she cramped, squeezed,
> pared, pruned, drew back, peeped through: so that with-
> out knowing precisely what made the evening disagreeable,
> and caused this pressure on the top of the head (which
> might well be imputed to the professional conversation,
> or the fatigue of a great doctor whose life, Lady Bradshaw
> said, 'is not his own but his patient's'), disagreeable it was:
> so that guests, when the clock struck ten, breathed in the
> air of Harley Street even with rapture; which relief, how-
> ever, was denied to his patients.

(MD, pp. 111-2.)

Bradshaw and his colleagues are not, Virginia argues, to be
viewed as a peculiar phenomenon independent of the social
order. They are, more correctly, an integral part of a system
bent on repressing all forms of deviance, a system which
seeks to maintain order by promoting uniformity of behaviour, at least among the classes which cannot afford the
luxury of eccentricity. Residing at the centre of a matrix of
power which includes legislators, judges, the police, the penal
system, psychiatry, and to some degree the church, Bradshaw

possesses a power which is almost entirely unchecked by the limits within which the others are obliged to operate.[18] Using the knowledge base of the profession as an argument against 'lay intervention', the doctor in Bradshaw's position was able to possess almost total power over his patient:

There in the grey room, with the pictures on the wall, and the valuable furniture, under the ground-glass sky-light, they learnt the extent of their transgressions: huddled up in arm-chairs, they watched him go through, for their benefit, a curious exercise with the arms, which he shot out, brought sharply back to his hip, to prove (if the patient was obstinate) that Sir William was master of his own actions, which the patient was not. There some weakly broke down; sobbed, submitted; others, inspired by Heaven knows what intemperate madness, called Sir William to his face a damnable humbug; questioned, even more impiously, life itself. Why live? they demanded. Sir William replied that life was good. Certainly Lady Bradshaw in ostrich feathers hung over the mantelpiece, and as for his income it was quite twelve thousand a year. But to us, they protested, life has given no such bounty. He acquiesced. They lacked a sense of proportion. And perhaps, after all, there is no God? He shrugged his shoulders. In short, this living or not living is an affair of our own? But there they were mistaken. Sir William had a friend in Surrey where they taught, what Sir William frankly admitted was a difficult art — a sense of proportion. There were, moreover, family affection; honour; courage; and a brilliant career. All of these had in Sir William a resolute champion. If they failed, he had to support him police and the good of society, which, he remarked very quietly, would take care, down in Surrey, that these unsocial impulses, bred more than anything by the lack of good blood, were held in control. *And then stole out from her hiding-place and mounted her throne that Goddess whose lust is to override opposition, to stamp indelibly in the sanctuaries of others the image of herself.* Naked, defenceless, the exhausted, the friendless received the impress of Sir William's will. He swooped; he devoured. He shut people up. It was this combination of decision and humanity that endeared Sir William so greatly to the relations of his victims.

(*MD*, pp. 112-13, my italics.)

When Holmes comes to take Septimus away, he leaps from his window on to the area railings. ' "The coward!" cried Dr Holmes, bursting the door open' (*MD*, p. 165).

Examining the works of Savage, Head, Craig and Hyslop in the following four chapters, we will see how chillingly accurate Virginia's picture of Holmes and Bradshaw is.

4

The Morality of Madness: Sir George Henry Savage

George Henry Savage (1842-1921) was one of the most eminent physicians of his day. He was a young man when Victoria was at the height of her reign, but at the time of his retirement the erosion of Victorian values and the emergence of revolutionary ideas in morals, politics and the arts and sciences had already begun in earnest.

Savage was born in Brighton, and educated at Brighton Schools, Sussex County Hospital and, finally, at Guy's Hospital, where he won the Treasurer's Gold Medal. Savage maintained throughout his life a successful private practice (his estate was valued at over £27,000 at the time of his death). Savage was, at various times in his career, Physician Superintendant at Bethlem Royal Hospital; President of the Medico-Psychological Association of Great Britain; President of the Neurological Society; Examiner in Mental Physiology, University of London; Lecturer in Mental Diseases, Guy's Hospital; and Consulting Physician to Guy's Hospital and the Earlswood Idiot Asylum. In addition to his professional interests and accomplishments, Savage was an active sportsman, and particularly enjoyed mountaineering, fishing and fencing.

Savage was especially known to his contemporaries as the author of *Insanity and Allied Neuroses*, a popular textbook prior to the turn of the century.[1] They also knew him as editor of the *Journal of Mental Science*. This journal was read by most practitioners of psychological medicine throughout the late nineteenth and early twentieth centuries in Great Britain. If we want to know, generally, what Savage's views were on the subject of insanity, we might find a succinct answer by describing what role the *Journal of Mental Science* played. In her study of the history of mental health legislation in Great Britain, *Mental Health and Social Policy 1845-1959*, Kathleen Jones has shown that:

> The *Journal of Mental Science*, being the official organ of the asylum doctors, was strongly pro-medical, inclined to resent any lay intervention in their field. 'Insanity is purely a disease of the brain,' wrote the editor [Sir John Charles Bucknill, 1817-1897] in the second issue. 'The physician is now the responsible guardian of the lunatic, and must ever remain so'.[2]

This is Savage's view as well. He writes, for example, in an article entitled 'Constant Watching of Suicide Cases',[3]

> The public will be better pleased with fewer suicides in asylums, it is said. I fear I do not care what the public think about it, as they are certainly the least fit to judge collectively of the good of the insane. . .
>
> (Savage, 1884c, p. 19.)

Savage was a prolific writer. He published more than one hundred articles in his lifetime, about forty-five of them dealing with insanity.

What role did Savage play in Virginia's life? It is possible to piece together some idea of the kind of treatment Virginia received by examining references to Savage in the Bell biography, Leonard's autobiography, and Virginia's own writings. Savage had long been the family physician at 22 Hyde Park Gate (along with Dr Seton), and when Virginia suffered a serious breakdown in May 1904 following her father's death, Savage was called in.[4] Aside from Quentin Bell's few remarks in the first volume of his biography, we know nothing of what happened from May through September of 1904, the summer of which Bell has said, 'all that summer she was mad' (Bell, 1, p. 90). Then, in September,

> Her letters to Violet Dickinson are optimistic — over-optimistic; she was impatient to start writing again and

believed herself to be more completely cured than she in fact was. Dr Savage, her specialist and an old friend of the family, insisted that she should live very quietly and, if possible, away from London.

(Bell, 1, p. 90.)

Virginia then, as we know, went to Cambridge to stay with her aunt Caroline Emelia, returning to Gordon Square early in the new year. The household to which she returned was, of course, the beginnings of the original Bloomsbury Group. When Thoby, Adrian, Vanessa and Virginia Stephen left 22 Hyde Park Gate for their new residence in Bloomsbury, Gerald Duckworth took the opportunity to depart. George Duckworth, however, decided to stay on and look after the social lives of his two half-sisters. Bell tells us that, in 1904, Savage learned of George's 'attentions' and confronted him with the matter.[5] There is no record of Savage having taken any definite action as a result of this knowledge, and it is quite possible that while he might have deplored Duckworth's actions on moral grounds, he failed to recognize the gravity of this behaviour in relation to Virginia's psychological state. If Savage had been able to 'connect', it seems likely that he would have spoken out against Duckworth's continued presence in the household. There is no doubt that George's insistence on remaining in the household was crucial.[6]

Apart from his involvement in the treatment of Thoby and Vanessa in 1906, Savage does not appear again in the Bell biography until 1912. Bell writes, 'At the end of January Virginia and Vanessa were discussing the question of whether Virginia should have children' (Bell, 2, p. 8). Leonard called in Savage, asking him whether he thought it would be advisable for Virginia to have children. Roger Poole has argued that 'Leonard lost confidence in Sir George Savage when Savage insisted that having children would do Virginia "a world of good". "So I went off and consulted two other well known doctors..."[7] The "so" has a logical force here. "*Since* Savage said that having children would do Virginia good, *so* I went to get opinions contrary to his." "[8] Bell writes,

Leonard talked to Dr (now Sir George) Savage, and Sir George, in his breezy way, had exclaimed that it would do her a world of good; but Leonard mistrusted Sir George; he consulted other people: Maurice Craig, Vanessa's specialist; T. B. Hyslop, and Jean Thomas, who kept a nursing home and knew Virginia well; their views differed but in the end Leonard decided and persuaded Virginia to agree that, although they both wanted children, it would be too dangerous for her to have them. In this I imagine that Leonard was right. It is hard to imagine Virginia as a mother. But it was to be a permanent source of grief to her and, in later years, she could never think of Vanessa's fruitful state without misery and envy.[9]

(Bell, 2, p. 8.)

Savage appears again in July 1913. Bell's chronology informs us that on 22 July Virginia accompanied Leonard to a Fabian conference in Keswick, where she fell ill (Bell, 2, p. 228). On 24 July they returned to London, and on the 25th Leonard consulted Savage:

Savage could see, as Leonard saw, that Virginia was very ill indeed, but I doubt whether he had more understanding of the causes or cure of her illness than Leonard. For him it was the same thing as usual, and the same remedy was prescribed. A few weeks in bed in Jean Thomas's Twickenham nursing home appeared to have cured her in 1910; it therefore seemed best, *in spite of her own remonstrances*, to repeat this treatment.[10] And since on that previous occasion the rest cure had been fortified by a holiday in Cornwall, Savage promised, if she now would do as he ordered, she might afterwards go with Leonard to Somerset on the holiday they had already planned.

(Bell, 2, p. 13, my italics.)

Virginia was an inmate[11] of Burley from 25 July to 11 August 1913. On 22 August, Leonard saw Savage in London, and told him he was afraid to take Virginia to Somerset in her present condition. Savage warned Leonard that he must take her, as to go back on his word at this point could be dangerous. They did go on holiday, to Holford. There, at the scene of the disastrous honeymoon, Virginia refused to eat.

They returned to London. Leonard, who had completely lost faith in Savage, consulted Henry Head on Roger Fry's recommendation.[12] Savage was annoyed with Leonard for having called in a second opinion without informing him first.[13] While Leonard and Vanessa were in Henrietta Street, explaining themselves to Savage, Virginia attempted suicide by swallowing 100 grains of veronal. At this point, Savage ceases to play an active part in the treatment of Virginia.

We are already familiar, from the last chapter, with Virginia's views on his treatment of her: the seclusion, and the ban on reading and writing. But what were Savage's views on the subject of madness? In discussing the writings of Savage and his colleauges on insanity I shall, in each instance, consider them in their relation to three main categories: diagnosis; aetiology; and treatment. In each case I will conclude the main exegesis with a discussion of other ideas relevant to this study which occur in the works of the doctors.

Diagnosis

In essence, much of Savage's writing on insanity is concerned with what he calls 'moral insanity'

In an article entitled 'Moral Insanity'[14] which appeared in the *Journal of Mental Science* in 1881, one year prior to Virginia's birth, Savage outlined a set of beliefs to which he adhered until 1891, the year which marks a turning point in his career, and in his attitude with regard to insanity.[15]

The diagnosis of moral insanity in England derives mainly from the work of Dr James Cowles Prichard (1786-1848), who was chiefly known for his work in anthropology. Prichard was concerned to involve the emotional and moral side of man in a more 'complete' diagnosis. Following the French theorist Pinel, Prichard observed a condition in which the intellectual part of the subject was unaffected while the moral side was disturbed. The diagnosis presupposed a whole battery of social and other expectations where correct behaviour was concerned. Neither Prichard nor his followers offered a positive definition of what was meant by moral insanity, preferring to cite individual examples of departure from established behavioural norms. The concept of moral insanity was essentially an eighteenth-century idea, and was, in one sense, a reaction against the rationalism of that period. The diagnosis was subsumed under more sophisticated nosological systems by the end of the nineteenth century. Savage and his followers may be regarded as the last practitioners of a century-old concept.

What is moral insanity? Savage begins his definition by drawing a distinction between the intellectual and moral parts of the mind:

> though I should not deem any person capable of being intellectually complete and yet morally defective, I would maintain that the defect on the intellectual side may be so little appreciated, or of so little importance in reference to the individual's relationships with the outer world, that it may be disregarded.
>
> (Savage, 1881c, p. 147.)

Savage views the moral side of man as an extension of the physiological. Hence, like well-formed limbs and smoothly functioning nervous systems, it is a product of evolution: 'I look upon the moral relationships, so called, of the individual, as among the highest of his mental possessions, that long after the evolution of the mere organic lower parts, the moral side of man developed' (Savage, 1881c, p. 147).

What is meant by the 'moral side of man'?

> the recognition of . . . right in property developed with the appreciation of the value of human life, so that the control of one's passions, and of one's desires for possession, and of one's passion for power developed quite late in man, and, as might be expected, the last and highest acquisitions are those which are lost most readily.[16]
>
> (Savage, 1881c, pp. 147-8.)

Let us pause for a moment and consider how many themes Savage has called up in this paragraph, and the manner in

which he does it. We start with the physical, then evolve to
the moral. At this point, while not daring to make a clear
and explicit assertion of logical and necessary connection,
Savage nevertheless implies, by his clever juxtaposition of
the physiological, the moral and the political, that the
foundations and motives of empire (power, property and
passion) are a logical and natural development of our moral
side. We may well ask what business medicine has in this
territory. (In *Three Guineas*, Virginia argued that politicians,
doctors, and the clergy are all best defined as priesthoods,
representatives and enforcers of various political *status
quo*s.) By enquiring into the presuppositions behind Savage's
remarks, we discover that, under the cloak of medicine,
Savage is engaged in an exercise which is not entirely what it
professes to be. From the start, we may see that the diagnosis
of madness has behind it an ulterior motive. This is borne
out when Savage ventures to give us an explicit example of a
case of moral insanity: 'The eccentric person who neglects
his relationship to his fellow men and to the society and
social position into which he was born must be looked
upon as morally insane' (Savage, 1881c, p. 148). What strikes
us as being immediately apparent, regardless of where our
own political sympathies lie, is that this 'diagnosis' is little
more than a tool for the preservation of class distinctions.
(It is in the light of thinking of this sort that *Three Guineas*
begins to make sense.) One needn't be a socialist to recognize
the nature of the presuppositions underlying this diagnosis,
and the master whom they serve. Furthermore, we must ask,
what are the ways in which one neglects one's social relationship to one's 'fellow men and to the society and social
position into which he was born'? In the article on moral
insanity, Savage neglects to inform us what they are. However, in subsequent texts (which we will consider shortly),
Savage maintains that this neglect can manifest itself in the
desire to become better educated (particularly in the case
of women and of the lower classes), and in the flouting of
social codes (of dress or behaviour, for example).

We may be disappointed by Savage's lack of rigour in
defining moral insanity. However, the obfuscations, contradictions and indecisiveness which we encounter in his writing

may themselves provide the means by which we may determine precisely what it is he believes. Indeed, they may be the only means by which his thought may be apprehended, for he consciously avoids clear explanations, and gives as a reason his belief that his audience already shares his assumptions:

> I hardly think it worth my while to make very elaborate distinctions between the varieties of moral insanity. I would take it for granted that all admit what I have already said — that there is a condition in which the moral nature or the moral side of the character is affected greatly in excess of the intellectual side. . .
> (Savage, 1881c, p. 148.)

The variety of moral insanity which Savage has discussed so far is referred to by him as *primary* moral insanity. In an attempt to define primary moral insanity more specifically, he writes,

> when speaking of 'primary' I would refer to those cases which, *from the first development*, have some peculiarity or eccentricity of character exhibited purely on the social side.
> (Savage, 1881c, p. 148, my italics.)

So one form of moral insanity has a decidedly social flavour. Here we note a contradiction which is characteristic of Savage. He previously stated, when speaking of evolution and morality, that the moral side was the last part of man's nature to evolve, and hence the first to disappear with the onset of moral insanity. But in the definition of primary moral insanity given above, he states that the characteristic peculiarity or eccentricity has been present 'from the first development'.[17]

Apart from this social brand of moral insanity (he has given us no indication of its cause), Savage maintains that there is also a hereditary form. Here, the ascendancy of the gene renders environmental factors inconsequential:

> Other cases seem from infancy prone to wickedness, and

I would most emphatically state my belief that very many so-called spoiled children are nothing more nor less than children who are morally of unsound mind, and that the spoiled child owes quite as much to his inheritance as to his education. In many cases, doubtless, the parent who begets a nervous child is very likely to further spoil such child by bad or unsuitable education. In considering these latter cases — those that from childhood show some peculiarity of temper and character — it is all-important to remember that inheritance of neurosis plays a very prominent part indeed — that, in fact, the inheritance of neurosis may mean that the children are naturally unstable and unfitted to control their lower natures; that they come into the world unfitted to suit themselves to their surroundings; and but for the conventional states of society, would soon lose their places and become exterminated.

(Savage, 1881c, pp. 148-9.)

What the 'conventional states of society' are remains a mystery; but, whatever they are, they are a mercy; for the morally insane infant owes his life to them.

Apart from primary moral insanity is *secondary* moral insanity, which Savage defines very loosely as 'secondary to some distinct attack of mental disease, or the condition may be secondary to some more general cause, such as intoxication; and in referring to intoxication it should be noted that not only is it a sign of moral insanity in many cases, but that it produces it' (Savage, 1881c, p. 149). Febrile disease[18] can also be a cause of moral insanity, and Savage remarks, 'I believe that I have seen one or two well-marked instances of moral insanity following an attack of febrile disease; so that a person, having suffered from a severe attack of rheumatic fever, became altogether morally perverse'[19] (Savage, 1881c, p. 149).

We find in Savage a serious difficulty with regard to his terminology. While asserting that moral insanity exists, and that it is a medical problem, he nevertheless uses, quite frequently, grossly moralistic and prescriptive terms in describing the conditions of his patients.[20] For instance, he describes a patient who has exhibited unusual behaviour following an attack of rheumatic fever as 'morally perverse'. Behaviour caused by febrile disease which is out of the patient's control is not the same as a wilful, conscious act of immorality — and apart from these considerations, Savage never defines what he means by 'morality'. Savage's alternation between medical and moral terminology tells us a great deal about his methods. Moral terminology replaces medical terminology precisely at that point where his empirical methodology based on a physiology of cause-and-effect is no longer able to account for the phenomena under consideration — and this includes a considerable number of the cases to which Savage refers. Consider the manner in which Savage describes a case of moral insanity in an infant:

> In cases of this kind it is not very uncommon to find some genius, or at all events, some precocity, and in some morally insane children, *one is disgusted* to find not only precocity in some lines of intellectual life, but a precocity of the animal passions also. Sexual desires are developed at an unusually early — in fact, sometimes at an infantine — age. The moral insanity may show itself before five years of age, though this is rare.[21]
> (Savage, 1881c, p. 150, my italics.)

Another example of Savage's moralistic terminology, brought into play where there are no empirical props to support an explanation, consists in the following:

> I have seen two cases, born of parents who were in Bethlem while they were pregnant, so that *the children were saturated with insanity while still in the womb*. The mothers told me *that these infants seemed to be perfect little devils from birth*.
> (Savage, 1881c, p. 150, my italics.)

On another occasion he writes, 'An insane parent may have an insane, idiotic, wicked, epileptic, or somnambulistic child.'[22] This confusion of the medical and the moral has profound implications where the rights and freedom of the patient are concerned. If a man is sick, he is to be treated. If he has broken the law, he is to be punished. If he is wicked, he is to be punished if his 'wickedness' violates civil codes. Savage's medicine seems to be partly therapeutic, partly punitive. In the article on 'moral insanity' he makes the following ominous declaration: 'I am not one who would allow every person who has lost self-control through disease to escape punishment.'[23] The solution of the problem of what to do with the morally insane lies, according to Savage, somewhere between the 'severity of the gaol' and the 'comparative luxury of the asylum' (Savage, 1881c, p. 150). He speaks of the morally insane as being 'constant obstructives to the discipline as well as to the cure of other patients' (Savage, 1881c, p. 155).

One other example of moral insanity which Savage gives may be of interest in relation to Virginia Woolf. This one has to do with 'lying':

> In one case I was consulted by a father, a most honest and straightforward man, who was almost heartbroken because his only daughter — he having four healthy and normal-minded sons — could not, as he expressed it, tell the truth; but when, on investigation, I enquired whether she told lies to her own advantage or to the advantage of other people, I found that nothing of the sort was the case, but that she had a habit of romancing, and on every available occasion would tell her parents the most extraordinary tales of her adventures, and of the people whom she had met, and what they said to her, without malice and without truth.
>
> (Savage, 1881c, pp. 150-1.)

Though Savage gives us few details, it is hard to think of this girl as insane. One wonders how Savage would have viewed Virginia's flights of fancy in conversation. One recalls Quentin Bell's account of Virginia's conversation while driving from Lewes to Sevenoaks one day: 'We met an elephant in the road here only the other day — I fancy they are common in this part of Kent. Why, there is another. Well, perhaps it is only an old sow, but you wouldn't usually find a sow that looked so much like an elephant in any other part of England.'[24]

Savage wrote many articles on the more general definition

and classification of insanity. In 1884 he made a few tenta-
tive attempts at definition in a paper read to the British
Medical Association at Belfast. He began by offering a
definition of mind: 'mind is but the organized result of all
the past experiences of the being, and therefore that mind,
being an ever inconstant and growing power, varies directly
as it is supplied by impressions from all parts of the body'.[25]
He makes an elementary distinction between disorder (of
function, where there is no organic change) and disease
(where actual organic change occurs). In 1887, Savage
turned his attention to insanity as a functional disorder
in an article entitled 'On Some Modes of Treatment of
Insanity as a Functional Disorder'.[26] This paper begins,

> I mean only to state that some, no⁺ all, cases of insanity
> are to be thus treated [i.e. as a functional disorder],
> and I would begin by asserting my belief in the existence
> of a large number of cases of insanity which rather deserve
> to be considered as depending on functional disorder than
> on disease of the brain or nervous system.
>
> (Savage, 1887b, p. 87.)

He then proceeds to state that, in his opinion, there are three
sorts of insanity:

> There are three very distinct groups of persons suffering
> from unsoundness of mind (1) those with disease of the
> brain; (2) those with the brain or nervous system badly
> nourished in one way or another, with insane symptoms
> as a result and, (3) those in whom the mind is unbalanced
> through some sensory or other disorder.
>
> (Savage, 1887b, p. 88.)

Savage mentions that he thinks the prognosis for the first
two sorts of insanity, treated by 'external' means, poor.
The third sort is amenable to 'reasonable treatment', though
he doesn't say on this occasion (or on any other, so far as I
am aware), in what this form of treatment consists.

In 1896 Savage develops further some of the thinking that
went into his 1887 article 'Moral Insanity'. In an article
entitled 'Insanity of Conduct'[27] he writes, in a manner

true to the editorial policy of the *Journal of Mental Science*,

> A man may smile and be a villain, and he may certainly be
> a precious talker and yet a pernicious person. We experts
> in lunacy recognize this, but the world, more especially
> the legal world, is loath to allow that insanity is often to
> be judged of by the acts of the individual rather than by
> his words.
>
> (Savage, 1896a, p. 1.)

It is important to note that Savage is at pains to include the
legal world in his definition of insanity of conduct. Again,
we are confronted with the problem of treatment versus
punishment. Savage re-emphasizes some of the more questionable views outlined in 'Moral Insanity':

> We do not want to form and name a fresh group of
> insanity of the Ethically Insane. The battle as to the
> existence of moral insanity is not over, in England there
> being still physicians of eminence who do not admit there
> is any such ailment apart from sinfulness.
>   We, on our part, wish to re-state our *belief* in moral
> insanity, and to go one step further and show that *breaches
> of the conventional as well as the moral laws of society
> may be but symptoms of disorder or disease of the higher
> nervous system.*
>
> (Savage, 1896a, p. 2, my italics.)

Savage's use of the term 'belief' is highly significant here. The
empiricist, when dealing with fact, *knows* rather than *believes*
(or so he claims). It is the man who adheres to a metaphysical
or religious faith who believes. Savage, the man of science,
would refer to religious or metaphysical faith as 'subjective'.
While asserting that his 'objective' world view is superior,
he fails to see that it too is little more than a subjective faith.
And that faith is more political than anything else. Savage's
use of the diagnosis of moral insanity shows that he is as
interested in being a legislator and adjudicator of social
conduct as he is in being a doctor.
    In 1905 Savage offers a further general definition of in-
sanity. In the Lettsomian Lecture, delivered before the

Medical Society of London in February of that year, Savage
said, in a paper entitled 'Functional Mental Disorders',[28]

> In mental disorder I include a great deal more than in-
> sanity as it is generally considered. The Right Hon. A. J.
> Balfour, at the meeting of the British Association for the
> Advancement of Science last year, pointed out the limita-
> tions of science; he pointed out that the organs of sense
> which were the gauges as it were of truth were them-
> selves but the results, the evolved results, of the experiences
> and the very impressions which they had from without.
> Therefore the senses that were supposed to be the ultimate
> judges of all truth were themselves but the outcome of the
> impressions which were received from the things which
> they were to judge. In the same way we talk about sanity
> and insanity and the gauge of sanity is exactly in the same
> position that the senses are in relationship with science.
>
> (Savage, 1905, p. 409.)

While not constituting, strictly speaking, a definition of
insanity, this passage is nevertheless relevant to the problem
before us for, in it, Savage shows himself to be partial to
those ideas of Locke which Blake so emphatically refuted in
'There is No Natural Religion'. It constitutes a total disa-
vowal of man as an actively intentional being. The one
positive result of Savage's adherence to the *tabula rasa* theory
is that it allows him to recognize that, in certain forms of
functional insanity, where there is no recognizable organic
pathology, the patient's environment might be considered
a causal factor. Savage can therefore write, concluding his
1905 lecture,

> I would repeat here what appealed strongly to my Guy's
> class of former years, the statement that there is no such
> thing as insanity. Insanity, mental disorder, depends as
> much on the surroundings as on the individual's bodily
> condition. If we were all turned out like American watches,
> by the million, all alike, with changeable machinery and
> parts, it would be different. In so-called insanity, and in-
> deed in humanity, we have to deal with constantly chang-
> ing environment, different powers of adaptation, and I
> therefore say at once that I cannot expect to have a clear

morbid pathology for all conditions which do not fall within the conventional lines of sanity.[29]

(Savage, 1905, p. 411.)

While this proclamation is certainly more hopeful and more useful than some of Savage's moralistic pronouncements, we must not confuse 'disbelief' in insanity with the kind of contemporary scepticism exhibited by critics such as Laing, Szasz or Cooper. We are still in the realm of the mechanical. Just as chemical imbalance or an organic deterioration may be the cause of insanity, so, as far as Savage is concerned, adverse surroundings may 'cause' or 'produce' insanity. This is not the same thing as saying that a person chooses a certain form of behaviour as a defence against what is an intolerable situation (what has been termed the 'double bind', for instance). Savage's methodology, whether in discussing organic disease or functional disorders, is always rooted in an aggressive empiricism.

In 1903 Savage published two articles relating to insanity and the law.[30] They are significant because they serve to underline what we have suggested above, that the diagnosis of insanity is often more an indictment than a medical judgement. One of Savage's main points in two of these papers, 'On Unsoundness of Mind and Insanity' (Savage 1903a) and 'Uncertifiable Insanity and Certain Forms of Moral Defect' (Savage 1903b), is that not all persons who are judged to be of unsound mind ought to be detained in asylums. Here he takes the lawyers to task for interpreting the Lunacy Act of 1890 in such a way as to ensure that all persons judged of unsound mind may be candidates for incarceration.[31] Savage's purpose in this article is to declare loudly and clearly to the legal profession that no rigid definition of insanity can or will be given. Savage concludes that:

Lawyers will ever arrange that they shall have a 'sign', and we must be careful not to provide them with what they want, which is a hard and fast definition of insanity. Insanity is, as I have already said, peculiarly a relative condition, so that what is sane in one man is insane in the conduct of another, and what may be sane at one period of our lives would be insane at another.

(Savage, 1903a, p. 24.)

From one point of view, Savage appears as a liberal trying to protect the public from over-zealous interpreters and enforcers of the law. From another point of view, however, Savage's article only represents an argument between the medical and legal professions over who shall have greater power over the fate of the individual in society. Savage's reply to the legal interpretation of the Lunacy Act merely substitutes one arbitrary set of criteria for another: 'The point comes, of course, to this — at what degree of unsoundness of mind is the individual no longer able to fulfil his duty, because of unsoundness of mind' (Savage, 1903a, p. 15).

The key word here is 'duty' — the fulfilment of which is the criterion of sanity. This is an idea put forward by Savage in 1887 in 'Moral Insanity'. Now, as then, he neglects to say what 'duty' is. In view of the relative nature of insanity (as Savage notes above), the judgement as to whether or not a man is fulfilling his duty — not to mention the necessity of first defining what that duty is — would seem to be an extremely difficult, if not impossible, task. (This difficulty must have been compounded by the sheer number of patients Savage saw each day, particularly as Physician Superintendant of Bethlem.) We remember Savage's proclamation in 'Moral Insanity' about 'the severity of the gaol' and the 'relative luxury of the asylum', and view this attempt to remove judgement from the hands of the law and place it in the hands of the doctors with suspicion.

The law may often be unclear, and no doubt many miscarriages of justice do occur; yet, when a man is accused before the law, he has a right to representation by someone well versed in the law and sympathetic to his case, he has a right to a public trial by jury, and he has the right to speak in his defence, and to call others as witnesses in his defence. If accused by means of a medical diagnosis — moral insanity, for instance — a man has no right of appeal, and he may find it almost impossible to find another doctor to examine him in the hope that he will overrule the initial diagnosis. Punitive treatment in the form of baths, purges, mechanical restraint, drugs and isolation (in our time, ECT, drugs and leucotomy replace these) may be prescribed by the doctor, who is not required to seek permission from any higher authority before enforcing this 'treatment'. Before the law, a man has certain rights which will usually be upheld. Before the medical tribunal, a man may be helpless, without rights, punished, deprived of his liberty and caused untold suffering because one man says it is necessary. The diagnosis of insanity as developed by Savage is a tool for enforcing personal and political beliefs, and social and moral expectations in an arbitrary and subjective fashion. It is also a question of expediency: 'And so the difference between insanity and un-soundness of mind may be a question of convenience as to where the patient can be placed' (Savage, 1903a, p. 18).

Savage is so unaware of the kinds of presuppositions which fire his method that he is capable of self-contradictions of the grossest proportions. We have seen how his vocabulary in describing the behaviour of his patients is invariably moral-istic: 'evil', 'devil' and other such terms are used without hesitation. Yet, in a 1906 lecture on 'The Treatment of the Insane'[32], he insists,

> I have said to many of you probably before that there are two words I should like to get rid of in the English language — 'asylum' and 'lunatic'. It will take a hundred years to do away with the stigmata implied in these words — the feeling that because a person is affected in his mind therefore he is alien and must be shut off, so that a man suffering from disease of his highest faculties is treated as an outcast.
>
> (Savage, 1906-7, p. 457.)

The very title of the lecture in which this statement was made — 'The Treatment of the Insane' — contradicts Savage's thesis. Savage gives the impression, in his first sentence, of having made this point with regard to stigmatizing diagnostic terminology many times before. We must assume that he made it privately, or in unpublished lectures, for it does not appear in any of his published works other than this one.

In a 1903 article on moral insanity, Savage is still capable of describing one of his patients as drifting 'from one evil course to another' (Savage, 1903b, p. 748).

In 1907, Savage delivered the Bolingbroke Lecture before the South-West London Medical Society, and he chose as his topic 'The Factors of Insanity'.[33] Savage was then sixty-five years old, and we may take the remarks made around this date as being among his final opinions as to what constituted insanity. He defines insanity thus:

> Insanity, I have said, I shall not define but shall consider it to be a disorder of mental balance which renders the person alien — that is, out of relationship with the surroundings into which he has been born, educated, and has hitherto fitted. The standard will thus be seen to be a purely personal one, the person being measured by his present and past conduct.
>
> (Savage, 1907, p. 1137.)

The first part of this definition we recognize from the 1881 paper, 'Moral Insanity'. The second half, which has to do with the personal criteria of insanity, comes from a later date in Savage's career, the 1903 essay 'Unsoundness of Mind and Insanity'. He states also in this lecture that 'It is not in my opinion possible for everyone to become insane, we are not all potential lunatics' (Savage, 1907, p. 1137). Savage shows that he has already forgotten the ban on the term 'lunatic' which he advocated less than a year previously. (The prohibition against considering the insane as 'alien' has also been lifted — if, indeed, it was ever really meant seriously.) He believes that one *must* be predisposed towards insanity to actually become insane. It is not possible for everyone to become insane. Yet, in concluding his lecture, Savage states that '*it is not possible for everyone to become sane*; there is no one standard of sanity and there is no one pathology. There is, therefore, the personal factor in every case of insanity' (Savage, 1907, p. 1140).

To my knowledge, Savage does not make another major statement with regard to insanity until 1903, in what appears to be his last published work. It is a long, untitled paper

which is a summary of his career and interests, and it is full
of suggestions aimed at younger colleages (Savage is seventy
now).[34] We have seen how the one form of insanity about
which Savage never had any doubt was moral insanity, and
that many of the contradictions in his 'system' result from
this. It comes as a great surprise, then, to read in his final
paper the following reflection:

> It must also never be forgotten that so-called mental dis-
> order is gauged in relation to conduct and that certain
> disorders depend more on the surroundings of the patient
> than on the patient himself. I have long been in the habit
> of referring to the social misfits which have depended
> upon the surroundings rather than on the patient. Social
> and mental disorders are nearly related, and one of our
> most difficult problems is to decide where the badness
> ends and the madness begins.
>
> (Savage, 1913b, pp. 19-20.)

A considerable change has occurred. Mental disorder, that
ill-defined concept which Savage nevertheless managed to
employ with great frequency, has now been called into
question: it is 'so-called'. But most importantly, there is
some recognition of the main shortcoming which has marked
all of Savage's work: his confusion of the moralistic and the
medical, terms which should be mutually exclusive.[35] Of
course, Savage is not unique in having been guilty of con-
fusing medical and moral terminology; it was a failing which
permeated sections of the medical profession during Savage's
lifetime, and which has only been fully identified and self-
consciously combatted in recent years.[36]
Though he managed to recognize, at the end of his career,
the distinction between madness and badness, Savage nevertheless retained his mechanistic view of consciousness. In
concluding his presidential address, he speaks of

> the undefined and not understood Consciousness which
> may be the result of the internal secretions. It pleased me
> to think of feeling and consciousness as the by-products
> of nervous action, and I could not help seeing in some
> instances of morbid mental states evidence that the idea

was not altogether wild.[37]

(Savage, 1913b, pp. 26-7.)

Aetiology

What did Savage believe to be the causes of insanity? Early on in his career, in the only book he ever published (Savage, 1884e) Savage presented a number of specific examples of what he felt to be causes of insanity.[38] Of particular interest in view of the fact that Savage was Virginia Woolf's doctor until her marriage is his belief that education for women is needless and wasteful, if not harmful. Indeed, it may be a major cause of insanity:

> A strong and healthy girl of a nervous family is en-couraged to read for examinations, and having distin-guished herself, is, perhaps, sent to some fashionable forcing house, where useless book learning is crammed into her. She is exposed, like the Strasbourgh geese, to stuffing of mental food in overheated rooms, and dis-order of functions results. Or if a similarly promising girl is allowed to educate herself at home, the danger of solitary work and want of social friction may be seen in conceit developing into insanity. It is in this manner that the results of defective education become often apparent in the case of the weaker sex now-a-days.
>
> (Savage, 1884e, p. 23.)

The tone of this passage is, of course, that of the solid, respectable, upper-middle-class Englishman of the late Victorian period. It expresses all the right sentiments, all the right prejudices, in precisely the right language. There is no longer good sport to be had from pointing up Victorian foibles; but what must be noted is the fact that this kind of glib over-generalization (all girls' schools feature mental force-feeding in overheated rooms) may be published in a medical textbook. Most of Savage's statements in *Insanity and Allied Neuroses* are the opposite of 'scientific'. There is no critical detachment, no verification, no hypothesis, experimentation, control, no logical conclusions — only highly subjective, opinionated proclamations. And when we consider that, during the years prior to her marriage, Virginia Woolf spent most of her time reading, studying Latin and Greek, and writing — precisely the sort of occupation which, according to Savage, may promote 'conceit developing into insanity' — we may guess what Savage might have had to say with regard to that case.

But it is not only the weaker sex who may succumb to insanity produced by education. Further on in the book Savage maintains that education, in itself, regardless of its recipient, can be a pernicious influence:

> With the increase of education are produced over-ambition, feverish pursuit of gain and pleasure, aggregation in towns, celibacy with vice of one kind and another, and the development of religious indifference and general unbelief, associated with neglect of general hygienic conditions.
>
> (Savage, 1884e, p. 23.)

What is astonishing is that this statement is in no way qualified. It is merely presented. But Savage wouldn't have been as successful as he was if he did not know what he could and could not write without incurring the displeasure or disbelief of his colleagues. Savage can publish this sort of opinion because it echoes the prejudices and assumptions of a large proportion of his profession at the time. But isn't there a contradiction inherent in Savage's denigration of education when he and his colleagues are themselves the products of a most lengthy and strenuous professional training? Not at all. There is fear and hypocrisy, but not (at least from their point of view) contradiction. This is so because most, if not all, of Savage's readers understand implicitly that he does not really mean that education is, in itself, pernicious; they realize that what he means is that education ought not to be encouraged among women, or among the lower classes. And this is not because education might be physically or psychologically dangerous for women or workers, but because the authority of the clergy, the politicians, the lawyers and the doctors would undergo a process

of de-mystification if those under their control understood
enough of what they were doing to criticize them. Their aim
is to limit the possibility of a book like *Three Guineas*
being written. But if we are looking for contradictions, for
plain, outright self-negation, that too is present in *Insanity
and Allied Neuroses*.

For instance, early on in the book, Savage declares the
urban environment that most likely to cause insanity: 'We
find that in the highlands of Scotland and in the rural parts
of Ireland and Wales, a general paralysis of the insane is
almost unknown, yet as soon as the same people migrated to
cities they seemed to enjoy no immunity from this disease'
(Savage, 1884e, p. 20). Thirteen pages later, he confidently
proclaims that 'the precarious conditions of the farmer's
life are eminently those to cause a mental break-down'
(Savage, 1884e, p. 33).

In 1887, in a paper on 'Alternation of Neuroses' Savage
wrote that:

> So far, then, we have considered the fact that from
> parent to child the insane or nervous disposition may be
> transmitted, and before leaving the subject I would only
> sum up my experience.
> An insane parent may have an insane, wicked, epileptic,
> or somnambulistic child.
>
> (Savage, 1887a, p. 486.)

A primary cause of insanity may be, then, heredity. In
looking through other papers on the subject in the same
period, we discover that a hereditary or evolutionary view
of the cause of insanity seems to be predominant.

In 1887, in the article entitled 'Some Modes of Treatment of Insanity as a Functional Disorder', Savage suggests
that insanity might be caused by 'unhealthy subjective
states' — that is, by isolation from, or lack of friction with,
other persons. Savage documents this cause by citing the
case of a man who,

> having against his father's wish gone in for electrical
> engineering, instead of following arms, as his friends

wished, gradually got more and more estranged from all near to him, and in the end took a foreign appointment where much of his time was spent alone, and in an unhealthy, subjective state. This led one way or another to the development of hallucinations of nearly all his senses, so that he was sure his father had detectives following and watching him, and ready to report anything to his disadvantage.

(Savage 1887b, p. 104.)

It doesn't occur to Savage that this man's 'unhealthy subjective state' may itself be a symptom rather than a cause. The distinction between cause and symptom in so-called insanity can be as arbitrary as its definition. Which symptom is finally labelled 'cause' depends on how far the doctor is willing to go in the study of his patient; or, it may depend upon what the doctor's 'model' of illness, his preconceptions, allow him to to recognize. In alcoholism or drug addiction, the drink or drug may be the cause of certain forms of behaviour; yet the taking of the drug is in itself only a symptom of an underlying personal difficulty with which the patient is trying, unsuccessfully, to cope.

In the case cited above, it seems that there is, on the one hand, a young man who has an ambition which is, in itself, admirable. On the other hand, the father and friends probably consider electrical engineering a socially unacceptable career, only a little better than trade or manufacturing, and therefore they see it as being in their interest to counsel the young man against this choice. The man's 'unhealthy subjective state' is almost certainly the product of the manner in which his family and friends have alienated him. What is most interesting in this case history (and in almost every case history that Savage relates) is the role played by relatives and friends. In almost every case, the patient has in some way displeased these people. When their attempts to bring the patient round to their own point of view fail, they call in the doctor, and the diagnosis of insanity is brought into play. Perhaps the most fundamental definition of insanity as Savage saw it is nothing more or less than nonconformity to the wishes of others.[39]

While the majority of the medical profession at this time looked upon insanity as, like any other disease, a problem which could be quantified and dealt with by empirical methods, we can nevertheless detect a contrary current in the thinking of some doctors, and this is evident in some of Savage's work. The possibility that insanity may be a product of environment, of a situation, is implicit in much of his early work. Education or alienation from society are situational causes implying functional disorder rather than a physical cause suggesting organic disease. In 1891, in a paper which marks a turning-point in Savage's career, 'The Influence of Surroundings on the Production of Insanity', this implicit undercurrent is made explicit. Savage opens this paper with a proclamation which, given what we know of Savage's work so far, might be viewed as startling:

> I shall endeavour to make it clear that insanity may, and frequently does, arise in families in which no neurotic weakness can be detected, and that certain members of otherwise healthy families become insane as a result of the conditions in which they live.
>
> (Savage, 1891a, p. 529.)

I should make it plain that, as we shall see, Savage's view is not the same as that of the existential or phenomenological theorist's view of insanity. We are still operating at the mechanistic level, where adverse surroundings actively impinge upon the patient's passive consciousness to such an extent that they 'make' him mad. Nevertheless, Savage's new approach tempers to some extent the vehemence of his earlier views. Having taken a critical look at the Darwinian concept of man, Savage denounces the hopelessly pessimistic view that it can generate:

> We have heard so long and so eloquently of the tyranny of the organization that it appears to me that the time has come when some protest should be raised against this gospel of hopeless pessimism.
>
> We are what we are in mind and body to a great extent as organic results of our forefathers, but that we are no longer naked savages is some evidence that progress and

development in the individual and the race may take place as the result of changing surroundings.

Favourable conditions both as to food and as to mental culture will lead to progressive improvement, if the laws of nature are observed, while unfavourable conditions will lead to degeneration.[40]

(Savage, 1891a, pp. 529-30.)

While this is certainly a more enlightened view of the causes of insanity than a purely 'Darwinian' one, it still does not account for the fact of intentionality. Proper food, 'mental culture' and observation of the 'laws of nature' do not represent the sum total of man's existential needs which, if thwarted or unfulfilled, lead to disorder. This view, for instance, could not conclude that the young man whose intention it was to become an electrical engineer rather than a soldier, is suffering from an unhealthy environment which is made unhealthy for him by those who profess to have his interests in mind.

Savage continues,

In practice almost daily one meets with good examples of the influence of surroundings in the production of insanity, and none of my hearers will deny that the character of the insanity greatly depends on education and conditions of life; yet many are inclined to doubt the potency of these in producing insanity *de novo*. Yet asylum statistics, however carefully collected, only show a small minority of the patients to belong to neurotic stock, though in these statistics the family history is made to embrace collateral as well as direct branches.

(Savage, 1891a, p. 530.)

Proceeding even further in his claim for the influence of surroundings, Savage suggests, on the basis of uncited statistical evidence, that *most* cases of insanity in asylums are due to the influence of surroundings rather than to heredity. But what is more remarkable — what is, in fact almost revolutionary about this paper — is the following statement:

I do not wish to discount the value of such tables [i.e. the statistics referred to above], but I would warn others, and accept the warning myself, that the mind having once acquired a bias is very ready to accept as evidence all which agrees with this, and to reject what may be in opposition to the favourite idea. The mind absorbs the similar and rejects the dissimilar. The idea that lunatics are born, not made, is a dominate idea, and has to be firmly faced.

(Savage, 1891a, pp. 530-1.)

What is remarkable is Savage's self-conscious criticism of the scientific method, and of the nature of scientific discovery — a criticism which has probably been available in a partially-formulated way to many thinkers in this century, but which was not fully outlined and its implications developed until T. S. Kuhn's great work, *The Structure of Scientific Revolutions*.[41] Here, Savage acknowledges (though perhaps not fully, with all of the implications this has for his own work) that all scientific enterprise, the work of doctors of psychological medicine included, has a deeply subjective motivation, and that the formulation of hypotheses, the methods by which they are tested, and the conclusions drawn from them are all influenced to a great degree by the experimenter's own expectations; and that, in adopting a hypothesis which he is eager to prove, the scientist may not so much disregard information which may exist to disprove his hypothesis, but he may actually be blind to it, because the conceptual framework he has adopted simply cannot accommodate it. It is not too surprising that, while Savage could formulate this revolutionary critique, he was, at the same time, unable to apply it to his own work, to his own deep-seated prejudices and assumptions. After all, as we have seen, he was capable of contradicting himself to the point of complete self-negation in the course of a single work.

The implications of Savage's new view, at least for him, include the following:

I do not accept fully the doctrine of the criminal anthropologists. I believe some criminals are made by their surroundings as surely as I do that others are be-gotten. Every one of us knows of something in his mind which has been acquired by the circumstances of his life. A man's school, his college, and his profession modify his normal type of mind, and may also lead to disorder. The organized faith of the honest believer is real, though incomprehensible to the scientific agnostic, and has grown with his growth and his surroundings.[42]

(Savage, 1891a, p. 532.)

In admitting that religious faith may be a reality Savage admits that there is a subjective reality separate from, but nevertheless as real as, the objective one. But while he can accept the faith of the believer, he has difficulty in accepting what he judges to be the delusions suffered by some of his patients. As we shall see in the section on treatment, these 'delusions' may also be interpreted as having a very important symbolical reality.

While the first part of Savage's paper may be seen as innovative, its conclusions are reactionary. While warning that 'if we do not admit the influence of surroundings our methods of cure are limited' (Savage, 1891a, p. 535), Savage nevertheless advocated the following cure:

If insanity is always the definite result of primary changes in the nervous tissues, and if these changes are the common result of hereditary nervous irritability, then we are very helpless as physicians. We know that in an asylum the insanity depending on real disease of the brain is very unfavourable in its type. The time may come when medication will alleviate symptoms, but I fear will do little more for such cases. If much insanity depends upon disorder rather than disease, then we may take it that our present method of treatment in asylums is satisfactory, and that restful, pleasant surroundings are more necessary than 'medicine out of a bottle'!

(Savage, 1891a, p. 535.)

We suspect that Savage's new conception of insanity is not based on the 'disease', but on the treatment. If the organic model of insanity has a poor prognosis, and if the profession requires success to justify its activities, then insanity can be viewed as functional, since this conception of it

admits successful treatment. Even so, no one could consider
Bethlem a restful and pleasant place; and during Savage's
reign there, it was even less pleasant. Force-feeding, purges,
packs, baths, mechanical restraint, experimentation with new
drugs and such treatment do not constitute a restful atmosphere.[43] If surroundings can produce insanity, then what
surroundings are more eminently suited to its production
than those of the insane asylum? Again, we see the kind
of division which existed in Savage's thinking. In the 1891
paper we have, on the one hand, a more liberal view of what
might constitute insanity, along with a criticism of scientific
method. On the other hand, there is the inability to consider
new means of treatment to match the new conception of
insanity.

In 1897 Savage succeeded Dr Hack Tuke, the most famous
of the asylum doctors against lay criticism, as President of
the Neurological Society. In an abstract of his inaugural
address, 'Heredity in the Neuroses',[44] we read that

> Dr. Savage traced at some length from the Darwinian
> period to that of Weismann the theories of the influence
> of heredity. He could not admit that there was no power
> of transmitting acquired capacities. He felt much mis-
> understanding had arisen from the idea that there might be
> transmission of fully formed powers or faculties, whereas
> all that could be transmitted must be a predisposition for
> developing a habit or power. The very existence of species
> which bred true and yet bore distinct relationships to
> other species was proof of a power to vary and of a power
> of slowly acquiring specific characteristics which might be
> transmitted.
>
> (Savage, 1897, p. 128.)

In short, neurosis or insanity may not be transmitted from
parent to child fully formed. All that may be transmitted is
a tendency which, to use one of Savage's favourite metaphors,
is like a seed, which will only grow if conditions are favourable.

Savage divided the causes of insanity into two main
groups: insanity caused by heredity, and insanity caused by
surroundings. Almost every case which Savage attributes to

heredity is a case of what he calls 'neurosis'. Before examining those papers in which he discusses heredity as a cause of
insanity, we must attempt to ascertain what Savage means
when he speaks of neurosis.

Most of us probably associate the term neurosis with
Freud; or, more specifically, with Freud and Joseph Breuer,
who jointly published *Studies on Hysteria* in 1903. In that
revolutionary work, Freud and Breuer claimed that neurotic
symptoms invariably had a sexual aetiology. Sexual energy
which was not allowed to find a release became repressed.
This thwarted sexual energy manifested itself in neurotic
symptoms such as paralysis, various losses of function,
pains, and so on. This theory is one of economics: until the
energy is spent in some fashion, or 'abreacted', the symptoms
persist. Charles Rycroft puts the term neurosis in its historical
perspective:

> This term, which dates from the second half of the eight-
> eenth century, originally meant a disease of the nerves.
> Then later, in the nineteenth century, it was used to
> describe 'functional disorders', i.e. diseases believed to be
> due to functional disturbances of the nervous system
> which were unaccompanied by structural changes. Since
> Freud's discovery that one of the neuroses, *hysteria*, was
> a disorder of the personality and not of the nerves, it has
> been used to describe precisely those mental disorders
> which are not diseases of the nervous system.[45]

In London in 1887, neurosis could mean something quite
different from what it meant in Vienna. Savage begins his
paper of 1887, 'Alternation of Neuroses', with the following
definition: 'It is only necessary to say that I use the term
neurosis in a very general way, thereby meaning any well
recognized disturbance of the nervous system which might
be considered due to direct inheritance, or might itself start
a morbid nervous series' (Savage, 1887a, p. 485). So, for
Savage, in 1887, neurosis was a physiological phenomenon.
It can refer to almost anything that is likely to go wrong with
a patient, and it is due to direct inheritance. In 1897, in an
abstract of the address delivered to the Neurological Society
of London, Savage had a different view. Now,

Neurosis was looked upon as morbid nervous instability which showed itself in a nervous expression of bodily states, this nervous expression being exaggerated or premature. Neurosis depended more on the general bodily state than on the states of nervous tissues primarily. . . . Certain neuroses are distinct, and seem to have little likelihood of becoming insanity.

(Savage, 1897, p. 128.)

In this passage the concept is still defined in a manner so hazy as to render it virtually useless as a serious diagnostic term. Eight years later, in the Lettsomian Lecture, 'Functional Mental Disorders', Savage further elaborated the definition of neurosis:

there are the so-called neurotic, the unstable people, you may say, who are pathological specimens from the first; possibly so; I can only say that the world works on two wheels, I believe -- the neurotic and the gouty — and I am inclined to think that the neurotic type has to be considered not as a pathological entity, but as a variety that may tend to be good, bad, or indifferent.

(Savage, 1905, p. 410.)

Finally, the last mention of neurosis in Savage's work is in an article entitled 'The Mental Disorders of Childhood', published in 1908.[46] Here, Savage states that:

It is a common experience when inquiring into the history of mental disturbance to be told that the patient has never been the same since a bad attack of whooping cough. This disease is so bound up with the nervous system that it may be regarded as a neurosis. . .[47]

(Savage, 1908b, p. 520.)

None of these definitions is really useful; they all serve to confuse the issue rather than to clarify it. However, these are Savage's views on the subject of neurosis, and it is on the basis of Savage's definitions that the term is used when discussing the role of heredity in the production of mental illness.

Savage's final position with regard to the role of heredity in mental illness is that a neurosis or other disorder may be inherited, but not fully formed; one initially inherits a tendency, which may be encouraged or discouraged, depending upon the surroundings. But who are the predisposed? Savage posed this question in 1907:

Who, then, are the predisposed? It is all very well to cover one's ignorance with a name but naming is necessary to enable us to go further. I say then that the essential or acquired neurosis is at the base of all insanity. By neurosis I mean the abnormal tendency to react too readily to the surroundings. Most neurotics are derived from parental neurosis of certain types, parental decadence, but this neurotic tendency may be self-induced by causes leading to brain degeneration, such as excess of alcohol and the like. The neurotic exhibit some special peculiarities. They may be unstable from infancy, being liable to motor defects of control as seen in convulsions or general restlessness, to defects of nutritional control seen in irregular temperature, and with development there is defect of emotional control as seen in the 'rages' of infancy and youth. There is a tendency to general instability, physical and nervous, seen in the development of disorders as soon as the stress of sexuality arises. With advancing years neurotic disorders are chiefly marked by their tendency to establish morbid mental habits, and I shall have to point out to you that the stronger the neurotic tendency the greater the tendency to establish such habits and to produce the chronic and recurrent types of disorder. I must, however, ask you not to be alarmed at the many evidences of neurotic tendency and of potentiality to become insane, for one has to remember no plants depend upon one condition alone, so there must be the seed, the soil, and the suitable conditions for growth to produce any result.

(Savage, 1907, p. 1137.)

This statement is in direct opposition to many of Savage's early pronouncements — particularly, and most importantly, the 1891 article on the influence of surroundings in the genesis of insanity. There he maintained that most insanity was caused by surroundings, and for that reason, the prognosis was good, for if removal of the patient to pleasant surroundings was the best medicine, then the profession had it within its power to effect cures. On the other hand, according to Savage, there seemed to be little immediate hope that the medical profession could devise means of contradicting genetic dictates. In this proclamation of 1907, most neurosis is acquired; and while, earlier, neurosis did not necessarily lead to insanity, it is now 'at the base of all insanity'. In essence, in the 1907 lecture, Savage has had to come back to the old problem with which he had to begin as far back as 1887: the problem of defining what it means to say that a person is mad, insane, neurotic, or lunatic. Despite the lack of any definite knowledge whatsoever, the business of diagnosing insanity goes on undisturbed:

There is insanity of evolution or by evolution as well as insanity of dissolution. There is no definite entity which can be considered the cause of insanity, and there is no definite set of symptoms always associated with certain lines of conduct which must be looked upon as mad. There are, as I shall point out, certain mental growths which are morbid but which do not depend upon any line of dissolution. When saying that there are forms of mental disorder which have no material pathology, I must not be misunderstood, for, of course, I admit that every action and every thought has its associated and appropriate nervous equivalent. Every result has a cause. . .[48]

(Savage, 1907, pp. 1137-8.)

And, in the end, Savage comes down on the side of the neurological school. The enthusiastic questioning of the tyranny of this view which Savage undertook in 1891 was short-lived and, by the end of his life, he had returned to the views held in the early articles.

In 1908, in his penultimate article on insanity, Savage discusses the mental disorders of childhood, and hereditary factors are seen as the most important and the most common causes of what he refers to (and this seems to be the only time Savage uses the term) as 'psychoses'. 'In most cases of juvenile psychoses there is a marked hereditary influence' he writes (Savage, 1908b, p. 519). Savage would most likely have viewed Virginia's madness as a result of heredity rather than environment. It seems certain that he would have been familiar with Leslie Stephen's early medical history. He certainly knew of Virginia's cousin's (James Stephen's) madness, having confined him to the asylum where he died.

Treatment

How did Savage treat Virginia? The history of the various periods spent at Burley are fairly well documented in Virginia's letters. Food, rest and the avoidance of intellectual stimulation were enforced.

Savage's writings on the treatment of insanity show the same degree of contradiction as do his writings on the more theoretical and speculative questions of definition and aetiology, though here the contradiction may be much more serious in its implications. Savage begins his writing career with three articles on the use and abuse of various drugs in the treatment of insanity. Throughout his later writings, there is a repeated warning to colleagues not to rely on drugs in the treatment of insanity. However, the veronal with which Virginia tried to kill herself in 1913 was obtained from Savage; and, more seriously, Savage's resignation from his post at Bethlem coincided with the public disclosure of irregularities of treatment there — including the frequent use of mechanical restraint and 'quietening medicines'. The issue became one of national interest, and was the subject of editorial statements in the major medical journals, and was hotly debated in the correspondence columns of *The Times*.

Savage's first paper on treatment by drugs was entitled 'Uses and Abuses of Chloral Hydrate'.[49] Chloral hydrate was then widely used for inducing sleep, and in the treatment of the insane. Savage begins his paper with a severe warning to the profession:

> I should begin by saying that, as a sleep producer, it is powerful, but sleep is not the one thing needful to cure insanity, and sleep may be obtained at too dear a price.

A recent writer said we had passed from a time of physical
restraint to one of chemical restraint. I do not think the
profession has passed, but I confess to believing that great
risk has been run, and that without energetic protest the
harm will be done.

(Savage, 1879c, p. 5.)

On the same page he goes on to say that: 'We must not
quiet our patients for the sake of quiet.' In his analysis of
the drug, Savage shows how, when abused, it may in fact
be a *cause* of insanity, rather than a cure. His final verdict
is not in favour of the drug:

chloral may produce physical ill health, hypochondriasis
and insanity. It may relieve epileptic furor, but cannot
cure epilepsy. It may produce sleep in some cases with
advantage, but more commonly disadvantageously. It may
be used as restraint rather than treatment in violent cases.

(Savage, 1879c, p. 8.)

The second major article on the use of drugs in the treatment
of insanity also appears in 1879, and is entitled 'Hyoscyamine
and its Uses'.[50] This article is even more critical of reliance
on drugs than the previous one. Savage begins by citing some
of the recent literature on the drug, and then goes on to
make the very important point that, while all of the writers
he had studied used the term 'hyoscyamine' to describe the
drug with which they were experimenting, there are in fact
three drugs which go by this name, and that an adequate
distinction had not, to date, been made among them. Savage
experimented with all three of these forms at Bethlem, and
this paper presents the results of these trials. They are uni-
formly horrifying.

With the variety known as 'hyoscyamia', a dose as small
as one twenty-sixth of a grain produced collapse. Other
symptoms were inability to read, loss of power in the limbs,
great mental depression and 'dread, so that the patients
would struggle violently rather than have a second dose'
(Savage, 1879a, p. 178). It also produced 'the feeling as if
death were imminent', confusion, hallucinations of sight
and of touch, and 'a dry, unpleasant feeling in the throat

which drinking did not relieve'. He notes further that 'the appetite always failed at once', and that these acute symptoms lasted from twelve to eighteen hours, 'the moral effect lasting much longer' (Savage, 1879a, p. 179). Savage used the drug on a number of patients who were noisy or who were 'dirty in their rooms': 'a quiet night and a clean room were the results' (Savage, 1879a, p. 179). However, despite the value of the drug as an expedient form of treatment, Savage wrote that he could have no good opinion of it. He also notes, in one of the brief case histories which he cites, that the subject of his experiments was 'violent and vindictive against me as a poisoner'. This is hardly surprising.

With another form of the drug, referred to as 'the extractive of hyoscyamine', the main result seemed to be serious loss of appetite. However, Savage is less unfavourable in his view of this form of the drug than he is of the one just discussed. He writes, 'On the whole I like the drug as a producer of quiet without much injury to the patient' (Savage, 1879a, p. 180). Despite the fact that he likes this form of the drug as a sedative, Savage concludes the article by saying that: 'I do not consider any of the above-named drugs as curative in any sense, and my feeling is strongly against all narcotics and most so-called nervine drugs' (Savage, 1879a, p. 183). Savage tells us that he gave his test cases daily doses of the drug for six weeks. Considering the nature of its effects, it seems unlikely that his subjects were willing, or that they escaped unharmed. We are not surprised when Savage tells us that they suffered from 'delusions' of persecution.

Despite the fact that Savage concludes his article with an unfavourable view of the drug, and an explicit statement against the use of narcotics, he nevertheless published, in 1881, a short paper entitled 'Case of Mania Greatly Improved By the Use of Hyoscyamine'.[51] The conclusion Savage reaches in this brief paper is somewhat at variance with his explicit statements against the use of narcotics in the previous papers, but not with the implicit approval which he expressed when he said that he liked the drug as a sleep-producing agent. In the 1881 paper we find that what he really means is that he doesn't think that narcotics can provide a cure for insanity, and that, while they should not be used regularly, he finds the prescription of them beneficial in some cases:

> I report this case, not as I at one time hoped, of a cure, but rather to point to the use I made of Hyoscyamine and allied drugs, not to produce quiet, but to break any tendencies to regularity of return in attacks of excitement. I feel very strongly against the regular use of narcotics, considering that they not only do not cure, but that they, in many cases, act injuriously, making possibly curable cases incurable.
>
> (Savage, 1881a, p. 62.)

It is impossible to ascertain for certain whether or not Savage prescribed hyoscyamine for Virginia. Certainly, every one of the side-effects of the drug correspond with the main symptoms of Virginia's breakdowns: inability to read or concentrate; depression; feelings of dread, as if death were imminent; confusion; hallucinations; failure of appetite; 'a dry unpleasant feeling in the throat which drinking did not relieve'; and loss of power in the limbs. We are already aware that Virginia exhibited all but the final two symptoms listed here. But her diary entry for 2 September 1930 recounts a fainting fit in which she experiences the 'unpleasant feeling' in the throat:

> I was walking down the path with Lydia [Keynes, née Lopokova, the ballerina who married J. M. Keynes]. If this dont stop, I said, referring to the bitter taste in my mouth & the pressure like a wire cage of sound over my head, then I am ill: yes, very likely I am destroyed, diseased, dead. Damn it! Here I fell down — saying 'How strange — flowers'. In scraps I felt & knew myself carried into the sitting room by Maynard, saw L. look very frightened; said I will go upstairs; the drumming of my heart, the pain, the effort got violent at the doorstep; overcame me; like gas; I was unconscious; then the wall & the picture returned to my eyes; I saw life again.
>
> (*Diary*, 3, p. 315.)

Among Leonard's papers in the Monk's House Collection at the University of Sussex is a document entitled 'Account of Fainting Attack, 11 August'.[52] Leonard does not make a note of the year, but it is possible that he is referring to an attack on 19 August 1925 which is documented in Virginia's diary (*Diary*, 3, p. 38). The occasion was Quentin Bell's fifteenth birthday. Again, the Keynes's were there. Among the symptoms noted by Leonard is a very bitter taste in the roof of the mouth. If a drug such as hyoscyamine were prescribed to Virginia, the chronology of her treatment reveals that it would probably have been done so under Maurice Craig's orders. As we shall see, Craig often prescribed a sleeping draught for Virginia, 'to take at the least wakefulness' (*Letters*, 2, p. 89).

In an address to the first meeting of the Section of Psychology at the annual meeting of the British Medical Association in Belfast in 1884, Savage proposed that, since insanity was generally divided into two main groups — functional and organic — different treatments were required for each variety:

> The treatment of disorder and of disease must surely differ entirely, and I think, therefore, that the diagnosis between disease and disorder is of the utmost importance for the welfare of the patient. Disease of the brain does occur in the insane, so that we find the finer elements of the nerve-tissue interfered with; but, on the other hand, it is astonishing to find how few mental symptoms may be present when disease of a coarse kind is presented within the skull.
>
> (Savage, 1884d, p. 239.)

Savage did not, however, in the course of that address, say in what ways treatment should vary for disorder and disease. Indeed, he did not mention what they were at that time, nor did he make any further reference to treatment whatsoever. We must wait until 1887 for Savage's first major statement on the treatment of insanity, in an article entitled 'On Some Modes of Treatment of Insanity as a Functional Disorder'. During this time, Savage was Physician

Superintendant at Bethlem, and in order to represent Savage fully and fairly, I must quote from the article at length, for it must provide the background to the story of the debate over the mechanical restraint of patients at Bethlem, its astronomical mortality rate, and Savage's resignation:

> Treatment of the insane at present comprises treatment by drugs, and the treatment by seclusion, *i.e.* by the removal from home and home associations. Before proceeding to my special points I must briefly refer to these. I believe that drugs in a few cases are very useful in breaking down habits of sleeplessness, restlessness, violence, or the like, but that they should be used with a sparing hand, and certainly not continuously. I believe that every patient of unsound mind who is being kept quiet and controlled by chloral, bromide, opium, or any other sedative or hypnotic is being badly treated. I would rather tie a patient down constantly than keep him always under the influence of a powerful drug. The term 'medical restraint' has been coined, and though I believe in some cases the term has been abused, yet I believe that on the whole the very opprobrium which is connected with the term 'restraint' will be of use and make a man think twice before he continuously treats patients suffering from insanity or any of its more marked symptoms with these 'restraint' drugs, potent in some cases for good, but in more for evil. Drugs, of course, must be used in cases where the insanity depends upon some condition of the body which may be relieved by medicine . . . . Cod-liver oil, steel wine, Griffith's mixture, mineral acids and tonics of one kind and another, form the staple drugs used in Bethlem Hospital.
>
> (Savage, 1887b, pp. 88-9.)

This article follows the form we have now come to recognize as characteristic of Savage. He begins with a fairly liberal statement, opposing what he knows many medical men to believe to be objectionable practices in the profession. But Savage was a seasoned writer, and an experienced orator. He knew how to handle his audience. It cost him nothing to placate potential critics at the beginning of a speech or an article, for he could always go on, as his text progressed, to subtly (and sometimes not so subtly) introduce enough exceptions to the golden rule initially outlined to give himself almost unlimited freedom.[53] So, after beginning the 1887 article in a liberal fashion, defending the rights of the patient, he goes on to say that

> although I follow as much as possible the principle of 'non-restraint', yet I should consider myself altogether unfit to take charge of a large asylum if I tied my hands by following the absolute system of non-restraint regardless of every condition which may arise among the insane. I would say definitely that restraint itself may in a few cases be of immense importance from the reasonable or rational point of view, and for that matter powerful drugs such as hyoscyamin [sic] may have a similarly useful effect. I have known a patient violent, destructive, and maniacal who, having assaulted his fellow-patients and destroyed property and threatened suicide, when he found himself completely controlled in a prolonged warm bath for three hours became convinced of the inutility of his violence and from that time became more amenable to more congenial treatment, and I have known a chronic case of insanity benefited materially by a few hours in the padded room or even an hour's restraint, so that habits of destructiveness, such as tearing paper from the walls, or jumping on chairs, have been checked, and the patient has been thereby less likely to injure himself and is rendered altogether a more hopeful case than before restraint.
> (Savage, 1887b, pp. 89-90.)

Having cited the exceptions to his own rule, Savage then goes on to justify himself by means of an unpleasant metaphor:

> The man with a badly broken leg requires rest (restraint if you like), removal of injurious influences, simple nutritious food, and little more. Many acute cases of insanity should be treated in precisely the same way. They are practically put into splints when they are sent to an asylum, and if in this splint it should be necessary from time to time to tighten the bandage I see no harm likely to follow.
> (Savage, 1887b, p. 90.)

This version of the asylum is not the idyllic one referred to in the 1891 article on the influence of surroundings, where the asylum is a 'restful' and 'pleasant' place.

In 1888, one year after the publication of this article, Savage came under severe attack not only from lay critics, but from some of his colleagues. In September and October of 1888 there appeared in the correspondence columns of *The Times* a number of letters protesting against the treatment of patients at Bethlem, especially against the use of quietening drugs and mechanical restraint. On 26 September 1888 Sir James Clark Lawrence, president of Bridewell and Bethlem Royal Hospitals, wrote to *The Times* in defence of these institutions and their officials, stating that the lunacy inspectors had made their reports for the year in August, and had found nothing out of the ordinary. On 2 October, Sir James Charles Bucknill[54] replied with a scathing attack on Lawrence and his methods. Bucknill alleged that Lawrence spent very little time at either of the institutions of which he was President, and that he had neglected to mention one very glaring irregularity noted by the lunacy inspectors in their report. The irregularity consisted in the fact that out of 264 patients resident at Bethlem in 1887, 38 of them had died that year in hospital — 14.4 per cent of the hospital's population. This figure compared unfavourably with the average in-hospital mortality rate of 7.28 per cent nationally in similar institutions. The inspectors' report also showed that, during the first twenty-six days of June 1887, 18 out of 264 patients had been restrained mechanically, as compared with only 25 cases of restraint recorded during the same period in all of the institutions in the United Kingdom combined. On 6 October, an editorial in *The Lancet* condemned 'the breeze which has been blowing of late in the columns of one of our daily contemporaries'.[55] The writer claimed that no layman had a right to interfere with or even comment on a professional medical matter. *The Times* has never made a policy of publishing unsubstantiated attacks on innocent victims in its columns, and Savage's position at Bethlem was not made more secure by the breeze which blew there. Savage wrote to the editor of the *Lancet*, and on 13 October a letter appeared in which he stated that he had not condescended to a debate in the daily press, and would continue to refrain from doing so.[56] Given that the medical profession had become, by 1888, autonomous enough not to be easily bullied by lay criticism, Savage's position was not seriously threatened at this point. It was threatened, however, when a colleague, Dr George Thompson, wrote to *The Lancet* accusing Savage of imprudent and excessive use of drugs as a means of enforcing quiet among patients at Bethlem. Savage, of necessity, did respond to this more serious threat to his position in a one-paragraph plea of innocence to *The Lancet* on 3 November. On 13 October he had published a very long letter explaining his position with regard to the use of mechanical restraint. Except for the fact that it is a plea of innocence, the letter is very similar to the 1887 article on 'Some Modes of Treatment of Insanity as a Functional Disorder'. After having reiterated all of the points made in that article, including the initial statement against the use of restraint, and then the advocation of it, Savage concludes,

I do not wish here and now to enter into all the cases of mechanical restraint which are recorded in the 'visitation book', though I am prepared to do this if need be. At present it must suffice for me to say that I felt for a time restrained from doing what seemed likely to be useful to my patients because of this so-called principle of 'non-restraint', but during the past two years I have gained confidence from experience, and I have tried the experiment with results which have justified my action, and, with Dr. Yellowlees of Glasgow, I would say that I acknowledge no principle of 'non-restraint', but only the higher one of humanity and humane treatment, which, if it mean anything, means the use of every method likely to restore health. The dread of the return of the use of fetters appears to me as groundless as though, because we use domestic servants, there should arise a scare lest slavery should re-develop. Service will last, and though the slavery of restraint is over, its service as a handmaid to the physician will continue to have its place and to be better understood.

(Savage, 1888a, pp. 738-9.)

In the letter, Savage describes the kinds of mechanical restraint which he used at Bethlem:

> The mechanical means used were — (*a*) 'Soft gloves', of which each hand is separate and padded to the thickness of about an inch, and which are fastened by a strap round the wrist with a screw button. (*b*) 'Strong dresses', made of stout linen or woollen material, and lined throughout with flannel. The limbs are free to move, but the hands are enclosed in the extremities of the dress, which are padded. (*c*) 'Side-arm dresses', made of the same stuffs as the last, but in these there are two attached pockets to the side of the body of the dress, into which the hands of the patient are placed. By this means, though the patient can walk about his room, such dresses being used at night, he cannot make use of his hands to injure or destroy. (*d*) I employ the wet and also the dry pack. The former is so commonly used that I need not describe it; but as the dry pack is seldom used with the insane, I therefore wish to point out that in this mode of treatment I have the patient wrapped in a sheet or a blanket, and if very restless a second may be used. The patient is then placed on a mattress, and retained there either by means of an attendant, or else by applying a sheet over the patient, which is fastened under the bed. In a few instances, in which there was exhaustion, with some bodily ailment as well, such as swelling of the feet, I have placed the patient in a side-arm dress, and then lightly packed him, so as to ensure the recumbent position, and in one similar case I had tapes applied to the side-arm dress and fixed to the bed. The result was the saving of the patient's life. I have used a belt once with attachment of the elbows to it, so that the patient, who was given to injuring himself by picking and rubbing, was thus prevented from so doing. I maintain that every physician with experience has a right to private judgement in the treatment of his cases, and that is practically what I claim and for which I suffer abuse.
>
> (Savage, 1888a, p. 738.)

On 2 November 1888 a testimonial dinner was held at the Café Royal in honour of Savage's retirement from Bethlem. The distinguished guests included Dr Hack Tuke, the main spokesman for the asylum doctors against lay intervention, and a prepared address 'referred to the exceptional ability and energy with which Dr. Savage had performed his duties'.[57]

When the patient's situation did not warrant drugs or mechanical restraint, what other means did Savage use? He practised a form of treatment which he referred to as 'moral treatment'. This consisted in the following advice which Savage offered to the young doctor:

> be perfectly straightforward in all your relationships with your patients, and by this I mean not the more conventional speaking as much truth as is necessary, but speaking as nearly as possible the whole truth to each individual case.
>
> (Savage, 1887b, p. 93.)

Savage speaks of the 'force of reason', which even the insane acknowledge. Use reason, Savage urges, and you will get reasonable results. However, as usual, there are exceptions, and in this case they are cited with the usual promptness. Savage refers to cases of delusions, 'cases in which the sensory impressions are so predominant that no reason affects them at all' (Savage, 1887b, p. 93). He cites one case which is of particular interest. It concerns a man whose general feelings regarding his treatment are of intense suspicion. He feels, as Virginia Woolf did, that there is a conspiracy afoot:

> at present there is a patient in Bethlem who is suspicious, and who believes that he has been kidnapped into Bethlem Hospital for some improper purpose. He hears voices at night telling him what is going to be done to him, and by day every movement of his neighbouring patients indicates to him some plot or conspiracy which is to do him harm. The doctors are to him not medical men at all, but jailors and torturers, who have control over the engines which are to work his destruction. By day and by night his senses are misleading him, and these sensory impressions are so vivid and so constant that other less impressive evidence given by outsiders is not accepted; but still, even in a case

like this, I seek every opportunity of upsetting his evidence.
If, for instance, he says 'there is a battery under my bedroom,' I say 'come and see for yourself the room under
yours;' or, if he says 'on the roof there is an apparatus,'
one brings evidence to show that no such apparatus exists.
(Savage, 1887b, pp. 93-4.)

Of course, Savage is right — from his own point of view. But
his advice to the young doctor never gets beyond self-
congratulation. Savage doesn't stop to inquire whether or not
the patient's 'delusions' might have some basis — if not in
empirical reality, then in a symbolical way. As for the empirical reality, we can be sure that the patient in question knew
of the means of restraint practised by Savage at Bethlem,
as the case history is published in 1887, the year during
which Savage used restraint in earnest. It is perfectly reasonable that, if the patient saw others being restrained, or if he
had been restrained himself, he should look upon the doctors
as 'jailors' and 'torturers'. But the crux of the matter is a lack
of communication. Savage insists on 'reading' the patient's
behaviour at a literal level only. Of course, there is no battery
under the floor, no engines on the roof. But what does exist
in a very real way is a severe threat to the patient's freedom,
and to his dignity as a human being. He feels, with every
justification, that he is being violated, humiliated, abused.
This is what his 'delusions' mean.

I am quite certain that there was a sufficient basis for the
'delusions' from which Virginia Woolf suffered, and that they
have a meaning: they are natural reactions to what she quite
rightly viewed as an impingement upon her freedom, a violation of her self. In the same way, her attacks upon Leonard
and her nurses are the reactions of a person with her wits
about her who feels she is being manipulated and forced.

Behind the golden rules prohibiting the use of drugs and
mechanical restraint lay, paradoxically, an advocation of the
use of those methods of treatment. Behind the determination
to tell the patient the truth, to be honest with him, lies
emotional blackmail and disconfirmation of the patient's
own experience. When Savage treats a patient, two points
of view come into conflict. The patient's point of view is

that of the madman, the point of view which doesn't tally with the majority. Savage's point of view is that of Reason, of proportion, of common sense and of good. Savage considers a patient's prognosis good if he is submissive — if he rejects his own point of view (his self) and comes over to Savage's side.[58] The patient must admit that he is sick. But he must do more than that. He must please the doctor, he must show that he is repentant, and that he is sorry for having caused so much bother.

For instance, a potential suicide is admitted to hospital. Until the time of his admission, the man's friends had looked after him constantly, but the expense and energy required became too great:

> On his arrival I told him that we had no such provision to prevent him from injuring himself as he had been used to, but that *I trusted he would not injure himself, as it would cause great worry and annoyance to us who wished to do a kindly act to him.*
>
> (Savage, 1887b, p. 95, my italics.)

No attempt is made to find out why the man is suicidal. The whole aim of Savage's moral method is to secure from his patients behaviour which contributes to the smooth running of the hospital. On another occasion, Savage's moral method consisted in letting a man have his freedom from the hospital for a day, provided that he adhered to a set of rules which Savage had laid down. Savage relates, '*to my disgust*, he broke every one of his promises' (Savage, 1887b, p. 92, my italics). The patient quite cleverly replies to Savage's complaint that, having treated him as a man of honour, he has gone back on his word: 'Quite so, I, as a lunatic, can give my word, but, as a lunatic, I cannot enter into a contract' (Savage, 1887b, p. 92). According to the current lunacy legislation, the man was perfectly correct — he could not enter into a binding agreement. Savage's disgust doesn't allow him to take the point made by the patient, or to recognize the grim humour of his logic. By assuring the patient that he is a friend, and that it is only through him that cure can be affected; and then by citing the patient's symptoms as

instances of gross neglect of his friendship, of personal insult
to himself, Savage bullies the patient into conforming to his
expectations. It is not surprising that Savage is an admirer
of Dr Yellowlees of Glasgow (to whom he refers in his letter
to *The Lancet*, defending his conduct at Bethlem), who

> makes a point of attracting the feelings and the sentiments
> in cases of masturbation, for he transfixes the prepuce in a
> slow, almost solemn way, at the same time that he
> preaches a very stirring sermon on the weakness of the
> vice and the probable results if the habit continued.
> (Savage, 1887b, p. 104.)

The OED defines 'transfix' as a transitive verb meaning to
'Pierce with a lance, etc.'. Another form of moral treatment
used by Savage consists in getting friends and relatives to
send letters to the patient disconfirming his 'delusions'.

In some cases, Savage combined the moral and the medical
modes of treatment. He describes an extraordinary case of a
suicidal and homicidal patient who suffered from various
hallucinations. The man was extremely intelligent, and
Savage got him to read about other cases of hallucination.
The man eventually began a book about his experiences,
and Savage thought his chances of recovery good. The
study and writing constituted the moral treatment in this
case. Savage adds that, 'It is only right to say that besides the
moral treatment I have tried other means. Thus, he has had
a blister over the scalp and setons through the neck . . . so
that this patient has been treated, on the one hand, by
reason and at the same time has not been neglected from a
medical point of view' (Savage, 1887b, p. 100). (The OED
defines 'blister' as 'anything applied to raise a blister.' A
'seton' is a 'Skein of cotton etc. passed below skin and left
with ends protruding to promote drainage etc.')

Most of the above discussion is based on Savage's paper of
1887, on 'Some Modes of Treatment of Insanity as a Functional Disorder'. It is not until 1906 that we get another
manifesto from Savage on the treatment of the insane. In his
article entitled 'The Treatment of The Insane', Savage re-
iterates the moral method of treatment: 'A man presents

himself saying the whole world is against him and he will kill himself. I say, "You feel you could kill yourself; very well, don't. It will be very inconvenient for your friends and for me" ' (Savage, 1906-7, p. 458). About the use of drugs, Savage has this to say: 'People nowadays are rather inclined to disparage drugs and drug treatment, but there is no doubt that they are essential in some cases of mental disorder. They may prevent a breakdown, or they may alleviate it in one way or another' (Savage, 1906-7, p. 459). He then says a very curious thing with regard to purges: 'I remember the day when patients were kept quiet by antimony and purges. They were made sick or they were purged, and thus kept quiet. We have got past all this, and it is absolutely necessary to remember that purges may be essential and necessary' (Savage, 1906-7, p. 460). Usually Savage waits for a paragraph or two before breaking his golden rule; this article is unique in that, during the course of one sentence, he asserts that we have 'got past' purges, and that they are 'essential and necessary'. Saline injections are also recommended.

It is interesting to note a shift in Savage's attitude towards the moral method of treatment. In the paper of 1887, Savage insisted that one must use the 'force of reason' in dealing with deluded patients. In 1906-7 he is adamant in saying that 'to reason with the unreasonable does little good' (Savage, 1906-7, p. 460).

Savage concludes his 1906-7 article with a note about prophylaxis — preventive psychological medicine. He declares, 'we are left with only two methods — ample provision for the poor unfortunates in institutions, or ... castration' (Savage, 1906-7, p. 460).

The last recorded statement made by Savage on the subject of insanity is this: 'I am inclined to think that the scourging of the lunatic in times past might have occasionally been a help to recovery' (Savage, 1913b, p. 20).

Conclusion

Virginia Woolf was speaking from experience when she referred to the 'dangerous and uncertain theories of psychologists

and biologists' in *Three Guineas*.[59] And she also knew what
she was talking about when she referred to the 'priesthood of
medicine' (*TG*, p. 231). It is perhaps in the light of *Three
Guineas* that the full implications of Savage's psychological
medicine become most apparent. For *Three Guineas* is the
work of an outraged individual who saw that the sanctity of
individuality, of the subjective life, was under universal
assault. Criticizing the 'objectivity' which many professions
claim for themselves, Virginia Woolf saw that: 'Since the
impersonal is fallible, it is well that it should be supplemented
by the personal' (*TG*, pp. 91-2). It is the personal for which
her writing stands, and Savage presented an immediate threat
to the personal.

The political argument of *Three Guineas*, which many
readers have found naive or cranky, was, in fact, a response
to a very real state of affairs. In conclusion, I would like to
examine Savage's views on the question of eugenics. Here,
Virginia's assertion that medicine can be a 'priesthood' and
a political force are convincingly substantiated.

In 1911 Savage published an article entitled 'On Insanity
and Marriage', which is followed by a long discussion on
eugenics, featuring contributions by prominent physicians
and lay persons, and which makes crudely explicit some of
the political undercurrents which we have noted in his work.[60]

We recall that when Leonard approached Savage on the
subject of Virginia having children, Savage said that it would
'do her a world of good'. In the article 'On Insanity and
Marriage', he gives numerous examples of cases in which
marriage should be forbidden by the doctor. He begins by
stating that:

In no case should it be allowed where there is a history
of periodical recurrences, and it is certain that there is a
very grave risk in those cases of adolescents who at
puberty and with adolescence have periods of depression
and buoyancy. I have seen a good many such cases in
which there has been marriage in haste with a leisure of
repentance. I think suppression of the facts as to such
attacks should really be a ground for declaration of nullity.

(Savage, 1911b, p. 98.)

He also notes, 'I would never allow marriage in any cases where there are fully organised delusions or hallucinations'; marriage is to be forbidden where 'there has been epilepsy with any mental symptoms', 'moral perversions', 'sexual perversion', or 'impotence' (Savage, 1911b, pp. 99-100). Savage declares that 'Marriage should never be recommended as a means of cure' — 'I would speak equally strongly against marriage as relief for so-called neurasthenia or hypochondriasis, and I have already said that for sexual disorder it is dangerous' (Savage, 1911b, p. 100).

We have seen how strong Savage's views are on a controversial subject such as mechanical restraint. On the subject of eugenics and marriage his views are equally strong, and they are shared by many of his contemporaries. In the discussion which follows Savage's paper, a Mr Crackenthorpe, who describes himself as a 'eugenist', deplores the fact that anyone may publish banns and be married without state control or hindrance. He hopes that with 'the growth of scientific knowledge on the one part, and of lay enthusiasm on the other, we should probably arrive within reasonable distance of the State requiring that there should be produced some *prima facie* testimony of fitness before people were allowed to marry' (Savage, 1911b, p. 102). A woman identified as 'Miss Dendy' makes a lengthy contribution to the discussion. The only background information she relates about herself is that she is mistress of a home for '225 feeble-minded boys and girls and young men and women' (Savage, 1911b, p. 104). What is relevant in her speech is her conception of the feeble-minded.[61] 'Happiness was the normal condition of the feeble-minded; they had neither remorse for what they had done, nor any apprehension concerning what might happen in the future. At Sandlebridge they built upon the weakness of the will factor. That was the factor which was common to all of them; they had practically no will-power' (Savage, 1911b, p. 105). Even if we assume that Miss Dendy's charges are very 'low grade' 'idiots' (to use the then current terminology), we must still contest the idea that they had absolutely no sense of time — no memory, no hope, no experience. Miss Dendy is concerned to reinforce the defects of her charges, to ensure that they will always

be happy idiots, and untroublesome ones. Miss Dendy's
farm is an Orwellian nightmare come true:

> Many of the children have been in the home over eight
> years; four were over twenty-one years of age, and she
> could assure the meeting at their coming of age party their
> only conversation was as to what they should do with the
> farm stock in future years. They had no wish to leave, and
> the only inclinations and ideas which seemed to exercise
> them were those which were put into their heads by the
> responsible officials of the home. Yet there were thousands
> of similar people abroad in the land, who were left to take
> their ideas from their evil-disposed associates. Such a state
> of things was the height of folly.
>
> (Savage, 1911b, p. 105.)

There is a sinister contradiction inherent in Miss Dendy's
account. She assures her audience that her charges are basic-
ally happy animals: for if they haven't memory, hope,
despair, desire or goals then they are no better than animals.
Yet, in their happy animal state, they have no sexual desire,
she maintains. One wonders how Miss Dendy contrived to
prevent sexuality from rearing its ugly head.

According to Miss Dendy, 'thousands of people abroad in
the land' should be rounded up and placed in homes like her
own:

> Many such people belonged to the unemployed. She
> wished to be careful how she spoke of such things, because
> some had accused her of saying that all unemployed
> people were feeble-minded. There were many more such
> people than were generally supposed. She herself had a list
> of over 3,000, and additions were pouring in day by day.
>
> (Savage, 1911b, p. 105.)

In conclusion, Dr Fletcher Beach

> thought all would agree with the statement that national
> progress could only take place when means were taken to
> increase the fit and decrease the unfit. Dr. Ewart then
> pointed out that the proper way to decrease the unfit was

to put them into permanent institutions for the feeble-minded . . . . But those institutions were only drops in the ocean; it was necessary to have a large number of them established.

(Savage, 1911b, p. 106.)

Beach concludes his contribution by proposing that the state control human reproduction, discouraging the unfit and rewarding those who produce healthy offspring:

He, the speaker, did not consider himself a pessimist, but he believed that we were travelling towards a fall, and that the only way in which that fall could be arrested was for the State to interfere to prevent the unfit getting married. Dr. Ewart also said that the State might honour and reward those in all ranks of life who could produce, and did produce, healthy and able children.

(Savage, 1911b, p. 106.)

These statements by various speakers make explicit one of the political issues which we have maintained to be involved in the diagnosis of insanity. In his closing speech, Dr Ewart brings the often obscure assumptions which underlie the diagnosis of insanity into sharp focus. He maintains that the purpose of this meeting of the Medico-Psychological Association of Great Britain is 'the hope that the collective wisdom of that body might evolve a practical scheme whereby a polluting stream might be dammed and great good thus accrue to the national health' (Savage, 1911b, pp. 111-12). He makes it clear that not only should the defective, the below-average, be controlled; but that the above-average, the genius, should also be, if not controlled, then regarded with suspicion in a healthy society. 'If a race is healthy, vigorous, and successful, the best citizens are those who approach the average':

They would have well-balanced nervous organisations, and they would hand on the same characteristics to their offspring, for if physical strength is transmitted, so must mental strength. These men would be more useful than geniuses who are individuals with a disproportionate development of some particular faculty, leading to a disturbance of mental equilibrium, psychopathic phenomena, and emotional spasm. Can such be designated as Nature's finest handiwork?

(Savage, 1911b, p. 112.)

These sinister words contain the same contradictions that we found in Savage's views on education, for the medical man is never the 'average'. In this frenzy of political sermonizing, rational thought and human responsibility are devalued.

Having identified the kind of people whom he thinks constitute the best population, Ewart suggests to his colleagues the means by which this medical utopia might be made a reality:

As to the methods to be adopted, the best might be the notification of those aments by the medical officers attached to the different schools to then be certified before a magistrate and sent to some colony until the age of twenty-one, when they would again be examined, and a decision arrived at as to whether they should be allowed into the outer world, be segregated for life, or given the alternative of sterilisation. The rich should be notified as well as the poor, and they might be allowed to create private colonies.

(Savage, 1911b, p. 112.)

Ewart's closing words confirm the view of mankind held by him and his colleagues: 'Grapes do not grow on thorns nor figs on thistles. Would anyone knowingly select either diseased seeds or diseased animals to breed from?' (Savage, 1911b, p. 112.)

5

A Sympathetic Empiricist:
Sir Henry Head

When it became clear to Leonard that Savage could be of no real help to Virginia, he turned to Dr Henry Head, on Roger Fry's recommendation. Head is unique among the four doctors discussed here in that he is the only one whose achievements have caused his name to be remembered by historians of medicine. Savage, Craig and Hyslop all enjoyed a degree of fame in their day, but none of them made contributions upon which contemporary medical or psychiatric thought is based; and, so far, none of them have proved important for historians of medicine. Head, on the other hand, developed hypotheses relevant to a number of neurological problems, and few modern textbooks on neurology, brain function or aphasia are without reference to him.

Head was born in 1861 in London of an old Quaker family. He was at Charterhouse, and then studied at the University of Halle prior to matriculating at Trinity College, Cambridge in 1880, from which he graduated with first class honours in the Natural Sciences Tripos. From 1884 to 1886 he studied under Ewald Hering at the University of Prague. He returned to Cambridge to complete his anatomy and physiology requirements, and did his clinical work at University College Hospital, London. He received his MB in 1890, and took his MD in 1892. His MD thesis, 'Disturbances of Sensation, with Especial Reference to the Pain of Visceral Disease', was of exceptionally high standard, and formed the basis of a series of papers now regarded as classical which appeared in the neurological journal *Brain* between 1893-6.[1] 'This piece of work established "Head's areas", the regions of increased cutaneous sensitiveness associated with diseases of the viscera.'[2]

After qualifying, Head held the following positions: house physician, University College Hospital and Victoria Park Hospital For Diseases of the Chest; clinical assistant, County Mental Hospital, Rainhill, Liverpool; registrar, assistant physician, physician, and, finally, consulting physician, the London Hospital. He was a Fellow of the Royal College of Physicians and of the Royal Society. He edited *Brain* from 1905-21, and the results of some of his most important research were published there. His other publications include *Studies in Neurology* (in collaboration with F. Holmes, G. Riddoch, J. Sherren, W. H. R. Rivers and T. Thompson)[3] and *Aphasia and Kindred Disorders*.[4] Head is also very well known for his work on shell shock and other disorders associated with the 1914-18 war.[5]

Head's most important work involved a courageous experiment in which he exposed and excised nerves in his own hand. The hypothesis of this experiment and the results obtained are described concisely and clearly by J. D. Rolleston:

The most interesting event in Head's life was the operation performed on him by James Sherren, an eminent surgeon attached to the London Hospital. At the time of the operation the circumstances were ideal. Head was then forty-two years old, in perfect health, he had not smoked for two years and no alcohol was taken during the time of the observation. The operation, the details of which are described by William Halse Rivers under the title of 'A Human Experiment in Nerve Division' (*Brain*, vol. xxxi, 1908), consisted in exposure and excision of small portions of Head's left radial and external cutaneous nerves. To facilitate regeneration of the sensory fibres the ends of the excised nerves were united with silk sutures. The following results were obtained: 'All forms of superficial sensibility were lost over the radial half of the forearm and the back of the hand. There was no interference with deep sensibility, as this is subserved by afferent fibres in the motor nerves. Head recognized two forms of superficial or cutaneous sensibility and called these "protopathic" and "epicritic". Protopathic sensibility, which returned about seven weeks after the nerve had been cut, included sensory response to pain, heat, and cold of a crude nature. Epicritic sensibility, which returned later,

was finer and more discriminating; degrees of temperature
could be distinguished, light touch was appreciated, and
the subject was able to locate accurately the point touched.'
Throughout the investigation the tests were applied by
Rivers, while Head, whose eyes were closed, was unaware
of the nature of the stimuli and of the correctness or
error of his replies.[6]

The results of this experiment are still discussed today.
Jonathan Miller includes an interesting gloss on the experiment in his book, *The Body in Question*,[7] in which he
raises a fundamental question about the 'objectivity' of
Head's discovery, for no one has since been able to reproduce the experiment and obtain the same results. Gordon
Rattray Taylor's *Natural History of the Mind* (1979) discusses Head's contributions.[8] As we shall see, Head was
truly devoted to the ideal of Objectivity, but recognized the
difficulties involved in this quest. Head's radical fidelity to
the ideal of Objectivity (as opposed to objectivism, or pseudo-
objectivity) together with a profound sense of honesty where
the limitations of medical enquiry are concerned gave his
work a rare sense of integrity. As we shall see, it is Head's
continual self-questioning and his refusal to accept 'pat'
diagnoses (like Savage's moral insanity) that makes him
unique among the four doctors whose work is discussed here.
  It is interesting to note the extent to which Head's work
has mattered to fields outside of medicine. I. A. Richards'
empiricist theory of literature espoused in *Principles of
Literary Criticism* is based largely on a physiological theory
of psychology, and he lists Head's work in his bibliography.[9]
There is an intertextual relation between Head's work and
my own work on Virginia Woolf, for Merleau-Ponty's *Phenomenology of Perception* contains nine references to Head,
most of them concerned with his theory of 'body scheme'
outlined in the MD thesis and subsequent papers.[10] The body
scheme has to do with the individual's perception of his body,
the image he has of it, and the role of the nervous system in
that conception. Kurt Koffka's classic text on *Principles of
Gestalt Psychology*[11] makes heavy use of Head's theory, as
does *Body Image and Personality*, an important contemporary

work by Seymour Fisher and Sidney E. Cleveland.[12]

In addition to his medical work, Head was a poet. He published two volumes privately, and in 1919 Humphrey Milford/Oxford University Press published *Destroyers and Other Verses*, which included poems from the two privately published volumes as well as a translation of Heine's *Songs of La Mouche*. The poetry is, on the whole, good, and in places Head achieves some very strong and moving statements in the imagist vein. In a sequence entitled 'Sun and Shower', Head presents a dialogue between parted lovers which, in its unpretentiousness and elegant simplicity, achieves a mood similar to that evoked by Pound in his translations from the Chinese in *Cathay*:

She. . .

Willows are white as a breath upon silver
    beneath the dark sky:
On a grey waste of waters the promise of
    summer
        Floats eddying by.

And the nest that we built in the grass by
    the river,
        The home of our dream,
Far from men, where we sang through the
    soft summer weather
        Lies under the stream.

Come quickly, the night will bring silence
    and darkness
        To cover my tears
And stars will shine brighter above the dark
    waters
        And shadowy weirs.[13]

This volume also contains a series of war poems simply entitled '1914-1918', in which Head considers his position as a man too old actively to serve his country (he was fifty-three when the war began), the passing of the old order, and the horror of the trenches. There is a particularly moving and personal tribute to the courage of the French, which contradicts Sassoon's and Graves's feelings on that subject. In places, Head compares very favourably with Sassoon.

During the last twenty years of his life, Head suffered from 'a true creeping palsy'.[14] His decline was slow and painful, and he finally died of pneumonia in 1940. J. D. Rolleston wrote, 'Head did not receive many distinctions; he was knighted in 1927, elected an honorary fellow of Trinity College, Cambridge, in 1920, and received the honorary degree of LL.D. from Edinburgh University, and that of M.D. from Strasbourg University.'[15]

Head became involved with Virginia's case after Leonard and Virginia's disastrous trip to the Fabian conference at Keswick on 22 July, following which Savage sent Virginia to Burley from 23 July to 11 August 1913. From 11 August to 22 August, Leonard and Virginia stayed at Asham.[16] On the morning of 22 August, the Woolfs returned to London, and this morning was the occasion of the interview during which Savage 'pooh-poohed' Leonard's fears about taking Virginia to Holford for the promised holiday.

When was he actually consulted? Bell's chronology[17] gives the following entry for 22 August 1913: 'Leonard takes Virginia to London to see Drs Savage and Head; they go next day to the Plough Inn, Holford. Virginia's depression, delusions and resistance to food increase' (Bell, 2, p. 228). However in the text of Volume 2 of the biography, Bell gives this fuller, but seemingly conflicting account:

> Leonard was by this time thoroughly frightened by the prospect of taking Virginia alone to Somerset and, when he saw Savage, he expressed his fears. Sir George pooh-poohed them, and insisted that, since this holiday had been promised as a reward, the promise must be kept; to break it would be psychologically disastrous. *Meanwhile Virginia had been at 46 Gordon Square with Vanessa.* 'Virginia,' she reported to Clive, 'seems to me pretty bad. She worries constantly and one gets rid of one worry only to find that another crops up in a few minutes. Then she definitely has illusions about people.'
>
> (Bell, 2, p. 14, my italics.)

In the chronology Bell says that 'Leonard takes Virginia to London to see Drs Savage and Head.' In the full version of the story given in the text, Bell says that while Leonard was seeing Savage, 'Virginia had been at 46 Gordon Square with Vanessa.'

At any rate, after Leonard saw Savage (without Virginia it seems, which means that any opinion Savage formed was based on Leonard's account, and not upon an examination of the patient), he

> was able to talk things over with Vanessa, and also with Roger Fry, who being himself a man of science and the husband of a mad wife, was able at least to suggest an alternative to Savage, in whom Leonard had now lost all faith. Henry Head, a very distinguished scientist and man of culture (he had translated Heine), seemed altogether a more suitable consultant. *Leonard arranged to see him at once.* But there was little that Head could do at this juncture. He had to agree with Savage that the promised holiday must be undertaken; it might possibly work a cure. If it did not, and Virginia's condition deteriorated, Leonard should summon help and, if it got worse still, they must return to London.
>
> (Bell, 2, p. 14, my italics.)

'Leonard agreed to see him at once.' It would seem as if Leonard saw Head, unaccompanied by Virginia. If this is the case, again, there is a serious contradiction between the account given in the text and that given in the chronology.

On 23 August the Woolfs went to the Plough Inn, Holford, and Virginia's condition, particularly *vis à vis* food, worsened.

Virginia's refusal of food, her hallucinations, and her rejection of Leonard grew so acute that they had to return to London. Immediately upon their return (9 September), Bell's chronology tells us, Leonard took Virginia to see Head and Maurice Wright: 'Virginia sees Drs Wright and Head; in the evening she attempts suicide' (Bell, 2, p. 228). These interviews, particularly the one with Head, immediately precede a very serious suicide attempt — to swallow a hundred grains of veronal is not to threaten suicide — and so they are of the utmost importance. This is Bell's account from

the time Leonard decided they must return to London to the
interviews with Wright and Head:

> At length Leonard determined that they really must go
> back and see a doctor. At first Virginia demurred, too
> afraid to go; but then, to his astonishment, suggested that
> they might see Dr Head, which was what he had secretly
> wanted. *She had not been a party to the discussion con-*
> *cerning Head at Gordon Square*, but no doubt she had
> been affected, as most people were affected, by the con-
> versation of Roger Fry. So, on the afternoon of 8 Sep-
> tember they travelled back with Ka [Cox] to London;
> by now his wife's condition was such that Leonard expected
> her at any moment to try to throw herself from the train.
> They arrived however at Brunswick Square, where they
> spent the night in Adrian's rooms. The next morning they
> went to see Dr Maurice Wright, whom Leonard had more
> than once consulted on his own account [regarding his
> trembling hands] and in whom he had considerable
> faith. Dr Wright told Virginia that she must accept the fact
> that she really was ill; and in the afternoon Dr Head re-
> peated this opinion, saying that she would get perfectly
> well again if she followed advice and re-entered a nursing
> home.
>
> (Bell, 2, p. 15, my italics.)

Here is Leonard's account of the decision to return to
London:

> I suggested that we should return to London at once, go
> to another doctor — any doctor whom she should choose;
> she would put her case to him and I would put mine; if he
> said that she was not ill, I would accept his verdict and
> would not worry her again about eating or resting or
> going to a nursing home; but if he said she was ill, then
> she would accept his verdict and undergo what treatment
> he might prescribe.[18]

This is his version of what happened when they saw Wright
and Head:

> I gave my account of what had happened and Virginia gave

hers. He told her that she was completely mistaken about her own condition; she was ill, ill like a person who had a cold or typhoid fever; but if she took his advice and did what he prescribed, her symptoms would go and she would be quite well again, able to think and write and read; she must go to a nursing home and stay in bed for a few weeks, resting and eating.[19]

Leonard's account makes two things clear. First, that Leonard was not content only to have his wife see a doctor (preferably Head) and to accept whatever opinion that doctor gave, but was concerned to present *his case* as well as allowing her to present hers. The question of madness must be seen in the context in which it actually occurs: it is a dispute between them over what meaning or explanation is to be attached to Virginia's rejection of Leonard and of food. Leonard believed that she was mad; Virginia believed she was not, 'that there was nothing wrong with her, that her anxieties and insomnia were due simply to her own faults, faults which she ought to overcome without medical assistance' (Bell, 2, p. 15). No attempt has been made by Bell, Woolf, Spater and Parsons, or the editors of the autobiographical papers, to follow this clue, to ascertain whether or not Virginia's formulation with regard to her mental condition might not have some validity. As I try to show in my reading of *Flush*[20], there were things about which Virginia did feel guilty, and which she found difficult to come to terms with. Secondly, the extent to which Leonard was concerned to win the argument may be ascertained from the fact that he did not, strictly speaking, keep the bargain made with his wife. Leonard's proposal was that they return to London and that Virginia should see 'any doctor whom she should choose'. When they arrive, she must see *two* doctors: Wright *and* Head. This manoeuvre is reminiscent of the one Leonard used with regard to the question of whether or not Virginia should have children. He sought Savage's opinion, Savage said yes; so he consulted Craig, Hyslop and Jean Thomas, the proprietor of Burley, from whom he got a majority verdict of no. Every single published autobiographical volume of Virginia's testifies to her lifelong desire to have children. It was the cause of a profound dispute between them, and Leonard won. He also won with regard to the question of madness.

Those who have maintained that Virginia was mad all agree on one point, that part of Virginia's madness lay in her belief that she was the victim of a conspiracy. Even a cursory examination of the facts suggests that she had every reason to feel this way, and it is not difficult to see why she was abusive and violent towards Leonard, Vanessa, and her nurses — another symptom of her madness.

So, while we have no detailed information as to what transpired during the course of the interviews with Wright and Head, we can make a well-founded guess as to what Virginia's state of mind was, and how she regarded these interviews. And since she chose the first opportunity following them — while Leonard and Vanessa were making apologies to Savage for seeing other specialists behind his back — to attempt suicide, it would not be arbitrary or irrational to suggest that the interviews with the doctors were the immediate cause of the suicide attempt, and that they constitute the final and intolerable instance of a series of invalidations of Virginia's personal experience.[21]

Head was primarily a neurologist, but he was rare among strictly empirically-minded doctors at the time in his sympathetic understanding of Freud's work on the unconscious, and in his grasp of the concept of repression. In other words, he had a firm belief in the reality of subjective experiences which could lead to disorder, and in the fact that many disorders could never be cured by traditional empirical means. He wrote comparatively little (in terms of volume) which deals directly with neurosis and psychosis (Head does not speak of madness), but what there is is important. The real value of Head's periodical publications lies in their critical examination of medical epistemology and methodology, and in their questioning of the presuppositions underlying the diagnosis of insanity.

Diagnosis

In an early article, on 'Some Mental States Associated With
Visceral Disease in the Sane',[22] Head puts forward the opinion that melancholia, hallucinations and delusions of suspicion
do not necessarily warrant the diagnosis of madness. Quite
the contrary, for it is not at all uncommon in cases of visceral
disease for the patient to suffer any or all of these symptoms
while being perfectly sane.[23] For Head, 'The mental disturbance seems to stand in direct relation to the intensity of the
pain and tenderness' (Head, 1895, p. 769). Savage would no
doubt speak of an 'insanity associated with visceral disease'.
Head grounds his approach firmly in scientific principles,
and spares his patient the stigmatizing diagnosis.

Head takes the business of diagnosis seriously, for he
realizes that the patient's subsequent treatment and experience will depend on it, and that the patient carries a
diagnosis with him from doctor to doctor. The extent to
which Head requires that diagnosis be *scientific* (as opposed
to Savage's moralistic or impressionistic diagnoses) may be
seen in the following criteria and example:

> Clinical diagnosis is a by-product of scientific investigation.
> It is impossible to expose every patient to laborious scien-
> tific examination, nor would it serve any useful purpose
> to do so; but the simple tests employed in the wards are
> valueless until they have been calibrated by more elaborate
> investigations. The man who says he can obtain all the
> information he wants, in cases of injury to peripheral
> nerves, by means of a pin and a piece of cotton-wool
> depends upon someone else to teach him the significance
> of these empirical tests. They have no scientific value
> until the data they yield are correlated with results
> achieved by methods capable of measurements.[24]

Head is speaking as a neurologist who was, throughout his
life, conducting detailed scientific researches, and he makes no
effort to conceal his disdain for the general practitioner who
does not take the scientific ideal seriously.[25] In a later article, he
elaborates upon this fundamental critique of diagnosis, this
time making explicit reference to 'mental medicine':

For another series of diagnoses the most elaborate bacteriological examinations are necessary, as, for example, 'paratyphoid A,' or 'paratyphoid B,' whilst in other cases that vague conscience-anodyne 'influenza,' or even the colloquial 'sore throat,' are sufficiently precise.

Think, too, of the intellectual confusion that can tolerate 'tremor,' 'paralysis agitans,' 'headache,' and 'hyperaesthesia' as correlative terms.

Mental medicine has always sinned grossly in this respect, and the permissible diagnoses under this heading are based indifferently on the cause, on the mental defect, or on changes of conduct. 'Alcoholic' insanity reveals nothing beyond the supposed cause; the patient may be excited, depressed, confused, or full of delusions. On the other hand, 'dementia' is an expression of loss of function, which may or may not be accompanied by positive manifestations of abnormal activity. *'Impulsive' insanity usually means that the trained attendant thinks he has to deal with a 'nasty' patient, whilst 'moral' insanity is a police-court diagnosis.*[26]

It is important to note that, in his objection to the diagnosis of 'impulsive' insanity, Head understands that the diagnosis is a function of the doctor's pre-judgement of the patient, of his expectations. Head carries his attack on his colleagues in this field much further when he writes of 'this acceptance of diverse and contradictory categories of belief, so common in all primitive cultures' (Head, 1919, p. 365). For Head, the 'science' of psychiatry is a 'primitive culture'. In the article on 'Disease and Diagnosis', Head presents what amounts to his final position on this subject, and the factors involved in diagnosis on the doctor's side:

Many diagnoses are based on no method of orderly reasoning; they are of no more intellectual value than 'spotting a winner' in a horse race. *Such guesses may bring financial reward to their maker, but add little to his intellectual credit.*

No one is more wedded to theory than the so-called 'practical' physician. He knows the 'cause' of each disease and the source and nature of the responsible toxin . . . . He shows a bold front where Science moves with bowed head and bated breath.

But the true clinician is a very different figure. *He walks humbly from one bedside to another, listening to each patient's story* and noting the diverse changes in function which form the disease he is called upon to treat. Much that he sees does not fit in with what he has been taught. It breaks his heart to know that he has neither the means nor the time to discover the significance of what he sees. To whom shall he turn for counsel?

This is the place of the man of science.

(Head, 1919, p. 366, my italics.)

Late in his career, Head turned his critical eye on the diagnosis of the psychoneuroses. Here, he extrapolates the ideals which he advocated with regard to the diagnosis of organic disease. In an article entitled 'Observations on the Elements of the Psycho-Neuroses',[27] he writes:

Face to face with the patient, it is futile to waste time in considering whether he is a case of neurasthenia, psychosthenia, anxiety neurosis, or hysteria. The war has unfortunately increased the universal love of labels. Medicine is particularly thought to be based on the principles of a penny-in-the-slot machine. Make a so-called 'diagnosis' and the rest follows mechanically. Hysteria is treated with electricity and massage; an anxiety neurosis needs a 'rest cure'; obsessions require fresh air and cheery companions. Nothing is more pitiful than the condition of the medical man who finds that these rules of practice break under him. *He is filled with mingled anger and despair, which frequently lead him to vent his impotence on the patient*; he expresses his opinion that 'the fellow is a rotter,' and he 'would like to see all his sort shot on the parade ground.' He has made no attempt to investigate the forces at work that produce the condition he does not understand. His 'diagnoses' are but camouflaged ignorance. The only diagnosis that is of the slightest value, or is worthy of the dignity of our profession, is the laying bare of the forces which underlie the morbid state and the discovery of the mental experiences which have set them in action. *Diagnosis of the psycho-neuroses is an individual investigation; they are not diseases, but morbid activities of a*

personality which demand to be understood. The form
they assume depends on the mental and physiological
life of the patient, his habits, and constitution.
                    (Head, 1920a, p. 391, my italics.)

Head's programme is radical. He calls for a questioning of
routine textbook diagnosis, a questioning of the neat categories into which the medical man is trained to put his
patients. 'Diagnosis of the psycho-neuroses is an individual
investigation', Head declares. This makes the doctor's job
difficult — he must exercise patience, sympathy, shrewd-
ness — but it puts the enterprise on the only footing which
can make it valid. Head rejects the idea of disease, and states
his firm belief in disorder. In other words, as far as the
psychoneuroses are concerned, the doctor is to treat the
patient and his unique history, not an objective entity called
'disease' for which the patient is merely the vehicle.[28]
Head gives a very clear example of what he means by the
distinction between disease and functional disorder. The
former involves organic change due to toxins, virus or whatever, while the latter involves a disturbance of the patient's
conceptualization of the world:

Loss of function can easily be recognized by its character.
It follows a conceptual and not a physiological or anatomi-
cal distribution. A patient with hysterical loss of speech
can write and read fluently, and one with complete
aphonia can cough loudly. When all power of recognizing
the position of one upper extremity appears to be lost, the
patient has no difficulty in finding the tip of his affected
forefinger with that of the normal hand; but he carries out
the reverse operation with difficulty, because it seems
natural to him to do badly with the 'bad' hand and well
with the 'good' one. But, when the sense of position is
disturbed from an organic lesion of the cortex, the condition is usually the exact opposite. The normal forefinger
cannot be brought into contact with that of the affected
hand because its position is not known, whereas the
reverse movement can be carried out without difficulty,
because the situation of the normal hand is accurately
recognized. It is easy to make fair shooting with a bad

rifle if we know the position of the target; but the best rifle in the world is useless if we are ignorant of the direction of our aim.

(Head, 1920a, p. 392.)

Head has a good insight into functional disorder — partly because he can easily recognize what is *not* functional disorder — and he understands the differences between them fully. He gives a few examples of ludicrous diagnoses made by anonymous colleagues who insist upon regarding simple conditions (which in the light of a very brief case history are made readily intelligible) as various complex organic conditions:

One of my patients suffered from no pain or loss of power in her hand until after her marriage, with the natural inference that her trouble was due to syphilitic infection . . . it was not until after marriage that she was forced to scrub the floor, to carry about a heavy baby, and habitually to perform other work necessitating continuous strain on the arms. Another patient, the son of a rich man, began to experience discomfort at about sixteen years of age, when he exchanged his quiet pony for a pulling horse. This was thought to be the hysteria of puberty. Again, a master baker, who consulted me during the war, noticed pain and wasting in his hand at the age of fifty. All his workmen had been called up, and for the first time in his life he was compelled, himself, to carry on the strenuous and exacting work of his bakehouse. This patient was thought to be suffering from 'neuritis' brought on by the air-raids.[29]

More seriously, however, Head was keenly aware of the possibility that physical symptoms could have an important psychological or symbolical value. Adopting Freud's concept of conversion neurosis, Head attempted to unravel the meanings of his patients' symptoms. He understood that, for example, 'If a soldier, unable any longer to face the horrors of the front, became paralysed in both legs, he was automatically relieved from the necessity of facing danger without the obloquy of running away.'[30]

Head's view on the definition and diagnosis of mental disorders is given definitive utterance in the conclusion of this 1920 article, 'The Elements of the Psycho-Neuroses':

> I have entered a plea for regarding the psychoneuroses as a disturbance of functions, common both to the nervous system and to the mind. The form they assume depends on the personality of the patient, and the nature of the emotions and ideas with which he has had to deal; it has nothing to do directly with the effect of external physical forces. Such expressions as 'shell shock' and 'neurasthenia' do not correspond categorically to the manifestations of the functional neuroses, which are in reality the forms assumed by the reaction of the patient to his individual mental experiences.
>
> (Head, 1920a, p. 392.)

Aetiology

In his 1895 article, 'Some Mental States Associated With Visceral Disease in the Sane', Head writes that melancholia, hallucinations and delusions which often occur in cases of visceral disease are caused purely and simply by pain: 'The mental disturbance seems to stand in direct relation to the intensity of pain and tenderness' (Head, 1895, p. 769).[31]

After the 1914-1918 war, in his articles on functional mental disorders, Head attributed most occasions of these to what may be termed situational causes. He writes, for example, that:

> No new morbid phenomena have been evoked by the war. The disordered functions of the human mind were manifested in exactly the same forms under the stress and strain of peace-time civilization. The one test of his conduct was, 'can he fight?' and the only reality to which he was compelled to adapt himself was a state of war.
>
> (Head, 1920a, p. 389.)

He makes this point about the war so that the following one regarding everyday civilian life will gain intensity:

On the other hand, in civilian life the factors underlying a psycho-neurosis are far more complex; they may lie in many different fields — thwarted ambition, business worry, or family anxieties, apart altogether from the disaccord between individual sexual desires and social convention.

(Head, 1920a, p. 389.)

Head recognizes just how complicated the events of 'everyday' life can be, and how significantly they figure in our psychological constitution. He recognizes (as Savage, Craig and Hyslop did not) the significance of the conflict between individual sexual desires and the constraints imposed by society, and he does so in a manner which does not obscure the subject with disdainful or moralistic language. He also recognizes the fundamental importance of the unconscious:

In the past, psychology dealt mainly with the intellectual factors of mental activity; the instinctive and emotional aspects of the mind were disregarded and the unconscious entirely neglected. But we have learnt to recognize that, outside the limits of the experiences which can be recalled to consciousness by an effort of the will, lie impressions capable of producing an active effect upon mental life.

(Head, 1920a, p. 389.)

Head realized that if symptoms were to be removed ('abreacted' in Freudian parlance), then the unconscious material must be brought to light and its energy discharged. Head's experience of treating the victims of trench warfare taught him about the nature of repression, and the absolute necessity of facing up to repressed experience. It also taught him that conscious material — traumatic experiences which have not been repressed (like Louis's experience of the unmitigable apple tree in *The Waves*) — could wield a negative power, and that facing up to the experience was an absolute essential of treatment:

Provided we can determine the process at work in the production of the psycho-neuroses, the causal factors

underlying a large number of the phenomena can be discovered without elaborate technique. In many cases,
especially during the war, the patient was conscious of the
experience which was at the bottom of his trouble, but,
because of the horror it engendered, he refused to face it.
This was particularly evident in cases of obsession. A man
who had seen some horrible or filthy sight naturally
repressed it whenever it appeared in consciousness. In
this he was encouraged by his medical attendants, who
advised him to 'go away and forget about the war.' 'Don't
think of anything you saw in France, but play games and
be with cheery fellows.' The evil of this advice has been
wonderfully expressed by Siegfried Sassoon in his poem
called 'Repression of War Experience':

> Now light the candles; one; two; there's a moth;
> What silly beggars they are to blunder in
> And scorch their wings with glory, liquid flame —
> No, no, not that — it's bad to think of war,
> When thoughts you've gagged all day come back to
> scare you.
> And it's been proved that soldiers don't go mad
> Unless they lose control of ugly thoughts
> That drive them out to jabber among the trees.

(Head, 1920a, p. 391.)

Head was right in recognizing that there is a place for
morality in psychological medicine, other than Savage's
sense of it. Rather, the morality consists in the patient's
courage to face up to, to confront courageously, the experiences which have contributed to his disorder. The doctor's
role is to assist the patient in this often very difficult task of
self-understanding. Head is right in calling his colleagues'
practice of exhorting the patient 'to forget' evil. Savage
prescribed a refusal to admit any of the unpleasant realities
which plagued his patients.[32] Virginia Woolf had to face at
least two pivotal crises which had a great moral significance
for her, and which were probably primary sources of disorder. These two crises are the experience of being molested
by her two half-brothers and her flirtation with Clive Bell,
her brother-in-law (the implications of which I examine in

my discussion of *Flush*). There is no record of any of
Virginia's doctors taking these events seriously (or even
knowing of them, although Savage knew what Vanessa had
told him of the Duckworths' attentions). It was left for
Virginia to undertake a form of self-analysis by writing
novels. In fact, one could say that writing saved her life,
until the old traumas returned with a vengeance and she
lost the heart, in the face of another war, to carry on. The
'evil practice' to which Head refers applies directly in the
case of Septimus Smith. Drs Holmes and Bradshaw seek to
cure the young man ruined by the war with porridge, sport
and the advice that he maintain a sense of proportion.

Finally, in the article entitled 'The Diagnosis of Hysteria',
Head considers a number of cases in which the symptoms of
disorder may be seen as the direct result of living in an untenable situation. Two of the examples correspond almost
identically with aspects of Virginia's case. We know that one
of the main symptoms of Virginia's disorder consisted in
her refusal of food. Food often had a profoundly personal
and symbolic meaning for her, and the rejection of it was
itself a significant act. The rejection of food by women is a
common phenomenon (though not always so severe as in
anorexia nervosa), and Head does not fail to recognize the
profound and fundamental importance of this symptom. He
writes, 'If, for example, a patient expresses to you a moral
repugnance to taking food, it is well to consider whether her
statement does not hide some real cause of moral doubt and
anxiety' (Head, 1922, p. 829). The other symptom which
Head discusses is the absence of sexual relations in marriage.
We know that soon after their marriage, the sexual side of
their relationship was abandoned. In her biography of
Virginia, Phyllis Rose writes, with profound naïveté, 'The
extraordinary fact is their marriage *was* a success. Whatever
pleasure Leonard got from this sexless union (and he was
known in Bloomsbury as a passionate man) we can only
imagine.'[33] Henry Head maintains, 'Marriage without physical
affection is an impossible human relation; one of the simplest
methods of escaping from such difficulties is the development of a physical illness' (Head, 1922, p. 829). We can only
wonder whether the discussion got this far when Virginia

and Leonard visited Head on the day of her suicide attempt.

Treatment

It is not difficult to infer, from what we have already learned of Head's views on diagnosis and aetiology, what his views on the subject of treatment might be. We would assume that the doctor's role would be to try and get at the experiences which have led to the patient's condition, and then to try and get the patient to come to terms with them — to help the patient become more conscious of his situation. This is in fact the case. Head's statements on treatment are infrequent, but they are marked by a great integrity. In 'The Elements of the Psycho-Neuroses' he writes:

> The majority of hysterical patients, like children, are unduly suggestible. But, in most instances, it is unnecessary to employ hypnotic suggestion. Provided the examination has been carried out carefully and sympathetically and nothing has been said or done to confirm the patient's belief in the severity of his disease, the physician will have acquired sufficient suggestive power to remove such physical disabilities as paralysis or loss of speech. Sometimes this suffices to produce a permanent cure; but it must not be forgotten that behind these obvious manifestations may lie a state of anxiety. This must be dealt with seriously and systematically, or the patient will relapse on the first occasion that his conflict is reawakened.
> (Head, 1920a, p. 392.)

While this programme is infinitely superior to the ones marked out by Savage, it is still, in some ways, unacceptable, particularly *vis à vis* the case of Virginia. It is certainly a mistake, at least in her case, to assume that she has the suggestibility of a child. We know from Virginia's letters, especially those in the first two volumes, that she objected strenuously to being treated like a child. Leonard, Bell, and the others who subscribe to the view that Virginia was mad all dwell on her 'childishness'. This has to be repugnant to anyone who has studied her work, and come to terms with its central themes. It is a peculiar critical intelligence which can assert the genius of works like *To The Lighthouse*, *The Waves* and *Between The Acts*, and also maintain that the author of those works was 'childish'. We must also doubt the assumption that, having acquired sufficient suggestive power over his child-like patient, the doctor can, with a few well chosen words, dismiss paralysis. We know from Freud's early work with hysterics that most of his patients were highly intelligent upper-middle-class women, some of whom had above-average linguistic and literary powers, and that while suggestion could sometimes remove hysterical symptoms, this was usually a long and painful process. We must also note, before moving on to Head's next statement, that he uses the term 'disease' to apply to neurotic symptoms, a term which, it will be remembered from the preceding section, Head maintained that he categorically rejected in favour of disorder or disturbance of function.

In his conclusion to 'The Elements of the Psycho-Neuroses', however, Head asserts the necessity (made plain in his discussion of repressed war experience, where he quotes the poem by Sassoon) for the patient to face up to repressed material, to confront it boldly, and to achieve a mastery of it by integrating it into his conscious life. Head makes this a fundamental aspect of treatment:

> Abnormal mental experiences must be brought into the main stream of the individual personality, and, if possible, the patient must be induced to regard them from a more favourable point of view. A terrifying object, that can be logically examined, tends to lose its fearful aspect. We dread the unknown; and to drag these half-appreciated horrors into the light of day may discharge the greater part of their emotional energy. If possible, a sorrow must be sublimed; the loss of some dearly beloved person should not be repressed, but be brought up to form an integral part of the sacrifice at the altar.
>
> (Head, 1920a, p. 392.)

This programme is admirably suited, to my mind, to Virginia's case. The kinds of repressed experiences with which she had to deal are precisely the sort to which Head refers. My reading of her novels as autobiography suggests that she did try very hard, and with a fair amount of success, to come to terms with this repressed material. (It was not repressed in the sense that she was completely unaware of it, for she did discuss it in letters, autobiographical writings and even in addresses to the Memoir Club. It was repressed in that she never seemed to grasp the full significance of it, or to understand the nature of the guilt she felt.) However, there seems to be no record anywhere of any other doctor actively pursuing this line of treatment with her. It would seem as though Head might have been just the man to do this. However, we don't know why he seems to have dropped out of the picture following Virginia's suicide attempt. It is likely that the conditions under which the interview prior to the attempt was held were highly unfavourable for a truly sympathetic relationship to begin. And it is very likely that the association — which must have lingered in Virginia's mind for the rest of her life — of the interview with Head and the horror into which she plunged herself only a few hours later, served to preclude any further dealings with him.

Head outlined his programme of treatment more fully in the 1922 paper, 'The Diagnosis of Hysteria'. I quote at length, for this is Head's final statement on the subject:

> I cannot close this discourse without saying a few words about treatment. If possible, the patient should be removed from the usual surroundings and new influences brought to bear. An attempt should be made to switch the dissociated part into the continuity of the patient's mental life. Every form of persuasion should be exercised to convince the patient that he is able to carry out the action he is convinced to be impossible. *Never bully him or accuse him of dishonesty. No one is a greater failure than the medical officer who wishes all hysterics could be shot at dawn.* On the other hand, the firm diplomatist with subtle and demonstrable reasons why the patient can stand, walk, or fall, often produces miraculous cures. But it must never be forgotten that in a large number of cases, especially in civil life, removal of hysterical symptoms is only a prelude to the discovery of an anxiety neurosis. The causes for the suppressed emotion must be

investigated, or the patient may be left in an even worse condition than that in which you found him.

To the medical man I would say, see that you do your patient no harm by antitherapeutic suggestion; carefully prune your conversation, and do not think your diagnosis aloud. Purge your mind of vague phrases, and avoid such words as 'neuritis'. *Some diagnoses, such as 'floating kidney,' are more deadly than the disease.* Avoid thinking in terms of surgery when dealing with functional neuroses. When you find that a patient is vomiting, do not let your mind at once leap to gastro-enterostomy. Be natural, but on guard; you will then be ready to deliver your blow at the moment required. At the same time, remember that your most brilliant conversation is useless with an hysteric; she is interested in herself, not you.

Nature's moral code, under which we work, is cruel and unrelenting. There is no forgiveness of sins; but, in the medical man, this knowledge should be tempered towards the patient by clinical curiosity and human sympathy. In conclusion, I would say to all who have to deal with these morbid conditions, *be as honest in thought as you would be naturally in deed.* Act without fear and never lose courage; finally, *call nothing common or unclean.*

(Head, 1922, p. 829, my italics.)

Head's advice to the physician is, needless to say, a model of integrity. This is especially true of his closing remarks, and his warning, 'call nothing common or unclean'. In Savage's work we saw how a moralistic attitude confused diagnosis and treatment and, ultimately, violated the patient. In Head's work we see the value of a judicious and reflective inclusion of moral considerations. To his credit, Head directs most of his moral points at the physician. But, by extension (and this applies most fundamentally in the situation where the patient needs to contribute the moral strength and courage to face up to certain repressed experiences), the moral points apply equally to the patient, and have a liberating rather than a constricting effect. Head does not take this point very far, though he is well aware of it. He implies it when he cites the following example:

in daily practice, the causes of much defective mental

harmony are not only more complex [than causes relating to the war], but are more difficult to elicit. A married woman is not likely to confess to her doctor that she is in love with another man, when the doctor's wife may any day drop in to tea with her. She may have absolute confidence in the discretion of her medical attendant, but the presence of his wife would instinctively remind her of the unpleasant conflict. On the other hand, she has no reluctance to confess what she knows in her heart to be the cause of her want of sleep and digestive troubles to a man living at a distance, whom she will in all probability never see again after her morbid condition has passed away.

(Head, 1920a, p. 391.)

Head cites this, of course, as a hypothetical situation, from which important general conclusions may be drawn. We must view Virginia's traumas primarily as existential problems, shot through with a moral content. From what we have seen of Savage's moralizing, we can be certain that these problems were not discussed openly with him. The work of Craig and Hyslop follows in the moralizing tradition of Savage, and so neither of them would present a suitable ear for Virginia's story. It would appear that Head was the perfect choice — but that the conditions were wrong. We remember that Virginia did not see Head by herself, but with Leonard, and that they both put their view of her case to him. We can be certain that Virginia would not bring herself to disclose the true sources of her disorder to a man she had never met before (though in time she might have, if the conditions were suitable), and she could never do it, no matter who the doctor was, while Leonard hovered over her. Given the enlightened and sympathetic views of Head, the fact that their meeting bore no fruit and was never repeated may be seen as a tragic event in the life of Virginia Woolf.

The question of where Freud should be placed in a discussion of Virginia Woolf and her doctors is a vexed one. With the exception of Head, the doctors largely ignored or ridiculed Freud's work. Virginia herself was close to some of Freud's earliest and most ardent disciples. Her brother, Adrian, and his wife Karin, both became medical doctors who pursued psychoanalytic training under Freud in Vienna. The Hogarth Press began to bring out James Strachey's translation of Freud, and Leonard reviewed *The Psychopathology of Everyday Life*. Virginia ridiculed her brother and his wife, and James and Alix Strachey, for their devotion to psychoanalysis. She wrote to Janet Case in 1921, 'The last people I saw were James and Alix [Strachey] fresh from Freud — Alix grown gaunt and vigorous — James puny and languid — such is the effect of 10 months psycho-analysis' (*Letters*, 2, p. 482). In 1924, when the Hogarth Press was in the middle of publishing Strachey's great translation of Freud, Virginia wrote to Molly MacCarthy,

> I shall be plunged in publishing affairs at once; we are publishing all Dr Freud, and I glance at the proof and read how Mr A. B. threw a bottle of red ink on to the sheets of his marriage bed to excuse his impotence to the housemaid, but threw it in the wrong place, which unhinged his wife's mind — and to this day she pours claret on the dinner table. We could all go on like that for hours; and yet these Germans think it proves something — besides their own gull-like imbecility.
>
> (*Letters*, 3, pp. 134-5.)

The question of whether or not Virginia might have benefited more from psychoanalysis than from an outdated form of psychological medicine must remain speculative. Certainly, in pursuing a sexual aetiology of neurosis, a Freudian would find much to work with in Virginia's case. Virginia herself remained sceptical to the end.

On 28 January 1939, the Woolfs visited the ailing Freud in Hampstead. Canny to the end, Freud presented Virginia with a narcissus.

Virginia Woolf 1902

Sir Leslie Stephen 1902

Vanessa Bell 1907

Leonard Woolf

Vita Sackville-West 1924

George Duckworth

Sir Henry Head

Dr Theophilus Bulkeley Hyslop

Sir George Henry Savage

Sir Maurice Craig

6

Enforcing Conformity: Sir Maurice Craig

Sir Maurice Craig was an almost exact contemporary of Henry Head. He was born in 1866, five years after Head, and died in 1935. Like Savage, he devoted most of his life exclusively to the study and treatment of mental disorders and, according to one colleague, 'he built up what was probably the largest consulting practice of his time in the speciality in which he practised'.[1] His career followed almost the same pattern as those of Savage and Head. He was educated at Bedford Grammar School before going on to Caius College, Cambridge, from which he graduated with first class honours in the Natural Sciences Tripos in 1887. He received his medical training at Guy's Hospital, taking his MRCS in 1891 and his MB and BCh in 1892. In 1897 he became a member of the Royal College of Physicians, and he was elected a Fellow in 1906.

Like Savage and Head, Craig rose quickly in his profession, and he made many of the same stops along the way, being particularly associated with Bethlem Royal Hospital. 'Before he gave himself entirely to private practice his experience of psychological medicine was gained principally at Bethlem Royal Hospital, where he was finally senior assistant medical officer.'[2] He was later appointed 'physician for psychological medicine to Guy's Hospital in succession to Sir George Savage'.[3] Craig held many key positions in the world of psychological medicine. He was Chairman of the Mental After-Care Association; Chairman of the Medical Committee at Cassel Hospital For Functional Nervous Disorders; Consulting Neurologist to the Ministry of Pensions; Governor of the Royal Hospitals of Bridewell and Bethlem; President of the Psychiatry Section, Royal Society of Medicine, 1928-29; Chairman of the National Council For Mental Hygiene; Vice-President (Great Britain) of the International Committee For Mental Hygiene. In addition to these appointments, Craig held various lectureships, and was a member of the War Office Committee on Shell Shock.[4]

Craig was a less prolific writer than Savage or Head, publishing only a handful of papers in medical journals. He published two books, *Psychological Medicine*[5] and *Nerve Exhaustion.*[6] The former was, like Savage's *Insanity and Allied Neuroses*, a popular textbook in its day. In many ways, it is little more than a modified restatement of the ideas Savage put forward in 1884.

What role did Craig play in the treatment of Virginia Woolf? We know that he was one of the doctors Leonard consulted on the subject of whether or not Virginia should have children. Leonard, who suffered from a violent trembling, especially in his hands, consulted Craig on his own account a number of times. It was Craig who signed the certificate declaring Leonard unfit for service during the 1914-1918 war.[7]

In Leonard's view, Craig was

the leading Harley Street specialist in nervous and mental diseases. He was a much younger and more intelligent man than Savage, and he not only took charge of the case during its acute stage over the next two years, he also, for the rest of Virginia's life, remained the mental specialist to whom we went for advice when we wanted it.[8]

Craig was called in after the veronal attempt of 1913, taking the place of Savage. By April 1914, Virginia had begun to recover enough to consider taking a holiday in Cornwall:

Maurice Craig, whom they now consulted and whose opinions and advice Leonard respected (Savage was by now only referred to as a matter of courtesy), agreed that Virginia was sufficiently improved to justify the undoubted risk of removing her from her familiar surroundings. They went for three weeks to Cornwall — to Lelant, St Ives and Carbis Bay. Leonard found the excursion a pretty nerve-wracking affair; Virginia was very fearful of strangers, still difficult over food, and liable to bursts of excitement or bouts of despair. But on the whole the holiday did her good; her nostalgic delight in the scenes of her childhood soothed her overwrought nerves, and her progress towards recovery, though erratic, was maintained during the summer months at Asham.

(Bell, 2, p. 19.)

Virginia frequently mentions Craig in her letters and diary from 1912 on. The first reference is a curious remark in a letter to Leonard in which she writes, 'Are you well? Shall you get any 'assions from Craig?' (*Letters*, 2, p. 12). The editors of the letters offer the following unlikely hypothesis as to the meaning of ''assions': 'The word 'assions may be a private word for contraceptives (*Letters*, 2, p. 12n). The next mention of Craig occurs in 1916, when she writes to Leonard that Craig has 'sent a message to tell me to stay in bed every morning, and always have a sleeping draught at hand, to take at the least wakefulness — and altogether to be very careful for a fortnight' (*Letters*, 2, p. 89). The editors tell us that 'the increasing vigour of Virginia's letters indicate her complete return to normality, and she was not to have another total mental breakdown until she killed herself 25 years later' (*Letters*, 2, p. 75). However, Craig kept a careful watch on his patient. Five days after his message, she received another: '(Dr) Craig sent a message to tell me to stay in bed till lunch' (*Letters*, 2, p. 90). There is no mention of him actually *seeing* his patient. On Christmas Day 1916 she writes to Saxon Sydney-Turner, 'I am quite well — I was rather depressed at being told to rest again, but it is very difficult to keep at the weight which (Dr) Craig thinks necessary — However, he was very encouraging about the future — if one is careful now' (*Letters*, 2, p. 131). The editors remark in a note about Virginia's reference to her weight, 'Virginia now weighed 11 stone, having lost a pound during this year' (*Letters*, 2, p. 131n).

Craig's treatment seems to have consisted mainly in getting his patient to rest, take sleeping draughts, and eat more than was probably good for her. The wisdom of requiring Virginia to eat so much that she weighed eleven stone, especially when we consider the delicacy of the problematical relation to food, is suspect. Virginia's weight is Craig's main concern at this point, and she writes to Vanessa two days later, 'I'm very well, but Craig thinks I've been losing weight too fast, and wants me not to walk much; and as I very much want to avoid having to go to bed, I am being very cautious' (*Letters*, 2, p. 132). The editors tell us that in 1918 Leonard 'went to see Dr Craig, who said that her weight was too low for safety'. Spater and Parsons give statistics with regard to Virginia's weight which lead us to ask what it was Craig was trying to do with his patient. They tell us that 'On September 30, 1913, three weeks after her suicide attempt, Virginia weighed 8 stone 7 pounds. Leonard's tabulation shows that she had gained more than a stone by January 13, 1914, and put on another three stone by the end of 1915 — a gain of roughly 60 pounds in little more than two years.'[9]

In addition to eating and rest, Craig prescribed sedatives. Virginia writes to Leonard on 17 April 1916,

> Precious Mongoose,
> This is just to tell you what a wonderfully good beast I am. I've done everything in order, not forgetting medicine twice. Fergusson came this morning, and said it was the best thing for me to get away tomorrow. He had been seeing Craig, who had sent a message to tell me to stay in bed every morning, and always have a sleeping draught at hand, to take at the least wakefulness — and altogether to be very careful for a fortnight. Fergy said my pulse was quite different from last summer — not only much steadier, but much stronger. I am to go on spraying my throat. He seemed very pleased with me.
>
> (*Letters*, 2, p. 89.)

Given that Virginia had attempted suicide only a few years earlier with veronal, it seems odd that she is to keep a sleeping draught at hand at all times. If she found bed rest and the prohibition against reading and writing an intolerable imposition, we can only guess what effect enforced unconsciousness had upon her.

Perhaps the most interesting passage in Virginia's autobiographical writings which has to do with Craig concerns a
young Bloomsbury satellite, H. T. J. (Harry) Norton. Norton
is introduced in an editorial note to the second volume of
Virginia's *Diary* as having been 'a brilliant pupil of Bertrand
Russell's at Cambridge and of whom much original work in
mathematics had been expected' (*Diary*, 2, p. 76n). We are
also told that he 'suffered increasingly from feelings of in-
adequacy and depression' (*Diary*, 2, p. 76n). Virginia first
mentions Norton in relation to Craig in a diary entry of
23 November 1930, which is a record of a conversation with
R. C. Trevelyan, the poet (and a close friend of Roger Fry):

The most amusing of his refrains was about Norton.
To hear Bob sigh & tread delicately like a hippopotamus
holding its breath one would suppose Norton suicidal &
maniac. The truth seems to be 'but you must discount
what I say — its very difficult to know what impression
I'm giving — yet one must say something to his friends; &
I *think* its going to be all right now; if we can get over the
next few weeks—' The truth is that he has given up mathematics ostensibly on Craig's advice, feels humiliated, &
daren't face his friends, poor devil, Gordon Square that is.
I think I can trace the crisis far back; his powers proving
not quite what he thought; worry; strain; despondency;
envisaging failure; thought of boasting; dread of being
ridiculous — all that, & then his appearance against him
with young women, morbid about sex, which clearly isn't
his strong line; culminating in a kind of breakdown on the
motherly housemaid's knee of good Bessy [Trevelyan's
wife]. There he sticks, afraid to issue out, without prospects, a man who has trusted entirely in intellect, & taken
his cue from that, given to despising, rejecting, & tacitly
claiming an exalted rank on the strength of mathematics
which cant be done, & never could be done, I expect.
(I quote Maynard [Keynes]) Such an egotist too; never
able to see any other face save his own; & worrying out
such laborious relationships always b(etw)een himself &
other people. Now, poor creature, for I pity him & know
his case from my own past, he translates stories from the
French, & a book said to want doing by Ponsonby. I can
imagine the kind of humility that must be on him, & how

he gropes this winter, for some possible method in the future.[10]

(Diary, 2, pp. 76-7.)

This passage is highly significant, for in it we find the seeds of one of Virginia's fundamental themes in her novels (which was a central tenet of her 'philosophy', to the extent that she may be said to have one): the impersonality of an over-zealous rationality, and its consequences in human terms. Here we perceive an echo of St John Hirst, the clever but spiritually puckered young graduate in *The Voyage Out*. The passage also looks forward to one side of the character of Sir Leslie Stephen as portrayed by Virginia in *To The Lighthouse*: the painful insecurity, the doubt suffered by the man who devotes his life to the pursuit of a perfectly rational and ordered world. It is also important to note the compassionate nature of Virginia's attitude towards this failed rationalist. It is not mocking. It is, in fact, a mini-portrait of a tragic figure, drawn with an abundance of understanding and sympathy: 'There he sticks, afraid to issue out, without prospects, a man who has trusted entirely to intellect, & taken his cue from that, given to despising, rejecting, & tacitly claiming an exalted rank on the strength of mathematics which cant be done, & never could, I expect.' Pitying him, and trying to put herself in his place, Virginia concludes, 'I can imagine the kind of humility that must be on him, & how he gropes this winter, for some possible method in the future.'

Four months later, Norton appears at Gordon Square, and proposes to live there. Virginia notes this in her diary, and observes the nature of Craig's treatment:

Norton has descended. Bob, of course, muddled it all up. Norton can lunch at any rate at 46 [Gordon Square]; & proposes to live there; yet is desperate; verging on suicidal; can talk of nothing but himself; & will, Nessa thinks, hang about them all like an old decomposing albatross. There's a new suggestion Dr who can make your hair curl, & unravel every knot in your nerves as far as 20 years back — but Norton can't be made to face him. So

Craig goes on rubbing in the suggestion that Norton can't work; & he can't work; & now proposes to get employment with the Webbs.[11]

(*Diary*, 2, p. 99)

What emerges from this tragic story is a clarification of Virginia Woolf's position with regard to empiricism — how it ought to be supplemented by feeling. We can be certain that this unsympathetic side of Craig contributed to Virginia's presentation of Drs Holmes and Bradshaw in *Mrs Dalloway*.[12]

Diagnosis

Craig's first publication was a textbook, *Psychological Medicine*, published in 1905, when he was thirty years old. The book's introduction tells us right away how the author intends to treat the subject of madness: 'throughout the following pages the student will be reminded to look upon mental disorders in the same way that he views diseases in general. This warning is very necessary as so many men regard the insane as if they were the victims of some strange visitation, and not sufferers from ordinary illness' (Craig, 1905, p. iii). Craig stresses the similarity between mental disorder and physical disease, and so part of the task faced by the student of Craig's thought is to determine how mental disorder *differs* from 'ordinary illness'.

When attempting to determine Craig's definition of insanity, we are faced with the same problem we confronted in Savage: he fails, in fact, to produce any coherent or consistent theoretical framework. As with Savage, definitions are based on 'cases' — examples (not complete case histories) chosen almost at random. He will write, for example, that:

The aesthetic sentiment is one that has no small interest to those who have the treatment of the insane, for it undergoes alteration in most forms of mental disorder. The acute maniac is often decorated to an extravagant extent, and as a rule sees beauty in objects which in sanity he would condemn as vulgar or common-place. Conversely,

the melancholiac will deplore that things which he for-
merly thought beautiful now appear gloomy and ugly.
Untidiness and want of personal cleanliness are characteristics of many of the insane.

(Craig, 1905, pp. 7-8.)

Of what use is this 'definition' to the student of medicine? If
we take the criteria of seeing beauty in what is thought ugly
or commonplace by the majority, or of being attired in a
gaudy fashion, or of being untidy or unwashed as constituting madness, we are giving the doctor *carte blanche* to
certify a very great number of harmless people. The criticism is not far-fetched. In the work of T. B. Hyslop, we find
a category of insanity — aesthetic insanity — which brands
Post-Impressionists, Cubists and others as thoroughly mad
and in need of treatment. This criterion has, of course, the
greatest relevance where the work of Virginia Woolf is
concerned.

Craig anticipated criticism of his lack of definition; but,
in one bold statement, he dismisses all criticism, and decides
to push ahead oblivious of the profound importance of the
debate, not only where the interests of the public are concerned, but where the integrity and credibility of his profession are concerned as well. 'Premising, therefore, that it is
impossible to define insanity, it is nevertheless necessary
for educational purposes to be dogmatic even at the risk of
being wrong' (Craig, 1905, p. 19). Claiming that it is impossible to define insanity, Craig proceeds to do the impossible,
and he declares: 'A person may be considered to be of unsound mind if 1) he is unable to look after himself and his
affairs 2) he is dangerous to himself or others, or 3) he
interferes with society' (Craig, 1905, p. 20). Again, it must
be pointed out that the medical establishment can view itself as an agency for the enforcement of civil laws. All three
of the above criteria are primarily legal ones. They are vague
enough to be open to almost unlimited interpretation and
application. But Craig soon goes on to give a specific example
of behaviour which may be classified as insane. Speaking of
social rules and civil laws he declares:

this code of laws determines what we may do and what we may not do; it lays down rules as to personal property, and creates the distinction between *meum* and *tuum*. Some persons fail to adjust themselves to these laws, and their conduct is disordered in that they fail to distinguish between their property and that of others.

(Craig, 1905, p. 21.)

If we were to accept Craig's guide as to what is the proper domain of the medical practitioner, we would have to ask what role the legal profession and the police had left to play in society. When a man exhibits the 'symptoms' Craig describes above, he is a thief, not a madman. It would be different if Craig were making a case for the diagnosis of kleptomania, but that is not the case.

Having authorized himself to define insanity for educational purposes, Craig presents further criteria for the diagnosis. He writes, 'the healthy-minded man is gregarious, the insane is solitary . . . . Some of the insane only believe their own opinion to be correct, not withstanding that it is unsupported by evidence and *contrary to the ideas* of everybody else' (Craig, 1905, p. 22, my italics). In one stroke, eccentricity, personal preference, and the freedom to think as one likes are outlawed. At this point we must pause and consider: we already know that, according to Craig, a very great amount of human behaviour is symptomatic of insanity — what sort of man, then, is sane? We already know that he avoids taking a position 'contrary to the opinions of everybody else', that, in short, he is a conformist. What else?

the healthy mind sees good in all men; to hate is almost alien to it, and even dislike is kept within narrow bounds. But the converse is equally true: in sanity, love is bestowed only on a chosen few, who, by ties of relationship or exceptional friendship, are its proper recipients. The insane are often bound by no such limitations, and are ready to thrust their affections on any who will receive them. The girl who in health is reserved and maidenly in her attitude, frequently becomes forward and immodest when insane.

(Craig, 1905, p. 23.)

Or, perhaps it is that she becomes insane when she is 'forward and immodest'. What Craig has erected as a model of sanity is nothing more than the character of a certain class of English male who flourished during the Empire (though he still exists). It is the man who is moderately educated, avoids controversy — and who is in some ways profoundly dishonest. Hatred is as native to the human character as love is. Dislike is as common as moderately friendly acquaintance (if not more so), and is the kind of negative response to others which is vital for self-definition and the erection of standards. Craig's criteria seem to discourage idiosyncrasy almost to the point of the destruction of character, or individuality.

Craig's prescription for social harmony reads very much like political propaganda:

> by insanity of mind is meant such derangement . . . as disables the person from thinking the thoughts, feeling the feelings, and doing the duties of the social body in, for, and by which he lives. Insanity means essentially then such a want of harmony between the individual and his social medium . . . as prevents him from living and working among his kind in the social organisation. Completely out of tune there, he is a social dischord of which nothing can be made.
>
> (Craig, 1905, p. 24.)

What Craig presents under the guise of 'education' in *Psychological Medicine* is a programme of propaganda aimed at developing 'right thinking'.

Eventually *Psychological Medicine* gets down to more generally accepted medical categories — hallucinations, delusions, and so on. He maintains, for example, that hallucinations do not necessarily indicate insanity, but that they are 'very valuable corroborative evidence' (Craig, 1905, p. 55).[13] He then goes on to offer as a guide to the medical student the following reflections on the nature of auditory hallucinations:

> They may be confined to one ear or both. The voice may be that of a friend or a stranger, male or female.

The sound may appear to come from above or below, or even from the abdomen. The conversation may be of a pleasant or unpleasant character; the words may be persuasive or commanding.

(Craig, 1905, p. 56.)

It is difficult to see what possible use this information could be put to. We would not tolerate for very long a weather man who employed such a self-negating discourse.

Delusions are an important symptom for Craig, but only (as in the case of hallucinations) as 'corroborative evidence':

Taken by themselves, [delusions] do not necessarily indicate insanity, but their presence is strongly indicative of mental disorder when they are found in conjunction with other evidence, such as failure of general conduct and neglect to conform to the ordinary rules of life and society.

(Craig, 1905, p. 64.)

In some respects, *Psychological Medicine* is not a medical book at all. In the diagnosis of madness, symptoms such as delusions, hallucinations, and other morbid phenomena play only a secondary role in determining who is mad and who is sane. The main criterion is always the patient's ability to conform to social expectations, and this is really a legal or political point. The diagnosis is dangerous because its fundamental criteria go undefined. While Craig fails to offer definitions for such terms as delusion or hallucination, we do not object strongly, because we think we have some idea of what it is he is referring to. The terms are comparatively simple, and the dictionary offers basic definitions upon which most people can agree. However, terms (or rather, concepts) such as 'failure of general conduct', 'ordinary rules of life and society', and the like are not simple terms at all — on the contrary, they are exceedingly complex and problematical. On the face of it, this might not seem to be the case, for the terminology is 'simple' in the sense that each word in the phrase is an everyday word which we can take for granted, and which passes without remark in the course of conversation. But, as with terms such as 'human nature', they can mean what each individual wants them to mean. It is seemingly innocent phrases like these that are the cause of so much error and confusion in so many discussions about 'man'.[14] Having acknowledged the presence of the two kinds of terminology employed in *Psychological Medicine*, we can take a brief look at the ways in which they are employed in the diagnosis of madness.

As for the simple medical terminology, while the terms have a relatively clear and accepted meaning, Craig fails to demonstrate how they are effectively used in the business of diagnosis, or how he himself defines them. His reflections on the nature of auditory hallucinations show one way in which Craig fails to employ the concept usefully. Other specific examples of cases demonstrate the gulf that exists between their general meaning and their specific manifestations in individuals. As Savage, while at Bethlem, was perplexed by his patient's delusions that the doctors were his jailors and torturers, so Craig is perplexed by the common delusion in which 'a man may believe that his head is open, and that his brains have been removed and replaced by some other material' (Craig, 1905, p. 61). If this situation occurred in a novel in which a doctor holding Craig's views treated a number of patients suffering from this 'delusion', most readers would be quick to point out what is being signified. Craig's understanding of this 'delusion' would amount to an indictment of his occupation, and so his perplexity is easy to understand. Craig cites another example which is intended to show a characteristic of delusions in general: 'The delusion needs no other support than the absolute conviction of the deluded. "I feel that I am lost forever!" is the cry of the clergyman, not withstanding that he has taught the way of salvation to his parishioners for years' (Craig, 1905, p. 61). What a parable may be contained here! Yet, as in the previous example, an understanding of the patient's complaint would lead to an intolerable self-criticism. Craig cannot imagine that the 'delusion' may express nothing less than the truth: that the clergyman *has* lost his faith; or, more difficult still, that he has acknowledged the fact that he never had any faith to begin with, that his previous state was the deluded one. It would seem that, in this case, Craig has forgotten one of his own maxims which he lays down early on in the book: 'It must not be forgotten that a disbelief is just as positive as a state of belief' (Craig, 1905, p. 7).

As far as the employment of the social criteria for madness is concerned, when he gets down to cases, we discover what the concept of 'society' really means for Craig. In the earlier sections of the book, society seemed a homogeneous concept — something to which everyone belonged, and into which everyone must integrate himself. But, as the concept is developed, we see that it is not homogeneous, but is divided into hierarchical groups. Aside from the obvious differences between the 'haves' and the 'have nots', there are also different criteria for the definition of 'social' symptoms of madness. Craig writes, for instance, that:

> The degree of education and the social status of a person whose conduct is under consideration are also important facts, for habits which would be regarded as decidedly eccentric in educated members of the upper classes, might pass unremarked in the lower grades of society.
>
> (Craig, 1905, p. 60.)

Like Savage, Craig insists that the individual refrain from behaviour uncharacteristic of his class. Conformity is enforced not only by the diagnosis of madness, but primarily (and with greater effectiveness) by the 'majority' of each social 'grade': 'Society, to use the word in its broadest sense, permits a certain amount of lassitude in obedience to its regulations; but, in the main, the views of the majority are paramount' (Craig, 1905, p. 60). The sort of discrimination which Craig employs in his definition and diagnosis of the social symptoms of madness is not confined merely to class, but has a clause with regard to sex as well. In the case of women, evidence for the social symptoms of madness consists in a deviation from the male view of what is acceptable or 'proper'. If a woman decides to deviate in some way from this code (for instance, by choosing a form of apparel which contradicts it), she is in danger of indictment by the medical court:

> The up-to-date woman may adopt the divided skirt,
> under the belief that it is a healthier form of apparel and
> permits a greater freedom of action; but should she in-
> dulge in so subversive a notion as to think the male attire
> even more hygienic, and carry her belief into practice, the
> arm of the law will be at once stretched out to warn her.
> If the warning is not heeded, society will place her in
> some safe keeping until she has learnt to conform to the
> ideas of the majority.
>
> (Craig, 1905, p. 60.)

It is difficult to accept that this kind of writing may be found
in a medical textbook. But, again, it must be kept in mind
that *Psychological Medicine*, like Savage's *Insanity and Allied
Neuroses*, is more a political treatise than anything else. It is
a programme for a utopia, a course in social engineering with
a decidedly legalistic tone. The proclamation which lays
down the law regarding sex roles is equally applicable to men.
Women are not to adopt the male form of attire, thereby
declaring themselves equal, and men are not to exhibit any
form of behaviour which may be construed as feminine.
Craig writes, for instance, 'as a general rule, a tendency to
outbursts of emotional weeping in men is a symptom of
grave import' (Craig, 1905, p. 68). Like all the social con-
ventions which Craig erects as evidence of sanity, this one is
particularly Anglo-Saxon. It could never apply, for instance,
in Mediterranean countries — the result would be a whole
people declared mad. The criteria for the definition of madness in the work of Craig and Savage have almost no basis
in medical science.

Towards the end of *Psychological Medicine*, Craig does
give a few more examples of what we may term 'medical'
symptoms of madness. For instance, he speaks of 'mania',
which may be divided into two varieties: simple and acute.
In both cases, he does not give a general definition, but
rather cites examples of the sort of behaviour a simple
or acute maniac might exhibit. A simple maniac 'usually
gets engaged to be married to several young women in quick
succession, as his ideas of marriage are ever changing' (Craig,
1905, p. 93). Craig defines acute mania at greater length,

but the 'definition' possesses the same utility as that for simple mania:

> These patients are frequently considered brilliant in their conversations. This is not actually the case, for when analysed *this seeming brilliancy will be found in large measure to be due to the unconventional character of their chatter*. They say quaint things which strike the hearer who is not used to home truths and personalities, as amusing. These patients are often more entertaining when ill than during health, for through loss of control they will in illness make remarks which they would in health perhaps think, but forbear to utter.
>
> (Craig, 1905, p. 94, my italics.)

Even when applying a medical concept, Craig still brings the social criteria into play. Any diagnosis of mania has, of course, to rely in some way on social evidence; but Craig's real reason for diagnosing acute mania as he does is that the patient's conversation is *unconventional*. The same disguised criteria operate in this elaboration upon the definition of acute mania:

> They are often considered almost superhuman in their strength, but in reality they are weaker than those in health. They appear to be strong, for they have singleness of purpose and use all their strength in one direction, and in this way differ from the sane person, as *the latter is constantly inhibiting his actions*.
>
> (Craig, 1905, p. 94, my italics.)

The logic of this statement is extremely confused. Craig makes a point with regard to the single-minded utilization of strength, then goes on to draw a conclusion which has to do with inhibiting one's actions. In fact, it is the conclusion which is the point of the statement, but the premises upon which it is based are absent. They exist, unacknowledged, in the mind of the writer. In concluding his discussion of mania, Craig writes, 'To sum up: all maniacs are capricious' (Craig, 1905, p. 95).

Craig's career as a writer on madness continued for twenty-

five years after the publication of *Psychological Medicine*. In
a 1911 article entitled 'What Is Meant By Insanity'[15], Craig
again makes the point that, in his view, there is no difference
between physical disease and mental disorder: 'Approach the
study of mental disorder in the same way as you would
approach any other branch of medicine, for there is really
no distinction between mental disorder and physical disorder' (Craig, 1911, p. 603). He prefaces that statement with
another which had no place in *Psychological Medicine*, a
warning to his fellow practitioners about the use of certain
terms: 'Never use the words "madness," "lunatic," or such
obsolete terms, as they convey an entirely different meaning
from what I hope to be able to show you is the real meaning
of mental disorder' (Craig, 1911, p. 603). (We recall that,
midway through his career, Savage offered a similar warning,
but went on using 'obsolete' terminology all the same. To his
credit, Craig does seem to abide by his rule.) He also restates
his belief that mental disorders cannot be defined, though,
as in the earlier work, he continues to discuss them with
confidence. He writes:

> Sanity itself is a relative term, and is equally indefinable.
> Every physician knows what he himself means when he
> speaks of a normal or healthy body, but would he care to
> state such an opinion in the terms of a definition?
>
> (Craig, 1911, p. 603.)

Of course, there can be no definition which is ultimate and
all-embracing. However, we must view with suspicion the
pronouncements of any doctor who is unable to define what
he means by health or illness. Craig makes an appeal to
common sense (another of those 'simple' terms which be-
devil inquiry) and concludes, 'Experience alone can furnish
us with a knowledge by which we can form a judgement of
what, for want of a better term, may be called a "normal
standard"' (Craig, 1911, p. 603). Of course, the appeal to
direct personal experience should play an important role in
all inquiry, but not in a haphazard way.

The paper of 1911 concludes with a further restatement
of principles contained in *Psychological Medicine*, and offers

an ominously legalistic metaphor by way of advice to the doctor as to how he should regard symptoms of insanity:

> In determining insanity, the evidence to establish it can- not be decided from one symptom. The symptom present may be regarded much in the same way as pieces of circumstantial evidence are during a trial. Each individual piece may denote nothing, but the chain formed by weld- ing the separate pieces together may be so strong as to compel one conclusion. So with the symptoms of insanity; each of them if present alone might be consistent with sanity, but taken together they might form so strong a body of evidence as to force the inference of insanity.
>
> (Craig, 1911, p. 605.)

In a 1922 lecture entitled 'Some Aspects of Education and Training in Relation to Mental Disorder', Craig elaborates further his view of insanity.[16] He writes:

> As I am addressing an audience largely consisting of lay- men, I must tell you that there are types of insanity which, like some physical diseases, are intrinsically part of the organism, and for which, with our present knowledge, little can be done either to prevent or to remedy.
>
> (Craig, 1922b, p. 211.)

He also writes, 'When one appreciates that in a given individ- ual nothing more than exaggerated and uncontrolled normal characteristics may constitute mental disorder, we realise how narrow is the margin between those whom we call the sane and the insane' (Craig, 1922b, p. 211). Craig writes here with an imperial disregard for the condemnation of the diagnosis which is implicit in his observations. In this article addressed to an audience consisting mostly of laymen, Craig confesses which symptoms are those likely to elicit a verdict of insanity when he is the judge:

> there is one symptom which appears early and which stands out in strong relief, and that is hyper-sensitivity . . . it is to me the symptom of all symptoms which gives rise to many others which in time may so disturb personality

as to occasion definite unsoundness of mind.
(Craig, 1922b, p. 212.)

Also, 'The normal child is extroverted' (Craig, 1922b, p. 224).
Extroversion is not defined by Craig, but judging from the
manner in which he has outlined normal social behaviour,
we may guess that it means nothing more or less than garrul-
ousness. What Craig calls 'phantasy' is also considered a very
suggestive symptom. Again, phantasy is not defined, but we
may extract a meaning from the following statement:

> The adult has day-dreams, but they ought merely to be an
> outgrowth of reality — a visualising of some ambition that
> is as yet far off but the contemplation of which affords
> encouragement in the present and a vision of hope for the
> future. On the other hand, phantasy which has no normal
> relationship to life indicates that an older child has either
> regressed or that his mind is not developing normally.
> (Craig, 1922b, p. 223.)

Daydreams which are 'merely an outgrowth of reality' are
fundamentally colourless and lacking in any dream-like
quality. The sort of daydream that Craig calls normal is no
daydream at all in the sense that it provides no respite from
hard reality, no momentary escape from the problems of
fully conscious social life. If daydreams are to be confined
to a future which is very definitely grounded in reality
(possibility), then there is little to differentiate them from
plans or ambitions. Craig's prescription for mental health
has much in common with the philosophy of Mr Gradgrind.
(How would Craig have viewed the work of Lewis Carroll,
one wonders?) This article is unique among Craig's writings
in that he anticipates the rebuttal of his position (perhaps
because he is dealing with a lay audience whose mind is not
already made up in conformity to prevailing professional
opinion). He continues,

> At this point I may be met by those who believe that
> 'self-expression' in whatever form it may take is the
> factor of overwhelming importance throughout a child's

life, and that what some may regard as phantasy is nothing more than the unfolding of a creative mind . . . . I agree, as I suppose most would agree, that self-expression has been sadly neglected in the past . . . . But because 'self-expression' has been a neglected factor in the past, there is no reason why it should be granted too free a place in the education of the future. Sooner or later the instinctive impulses of the child must meet and, if untrained and unconditioned, must clash with the social *regime* . . .

(Craig, 1922b, p. 223.)

Instead of imagination, what is required is that 'Right thoughts should become associated with proper actions' (Craig, 1922b, p. 225). In what appears to be the last paper written by Craig, he elevates this remark to a major theme. In this paper, 'The Importance of Mental Hygiene in Other Departments of Medical Practice'[17], given at the First International Congress on Mental Hygiene on 8 May 1930, in Washington D.C., Craig summed up his arguments on that occasion, and his life's work, by saying:

Some weeks back there was an article in the London *Times* on 'The Gradualness of Inevitability', and I am in cordial agreement with the writer of it, for it is an attitude to life that has long appealed to me. As the author so truly expressed it, 'the emergent character of a good man is inevitable. In retrospective analysis it is truly seen as the slow accretion of singly inconspicuous units of right thinking and right doing, each of which in its little moment might have been something different'. Now this is the very essence of mental hygiene. . .

(Craig, 1930, pp. 578-9.)

'Right thinking', 'right doing', 'sanity', 'madness' — all of these have been discussed, but we are still no clearer as to their meaning. We have, however, seen what master these terms serve, and to what ends.

Aetiology

It is clear that any discussion of the causes or treatment of a condition must follow from some clear notion of what the condition consists in. If the definition of the problem is hazy, then the aetiology is bound to be constructed on shifting sands, and any programme of treatment is bound to be questionable. In *Psychological Medicine*, statements about the cause of mental disorder are random shots in the dark. We are told that 'autotoxins of the alimentary tract may produce insanity' (Craig, 1905, p. 28).[18] Similarly, 'Constipation is not only a common symptom in the insane, but it is the rule rather than the exception to find a history of prolonged constipation before the mental disorder super-vened' (Craig, 1905, p. 29). This alleged cause (which doubles so well as a symptom of what is termed a 'greedy colon', a spastic colon, lack of tone in the colon muscle, or a diet which hasn't enough roughage) is not presented in a relevant context which justifies its inclusion. The history of regarding constipation as a cause of insanity initally existed outside of medical history, in the realm of demonology, in the popular imagination. Joseph Berke writes:

> Any explanation must take into account the values, expectations and beliefs common to the society in which they are employed. For example, in Europe in the Middle Ages and for hundreds of years thereafter it was common practice to prescribe emetics to induce vomiting, and cathartics to induce diarrhoea, for the mentally disturbed. By inducing vomiting and diarrhoea, people had the idea that the sick person could be induced to get rid of the evil spirits, demons and devils which were thought to have entered body and mind and taken possession of his faculties.[19]

The fact that a diagnosis and aetiology based upon medieval superstition can survive in serious medical writing in the twentieth century should be a guide to the sort of critical approach which is necessary when discussing some of the central texts of psychological medicine.

Another cause of insanity is 'unsuccessful work': 'Successful work, as long as it is not too successful, seldom leads to mental disorder; but unsuccessful work shows a very different record' (Craig, 1905, p. 29). Alcohol is also a major factor:

> from the social standpoint, alcohol is the curse of the British race, and is slowly but surely undermining the moral energy of the nation .... To sum up, alcohol deranges the nervous system and leads to early decay of the intellectual faculties of the individual, it produces degeneracy in the offspring, and finally extinction of the race.
>
> (Craig, 1905, p. 32.)

Following Savage, who claimed that 'social climbing' was a cause of insanity (especially among women and the lower classes), Craig maintains,

> Again, it is not uncommon to meet persons of humble origin, who by means of incessant work manage to raise themselves into some position higher in the social scale. They reach their ideal only to find they must be failures, as they lack the attributes which are necessary for success. Governesses, to some extent, belong to this class. The calling of a governess is always precarious, her salary is often a mere pittance, and as years go by, she finds herself with no savings, her accomplishments out of date, and nothing but the workhouse to look to.
>
> (Craig, 1905, p. 30.)

An appeal to fairness and human sympathy ought to demand compassion for the woman, not a diagnosis of insanity. If anyone is to be blamed for this situation, it must be the social order which is responsible for the creation of the calling and its pitfalls.

Finally, Craig dismisses all serious consideration of causes as 'groping in the dark', or mere 'metaphysics':

> Perhaps after all, the cause of much mental disorder is not so intricate and complicated as has been supposed; and it may be that while we have been groping in the

dark with metaphysicians, the key to the problem has
been lying under our very hands. Let there be no mis-
apprehension . . . . May it not be that much of the growing
increase of mental disorder is to a certain extent due to
our mode of living; no time for proper meals, no time for
necessary exercise, no time for attending to health; the
race for life is too keen, until finally we perish in the
product of our own metabolism?

(Craig, 1905, p. 29.)

Craig's comments are almost precisely those of Drs Holmes
and Bradshaw in *Mrs Dalloway*, a kind of scout leader's view
of things. Of course our 'style of living' has a lot to do with
the prevalence of mental disorder: but any serious discussion
would consider things like the blind pursuit of material gain,
our inhumanity to one another, and other phenomena as
symptoms/causes of a mentally unhealthy style of living.

In the 1911 article on 'What is Meant By Insanity', Craig
writes that 'mental unsoundness may be either due to failure
of evolution or a result of dissolution' (Craig, 1911, p. 605).
The 1922 paper on 'Mental Symptoms in Physical Disease'
tells us that emotion may be the cause of mental disorder
(Craig, 1922a, p. 946). In 'Some Aspects of Education and
Training in Relation to Mental Disorder', Craig says that
many children may be predisposed to mental disorder.
Often, poor health can push the borderline child into mental
disturbance. Aside from these few observations, Craig has
little else to contribute to the aetiology of mental disorder.

Treatment

Considering the broadness and inconclusiveness of Craig's
definitions of madness, it is not surprising that he will maintain that large numbers of the public may be in need of
treatment. Many statements in *Psychological Medicine*
demonstrate how easy it is to fulfil the requirements for
admission to the asylum. He writes, for instance:

If a man gives way to an outburst of temper, his friends
may regret it, but they do not consider it a symptom of

of insanity; but suppose his bad temper becomes chronic, and he is persistently irritable, the probability is that a physician will be called in to examine his mental condition.

(Craig, 1905, p. 50.)

Even in the case of what Craig terms 'mild disorder', 'there is no objection to informing the patient and his relatives that the symptoms complained of are nervous in origin, *and require very decided treatment*' (Craig, 1905, p. 51, my italics). It would be uncritical to fail to ask whether or not this eagerness to 'treat', to hospitalize, is not bound up with the fact that, according to his obituary in the *British Medical Journal*, Craig's 'was probably the largest consulting practice of his time in the speciality in which he practised'. Aside from this practice, Craig also ran an asylum in Carmarthen with a colleague, Dr Stodart, and his brother, Norman Craig, a barrister-at-law. He also helped to found a private hospital for wealthy patients afflicted with mental disorders.[20]

Again, in his remarks on the diagnosis and aetiology of mental disorder, there is no adherence on Craig's part to scientific principles. There are, as with regard to the other two problems, only random reflections based upon superstition, or moral, social, or political prejudice. Craig's prescription for the treatment of masturbation is a good example of the way in which the medical man can make concessions to social morality at the expense of honesty and scientific integrity:

With care it is quite easy in a conversation to see if a boy understands what is being referred to and if it is noticed that he is ignorant, the subject can be changed at once . . . . It should be clearly pointed out to the boy that to continue masturbation is to run the risk of undermining his whole constitution, and ruining himself in mind and body. On the other hand, his mind should be set at rest by telling him that up to the present no permanent harm has been done, and that if he conquers the habit he will be strong and well again.

(Craig, 1905, p. 70.)

What is the rationale behind this next prescription for the

treatment of suicidal patients? 'Suicide is most likely to occur in the early morning between 5 a.m. and 10 a.m. Between these hours the melancholiac is most depressed, and ought to be kept under strict observation' (Craig, 1905, p. 73).

The only real practical 'medical' treatment which Craig suggests in the course of his work is the prescription of veronal. Craig was contemptuous of all critics of hypnotic drugs, and in view of the fact that one of his most prominent patients made a very serious attempt on her life with the drug, the following comments may be viewed with concern:

> Most of us have been taught to eschew the use of those drugs which are commonly spoken of as hypnotics, and text-books and writings tend to emphasize their deleterious effects rather than their medicinal values. Some urge that drugs such as sodium veronal should be placed under the Dangerous Drugs Act, and give the reason that these drugs have been used as a means of self-destruction. If this argument is seriously intended, then razors and all sharp instruments must be scheduled, and gas must only be supplied in cylinders after much signing and countersigning. It would be interesting to know the proportion of persons for whom sodium veronal, for instance, has been prescribed and who die from taking an over-dose; the number must be infinitesimally small . . . . The fear of drug addiction is, in my opinion, much exaggerated.[21]

Craig's logic betrays a deep lack of understanding of the mind of the potential suicide, especially the female. Veronal is a most easy and painless means of committing suicide. The question should not be how many people have died from an overdose of veronal, but how many people have attempted to take their lives with the drug. Craig's disbelief in the phenomenon of drug addiction is equally naive, for the Dangerous Drugs Act in itself testifies to its existence, and a whole generation of Victorian novelists made it a recurrent theme, not least among their more genteel, female, elderly characters.

Speaking to an American audience in 1930, Craig maintained that alcohol — even a 'nightcap' — is a much more pernicious means of obtaining sleep than the taking of narcotics:

Your country is protected against at least one dangerous form of treatment, and that is taking a nightcap of alcohol, which usually grows bigger and not less as the weeks pass. To me it is one of the most pernicious 'remedies' for insomnia. . .

(Craig, 1930, p. 576.)

But finally, as is the case with Savage, Craig's real prescription for mental health is the maintainance of a moral, political and social *status quo*, and the preservation of class boundaries:

There is another group of cases which are particularly sad, as it is often the break-up of a life which from the earliest of days has been devoted to close application to work; this group includes those who have risen from the ranks and who through scholarship or unceasing study have acquired some good position, only to find that their personality is unsuited for the post. The issues of life cannot and must not be lightly faced; phrases like 'equal opportunity for all' have a fascinating sound to the uncritical mind, but if you carry this assumed truth into general practice, your kindly attention will bring about the mental downfall of many of those whom you intended to help . . . the majority must be content to move within narrow limits. Evolution is at all times slow and to attempt to hasten it is not only unwise but disappointing.

(Craig, 1922b, pp. 226-7.)

When the medical profession takes it upon itself to judge that a man who has reached a high position through native ability, diligence and perseverance (whatever his social origins may be) should not really be there because his 'personality' is not suitable, then it has clearly overstepped what should be its rightful boundaries. However, the fact remains that sections of the profession did think in this manner, and this is precisely the sort of thing against which Virginia Woolf was writing in *Three Guineas*, a work which was dismissed as shrill, naive, misinformed, offensive.[22]

Craig's final summing up in his article on 'Some Aspects of Education and Training in Relation to Mental Disorders' advises that 'The country is learning that the greatest asset to a nation is good health and that a small number of A1 men count for infinitely more than a crowd of the C3 class' (Craig, 1922b, p. 228). This reductive view of humanity is the one held by Craig, and, despite her own intellectual snobbishness, Craig's attitude is in fundamental opposition to that of Virginia Woolf. We can be certain that doctor and patient were hopelessly at odds, and that nothing of positive value can have ensued from their relationship.

7

The Madness of Art:
T. B. Hyslop

Symbolism is rife in the insane.[1]

I find gratification in the belief that post-impressionism,
futurism, cubism, and some of the other morbid manifestations of art are perhaps becoming more fully estimated
at their true value.[2]

In discussing the work of Savage and Craig we uncovered
many of the presuppositions underlying a medical paradigm
of the time in its approach to madness, and we discovered
that their diagnosis of insanity was essentially a moral judgement made by a secular priesthood. This phenomenon has
been discussed in its historical context in great detail by
Michel Foucault in *Madness and Civilization: A History of
Insanity in the Age of Reason*, and it is clear that the doctors
under discussion here are working in the tradition inaugurated
by Samuel Tuke at the beginning of the nineteenth century.[3]
Foucault traces the history of madness from its visible
presence in society during the Renaissance to its suppression and confinement during the Enlightenment, and its
final 'liberation' by Pinel and Tuke at the end of the eighteenth century. Tuke's 'retreat' did away with chains and
tortures (though they still had their place — Savage's story
testifies to this). They were replaced, Foucault shows, by
inculcating within the patient a profound sense of guilt with
regard to his condition, which had the effect of controlling
him as effectively as, and with less bother, than the various
punishments which had prevailed throughout the previous
century. The asylum became 'a religious domain without

religion, a domain of pure morality, of ethical uniformity'.[4]
As we have seen in the work of Savage and Craig, the insane
are always *guilty* -- of some transgression against society and
the prevailing codes of that society. The behaviour that these
doctors describe is, from their point of view, shameful — that
is how they regard their patients. Foucault describes the
nature of the medical profession's shift towards a moralistic
means of dealing with madness:

> Henceforth, more genuinely confined than he could have
> been in a dungeon and chains, a prisoner of nothing but
> himself, the sufferer was caught in a relation to himself
> that was of the order of transgression, and in a non-
> relation to others that was of the order of shame. The
> others are made innocent, they are no longer persecutors;
> the guilt is shifted inside, showing the madman that he
> was fascinated by nothing but his own presumption; the
> enemy faces disappear; he no longer feels their presence
> as observation, but as a denial of attention, as observation
> deflected; the others are now nothing but a limit that
> ceaselessly recedes as he advances. Delivered from his
> chains, he is now chained, by silence, to transgression and
> to shame. He feels himself punished, and he sees the sign
> of his innocence in that fact; free from all physical punish-
> ment, he must prove himself guilty. His torment was his
> glory; his deliverance must humiliate him.[5]

This, then, is the nature of the revolutionary compassion and
humanity of Tuke and his colleagues in liberating madness,
in bringing it out of the seclusion into which the age of
reason had driven it.

This historical fact has great relevance for our purposes,
because without an understanding of it, we cannot begin to
deal with madness in the nineteenth century and in our own
time. The doctors we have discussed so far — with the exception of Henry Head — do not deal in medical categories,
nor are their methods based on natural science. The whole
enterprise is *magical* in nature, and depends upon the doctor
securing a certain power over his patient, upon his gaining the
patient's complicity. As Foucault concludes, the so-called objectivity of the medical profession in its dealing with madness

was from the start a reification of a magical nature, which could only be accomplished with the complicity of the patient himself, and beginning from a transparent and clear moral practice, gradually forgotten as positivism imposed its myths of scientific objectivity; a practice forgotten in its origins and its meaning, but always used and always present. What we call psychiatric practice is a certain moral tactic contemporary with the end of the eighteenth century, preserved in the rites of asylum life, and overlaid by the myths of positivism.[6]

The 'forgotten practice' to which Foucault refers is most easy to recognize in Savage. In Hyslop's work, the forgotten practice is less recognizable, perhaps because Hyslop is a better rhetorician than Savage. Savage's writing has a certain innocence about it, and while his presuppositions may be unstated, they come through loud and clear. Hyslop, however, is a different case. His judgements are cooler, more reasoned, and his rhetoric is seductive. He is, aside from Head (whose genius was truly scientific), the most gifted of the doctors who treated Virginia Woolf.

Hyslop's *oeuvre* has a profound importance for the study of her madness, for he himself was an accomplished musician and painter (he was the author of a number of orchestral works, and his paintings were exhibited at the Royal Academy), yet he was able to denounce Post-Impressionism, Cubism, Futurism, and other modern movements in the arts as insane. Hyslop believed that the practitioners of these degenerate art forms, along with the critics who wrote favourably on their behalf, were in need of treatment: confinement, purges.

Theophilus Bulkeley Hyslop was born in 1864 and died in 1933. He received his medical education at Edinburgh, London and Paris, graduating from Edinburgh in 1886. He was, at the age of twenty-five, and before he took his MD, Assistant Medical Officer at Bethlem, becoming Medical Superintendant there ten years later. Hyslop was also a prominent lecturer, and his lectures on insanity at St Mary's Hospital in London were very well attended, as were the various public talks he would give on aspects of insanity, particularly in relation to art.

Looking at Hyslop's entry in *Who Was Who 1929-1940*, one tries to imagine the kind of man Hyslop was in the flesh, for on paper he is something of a superman: an accomplished athlete (he later wrote a book on *Mental Handicaps in Golf*); a painter who exhibited at the Royal Academy and the Royal Institute; a composer and playing member of several orchestras; a successful doctor; and a prolific author (his main works being *Mental Physiology*,[7] *The Borderland*, *The Great Abnormals*,[8] and *Mental Handicaps in Art*).[9] He was also a great diner-out and raconteur, being at one time President of the Omar Khayyam Club. A colleague, Dr W. H. B. Stoddart, wrote in the *British Medical Journal* following Hyslop's death:

he achieved outstanding merit in everything he touched. He was a man of fine physique, and in early life was a noted pole-jumper. He played cricket well in any part of the field, and with his keen vision was up to county form as a wicket-keeper. He excelled at tennis, and, if I remember rightly, his golf handicap was plus 2. He was an expert at billiards, and I have often seen him put up a break of 100 or more. He was a first-class musician; he could play the piano and violin magnificently, and several other instruments to some extent. He composed quite a lot of music, including a number of orchestral pieces, some of which have been played at promenade concerts. He painted hundreds of pictures, and three of his larger canvasses were hung at the Royal Academy. I remember his taking to sculpture at one time, or rather modelling in wax, and he produced several beautiful little things. He once published a book in imitation of Swift (*Laputa*) in which he satirized present-day customs — or rather, customs of twenty-five years ago. Another publication was a little book of poems, not perhaps above criticism, but quite good in their way. One year, for our annual show at Bethlem, he dramatized a book by T. S. Clouston, and produced a very amusing play .... *if he had been able to keep to one channel there is not the slightest doubt that he would have been a very great man indeed. His latter days were saddened by something in the nature of a neurosis. He developed an anxiety state in consequence of air raids during the war. Later this became manifest in a sort of*

*tic of the shoulders and face, and ultimately the malady
bore a strong resemblance to paralysis agitans.*[10]

It is significant that the writer of this obituary, a junior
colleague and former student of Hyslop's, should be so
critical of his mentor at the end of the piece. It is not the
only occasion on which a colleague has commented about
Hyslop's 'mental health'. In 1918, Hyslop wrote a paper
entitled 'Degeneration: The Medico-Psychological Aspects
of Modern Art, Music, Literature, Science and Religion'[11]
which he was to deliver at a meeting of the Medical Society
of London. Hyslop fell ill and could not attend; the paper,
which had been prepared in advance, was read by Sir George
Savage. After reading the paper (in which Hyslop charges
almost every contemporary artist, composer and writer of
note with insanity), Savage declared that he 'could not go
quite so far as Dr. Hyslop, who seemed to think that every
artist of distinction had at least "a bee in his bonnet";
otherwise he feared the author himself might be considered
as having more than one' (Hyslop, 1918, p. 293). Savage
went on to say that: 'He feared the Orator had been kept
away from the meeting by a neurosis, but not at the upper
end; he believed it was sciatica' (Hyslop, 1918, p. 293).
    Quentin Bell tells us that Hyslop, along with the other
doctors under discussion here, was one of the people to
whom Leonard went when 'seeking advice' about the question of children.
    Hyslop was something of a public figure, and wrote in
popular journals such as *The Nineteenth Century* as well
as for medical ones. His opinions were probably more widely
known than those of the other doctors, and they are more
antithetical to Virginia's than those of the others.
    In discussing the work of Hyslop, I shall follow the same
procedure employed in the previous chapters, looking at his
views on the diagnosis, aetiology and treatment of insanity.
However, Hyslop's remarks on the medical treatment of
insanity are few and far between, and do not constitute a
body of material large enough to criticize in a responsible
fashion. There is a *de facto* prescription to be inferred from
the writings we will examine, especially those which deal

with trade unions, women and education. Hyslop's approach to insanity was, to use his own term, 'sociological'.[12] He was concerned with broad social and political issues relating to madness rather than with clinical preoccupations. Of the cultural issues with which he concerns himself, two stand out as being in need of examination and elucidation: his views on the morality of eugenics (and the role of religion in medicine and society in general), and on the nature of certain schools of art, literature and music. The remainder of this section will therefore deal with these two issues.

Diagnosis

Hyslop's first book, *Mental Physiology*, was published in 1895. Like Savage's textbook it is noteworthy in that it offers very little in the way of real, verifiable scientific information; like Savage's book, it is merely the expression of an opinion, often unsubstantiated, on the nature of madness and sanity. It is interesting to note the connections which existed among Hyslop and Savage and Craig. *Mental Physiology* is dedicated 'To George H. Savage, Esq., M.D., F.R.C.P., in grateful acknowledgement of many acts of kindness, and as a mark of appreciation of his teachings and wideness of view this book is dedicated by his friend and pupil, THE AUTHOR.' The index of *Mental Physiology* was prepared by Craig.

What Hyslop has in common with Savage and Craig is the tendency to ignore any data which might be called 'metaphysical'. He writes, 'If we regard our science ... as an empirical one, we may with great advantage be allowed to be ignorant of what is useless' (Hyslop, 1895, p. 4). What is useless? For Hyslop, it is anything which smacks of metaphysics or subjectivity, and is therefore unquantifiable and 'unknowable'. That there was a widespread epistemological crisis in sections of the English medical profession (insofar as it had to deal with insanity) during the early years of this century is now evident. Savage and Craig recognized what was difficult to know, and decided it was not worth knowing; Henry Head presented a fine example of how the truly scientific mind could approach difficult areas of inquiry; and in Hyslop, we revert to the ways of Craig. 'What is mind?' Hyslop asks, 'and how can we explain it? Our answer is, *and must ever be*, we don't know. *And we can never know*' (Hyslop, 1895, p. 8, my italics). Yet, not knowing what mind is, Hyslop presumes to study it over almost 500 pages. He writes that we can study the growth of mind 'by examining the individual mind in the higher races of today' (Hyslop, 1895, p. 150). For Hyslop, the English race constitutes the furthest point of evolution, and his preoccupation with the deleterious effects of women's suffrage, alcohol and other socially disruptive phenomena on the race may be seen as a political belief preached and practised (by means of the diagnosis of insanity) in his capacity as a medical practitioner.

By 1905, these beliefs had assumed a radical, almost fanatical, character, and found their most vehement expression in an article entitled 'A Discussion of Occupation and Environment as Causative Factors of Insanity'. Hyslop begins his paper by saying that, in the course of writing it, he found that there were not nearly enough statistics available regarding those certified as insane; so he broadened his definition of insanity to include a more substantial portion of the population, thereby making his task easier:

At first I was prompted to deal seriatum with various trades and occupations as causative factors of insanity; but, when I began to search the records available for statistics, I found that my observations would have to depend mainly upon the records of those who were under official cognizance as certified lunatics. A little thought, moreover, convinced me that such observations would not be of sufficient value unless supplemented by observations based upon records of those who are *not yet* under official cognizance, yet who are incapable by reason of mental perversion or defect from taking active part as citizens. It also appeared essential to take account of *those who remain as citizens, yet who are incapable of aiding in their own survival, or of adding to the vigour of the race, and those who by reason of mental hebetude or other psychological factors are unable to support either themselves or their progeny, and who fall into the category*

of the 'unemployed' or 'unemployable'.
(Hyslop, 1905, p. 941, my italics.)

It is clear that when Hyslop speaks of 'those who remain as citizens', those who 'are not yet under official cognizance', he is saying two things: that those who have been certified as insane are no longer to be viewed as citizens, that they have been deprived of their rights; and that many who still retain their status as citizens should not do so, by reason of their failure to add to 'the vigour of the race'. It is this vigour and its continuance to which Hyslop's life and work are dedicated. Hyslop approved wholeheartedly of a speech given by the Bishop of Ripon in the House of Lords, in which the Bishop

> gave it as his opinion that the facts revealed in the report of the Interdepartmental Commission on Physical Deterioration were pregnant with danger to the empire. He contended that, unless some steps were taken, the British race would no longer be able to maintain its position as a colonizing and as a ruling power.
(Hyslop, 1905, p. 941.)

What are the symptoms of this deterioration? As in Savage, the desire to educate oneself; also, the growth of popular movements such as trade unions. Hyslop maintains that 'we are faced, on the one hand, by the problem of over-education and the possibility of a false economy in the brain system of the nation, and, on the other hand, the problem of the trades unions and other agencies as affecting the vital energies of the people' (Hyslop, 1905, pp. 941-2). It is interesting to try and imagine, as Hyslop clearly wants us to, the extraordinary imagery which he employs in discussing his medical view of the nation — the 'brain system of the nation'. Who are 'the nation'? Hyslop speaks of trade unions as some malignant entity forced upon the workers from outside, a kind of virus. That may be true of the unions as we know them today in England, but in those early days (and in 1905 working conditions were not much different than in Dickens's day; the legislation of 1911 was still a long way off), they were a truly necessary and democratic institution. Not a gang of politically ambitious self-seekers, but a concerted effort to alleviate the inhuman conditions in which people had to work, to combat the view that unemployment was a medical phenomenon — 'shamming', or 'malingering' — to be treated or punished, and to demonstrate that it was an economic phenomenon, a by-product of the new law of supply and demand. Prior to the legislation of 1911 which provided national insurance and health benefits for those injured at work, or those who lost their jobs because of economic factors out of their control, the unemployed not only had to suffer the hardship and humiliation of unemployment without 'dole', but often had to endure a stigmatizing pseudo-diagnosis by sections of the medical profession. Some became candidates for Miss Dendy's farm.

Hyslop saw the growth of trade unions as 'the process whereby the standard of physical and mental energy is turned to the level of the least fit', and he believed that it did much 'to vitiate and render inert the vitality of the British unit' (Hyslop, 1905, p. 942).

But, for Hyslop, this is a minor problem when compared with the wholesale defection of women from their role in the scheme of things:

> the removal of woman from her natural sphere of domesticity to that of mental labour not only renders her less fit to maintain the virility of the race, but it renders her prone to degenerate and initiate a downward tendency which gathers impetus in her progeny . . . . her mission is not only familial but social also, with a duty to perform toward her fellow-creatures and to help the destiny for which she was created. We grant her the right of being a great civilizing agent as well as an ornament, but, intending woman to be mother, Nature fashioned her destiny for her. The departure of woman from her natural sphere to an artificial one involves a brain struggle which is deleterious to the virility of the race . . . . It is true that the more our women aspire to exercising their nervous and mental functions so they become not only less virile, but also less capable of generating healthy stock. Now not only is this a question concerning the virility of the race, but it has very direct bearings upon the increase of our nervous

instability. In fact, the higher women strive to hold the torch of intellect, the dimmer the rays of light for the vision of their progeny.

(Hyslop, 1905, p. 942.)

The tone of this passage is that of the worried coloniser: 'our women', 'healthy stock', 'virility', 'progeny', and so on. Hyslop sees the self-improvement (not liberation — that is eras away from where Hyslop is positioned) of 'our women' as nothing less than mutiny, the worse that could happen. The spurious evolutionary arguments with which Hyslop concludes his remarks on women are as far from scientific truth as they could be. How can it be that a man's education, his harnessing of nature, his ordering of the world can lead to a higher stage of evolution, an increase in the brightness of the 'torch of intellect', while development of the female intellect dims it?

In the discussion which followed Hyslop's paper, many of his colleagues were in agreement with him. One, James Stewart, added his highly idiosyncratic view that 'the number of women who entertained the idea of matrimony was decreasing, partly because young women of the present day engaged in gymnastic exercises to such an extent that their mammary development was reducing their figure to the flatness of the male' (Hyslop, 1905, p. 945).

Hyslop is zealous in his ascription of lunacy to broad social movements with which he disagrees; but, considering his views, and those of some of his colleagues (and the earnestness with which they preach them), we really must pause and ask, who is mad?

Aetiology

In the 1905 paper 'A Discussion on Occupation and Environment as Causative Factors of Insanity', Hyslop states that insanity may be caused by factors 'which are internal — that is, either due to inheritance, or to the existence of some fundamental capacity which cannot be explained as the result of immediate ancestry' (Hyslop, 1905, p. 941). But it may also be due to what Hyslop terms 'sociological factors, or, in other words, to the social environment' (Hyslop, 1905, p. 941). These factors may include over-education, the liberation of women, the rise of trade unions and so on. Following Savage, Hyslop also views migration from rural to urban environments as an important factor in the causation of insanity. We recall that Savage was self-contradictory in this matter, claiming that rural life was eminently suited to sanity, and then adding that it led to mental disturbance. Hyslop does the same thing, claiming that:

> The transplantation of pauper children from the gutter or the field to the Board school at an age when their little lives cry out for freedom and expansion, while suggested as being necessitous, is not in itself an unmixed good. The gutter of the pauper child is its parentage, and a heritage of disease brought about, in part, by abuse of alcohol and other things. The mere transplantation in such instances only too often serves but to expose *the corruptions of the soil, and the sins of the parents are but paid for in full by the ratepayers who contribute to the maintenance of our asylums.*
>
> (Hyslop, 1905, p. 941.)

What are the 'corruptions of the soil'? Here Hyslop launches a venomous attack on those who are supposedly under his 'care'. Foucault's study deals at length with the pernicious argument that condemns the inmate for residing in the asylum (as if he were there voluntarily!) and for placing such a burden on the pocketbooks of the public.

Education is perhaps the greatest cause:

> Pupils and teachers have increased a thousand-fold; standards have been raised; competition as determined by examination, has become more than ever a test of memory of acquired knowledge. Everywhere we meet the same struggle for mental culture, until we have become brainy and unstable to a degree that threatens the possibility of a reversion.
>
> (Hyslop, 1905, p. 941.)

Hyslop also maintains that, without religion, there can be no such thing as a healthy mind. He repeats this dictum, word for word, throughout his published work: 'a true and philosophical religion raises the mind above a mere incidental emotionalism, and gives stability. With no religion and no moral obligation, the organism is apt to become a prey to the lusts of the flesh and their consequences' (Hyslop, 1905, p. 943). The third part of this chapter deals with Hyslop's peculiar definition of religion, and its role in the diagnosis of madness.

The only statement that Hyslop appears to make in his periodical writings on the cause of insanity which is of a genuine medical nature is the following:

> Speaking generally, it may, with a certain degree of certainty, be stated that all the rhythmical, alternating, and intermittent psychoses are due to faults in the mechanism of waste and repair as determined by the various organs of secretion and excretion. Since advancing this theory in a paper read before the Harveian Society some years ago I have become more and more satisfied with its truth, and I do not think it is too positive an assertion to make when I state that every form of psychosis which is rhythmical or alternating in its occurence is somatic and extracranial in its origin.[13]

Treatment

Medicine and Religion

Michel Foucault has noted how, largely due to the efforts of Samuel Tuke, the diagnosis and treatment of insanity assumed a moral or religious complexion in England. In Tuke this change from external to internal control of the patient is subtle: it is not explicitly stated or advocated. By the time Hyslop is writing, this new practice has become the norm, and he takes it one step further by advocating an explicit collusion between the Church and the medical profession (and the state with its legal machinery) in an effort to promote normalcy. In an essay entitled 'Faith and Mental Instability',

Hyslop employs a clever and logical rhetoric in an attempt to claim for his enterprise the backing of the Church:[14]

> If the Christian religion is a true philosophy, it is the duty of all who profess Christianity to assist in the practical application of its precepts, where such can be judiciously and safely applied, taking religious things perforce as they find them, and utilising their own special knowledge to the best possible advantage, according to the conditions they find.
>
> Is a person with deep religious convictions better equipped to face the stress of life than an unbeliever? An answer to this question was given by the writer in a paper read at the annual meeting of the British Medical Association held at Leicester in 1905. In stating that 'a true and philosophical religion raises the mind above a mere incidental emotionalism' he used the word 'religion' in its literal sense, as derived from *re* and *logo*, to gather and consider, as opposed to *negligens*. He in no way extended its connotation so as to include demonstrations of incidental emotionalism, superstition, or fanaticism. *Religion and moral obligation he considered to be almost convertible terms, both equally compatible with institutionalism, utilitarianism, or any other 'ism' derived from the study of the laws of life and mind.* Moral laws are generally principles of thought and action, which an intelligent being must apply for himself in the guidance of his conduct, and the translation of such general principles (expressed either in general abstract form or in the form of a command) into particular actions. Conformity with such precepts of morality may with reason be regarded as a safeguard against the 'lusts of the flesh'.
>
> (Hyslop, 1910, pp. 106-8.)

It takes more sleight of hand than Hyslop musters here to demonstrate that religion (or 'moral obligation') is necessarily compatible with utilitarianism. As for its being compatible with 'institutionalism', Hyslop seems to be making a non-statement. The OED defines 'institutionalism' as 'the system of institutions; attachment to such a system'. While this is a vague and nebulous term, we can guess what Hyslop means by it, given his position of seniority as Bethlem. More generally, the institution which Hyslop is promoting is the tradition of rationality and empiricism, in an attempt to discourage abnormality, eccentricity, irregularity, subjectivity, intuition, mysticism, or 'otherness'.

In a further attempt to yoke the Church and the medical profession together, Hyslop writes:

> It ought to be our object as teachers and physicians to fight against all those influences which tend to produce either religious indifference or intemperance, and to subscribe as best we may to that form of religious belief, so far as we can find it practically embodied or effective, which believes in 'the larger hope', though it condemns unreservedly the demonstrable superstition and sentimentality which impede its progress and power.
>
> (Hyslop, 1910, p. 111.)

Why does Hyslop court the Church in this fashion? It might appear at first that he is simply a pious man who wants to ensure that what he feels to be the truth is given a fair hearing. As we read though all of his writings which make reference to the Church, however, we discover that there is an ulterior motive: that Hyslop is courting the Church in the hope that it will, in turn, sanction the 'moral' conclusions which he and some of his colleauges arrive at with regard to the diagnosis and treatment of certain groups of people. Turning to his book of 1924, *The Borderland*, we read:

> The question as to whether people who are known to be sterile should be allowed to marry is too wide for present discussion. Of course there is always the difficulty of knowing when a person is really sterile. I believe that the Church would willingly fall in with any scheme which would relieve it from its responsibilities in sanctioning the marriage and propagation of the biologically unfit.
>
> (Hyslop, 1924, p. 267.)

Hyslop begins by speaking of the morality of allowing sterile persons to marry (is this because they might indulge in sexual intercourse with the knowledge that the ultimate purpose of the act would not be procreation?), but concludes by discussing the desirability of allowing the 'propagation of the biologically unfit'. Damned if you can, damned if you can't. Hyslop's courting of the Church may be clearly seen as a prelude to a takeover bid. Here, his judgement is extremely suspect. It is highly unlikely that the Church would 'willingly fall in' with Hyslop's schemes (although sections composed of people like the Bishop of Ripon might support him). This scheme is similar to Savage's eugenistic plans, and involves involuntary sterilization and incarceration. In an article which demonstrates the eagerness of Hyslop and his colleagues to gain the political power necessary to enforce their proposals, he writes of 'persons unfit to procreate', 'those who are to be deprived of the opportunity of procreating children', and 'deprivation of liberty of the subject' (Hyslop, 1912, p. 553).[15] Here, two years after Hyslop attempted to show that religion and utilitarianism are compatible, is a clear example of what that assertion really means:

> In the history of every prophylactic measure adopted *for the benefit of the greatest number* there has ever been much opposition and delay owing to fetish worship of the liberty of the subject, and, in this instance, in spite of overwhelming evidence of the existence of much evil inheritance that tends to destroy the vital energies of the nation, there are many who will raise their voices in indignant protestation. One point for our consideration is whether this matter of preventing procreation by the mentally defective is of equal urgency to the other matters referred to in the Bill. I, for my part, believe that it is one of the most important and farthest reaching of the benefits proposed, and that this sub-clause alone raises the principle of the Bill to a higher plane than does any other item in it.
>
> (Hyslop, 1912, p. 555, my italics.)

It is difficult to imagine what sort of religion would be agreeable to Hyslop's proposals (we know what sort of political system condones them), in which human freedom is discarded as a useless and foolish notion, and in which unspeakable tampering with the human mind and body is elevated to a transcendental form of activity.

These passages, more than any others which occur in Hyslop's work, point out with absolute clarity what it was Virginia Woolf referred to when she wrote in *Three Guineas* of the 'dangerous and uncertain theories of psychologists and biologists' (*TG*, p. 33). Criticizing the attitude which Hyslop represents, Virginia quotes three letters to the press which lament the fact that women are employed outside of the home, doing work that men should be doing, 'compelling men to be idle' (*TG*, p. 94). She holds these quotations up for inspection, and concludes,

There, in those quotations, is the egg of the very same worm that we know under other names in other countries. There we have in embryo the creature, Dictator as we call him when he is Italian or German, who believes that he has the right, whether given by God, Nature, sex or race is immaterial, to dictate to other human beings how they shall live; what they shall do. Let us quote again: 'Homes are the real places of the women who are now compelling men to be idle. It is time the Government insisted upon employers giving work to more men, thus enabling them to marry the women they cannot now approach.' Place beside it another quotation: 'There are two worlds in the life of the nation, the world of men and the world of women. Nature has done well to entrust the man with the care of his family and the nation. The woman's world is her family, her husband, her children, and her home.' One is written in English, the other in German. But where is the difference? Are they not both saying the same thing? Are they not both the voices of Dictators, whether they speak English or German, and are we not all agreed that the dictator when we meet him abroad is a very dangerous as well as a very ugly animal? And he is here among us, raising his ugly head, spitting his poison, small still, curled up like a caterpillar on a leaf, but in the heart of England. Is it not from this egg, to quote Mr. Wells again, that 'the practical obliteration of (our) freedom by Fascists or Nazis' will spring? And is not the woman who has to breathe that poison and to fight that insect, secretly and without arms, in her office, fighting the Fascist or the

Nazi as surely as those who fight him with arms in the limelight of publicity? And must not that fight wear down her strength and exhaust her spirit? Should we not help her to crush him in our own country before we ask her to help us to crush him abroad? And what right have we, Sir, to trumpet our ideals of freedom and justice to other countries when we can shake out from our most respectable newspapers any day of the week eggs like these?

(*TG*, pp. 96-8.)

The ravings of a mad woman?

It is eminently clear, in the light of the work of Savage, Craig and Hyslop, that Virginia knew precisely what she was talking about, and knew firsthand. *Three Guineas* places the confrontation between her world of subjectivity and the doctors' world of 'Objectivity' precisely where it belongs — in the public arena.

Medicine and Art

Hyslop's *oeuvre* contains three major statements on art as seen from the point of view of the doctor of psychological medicine: 'Post-Illusionism and Art in the Insane'; 'Degeneration: The Medico-Psychological Aspects of Modern Art, Music, Literature, Science and Religion'; and *The Borderland*. All of these writings employ the diagnostic category of 'aesthetic insanity'. Part of our task will be to determine what Hyslop meant by this term, and to try and ascertain what his judgement would be where Virginia's work is concerned.

'Post-Illusionism and Art in the Insane' amounts to a condemnation of the work of the Bloomsbury painters as well as a declaration of their collective insanity. Hyslop's weak word play in the title of his article refers to his comparison of an exhibition of patients' work held at Bethlem and the First Post-Impressionist Exhibition held in London in 1910. Hyslop dismisses Post-Impressionism thus:

the only criticism with regard to post-impressionism now offered is a quote from an insane person who informed the writer that, in his opinion, only half of the post-

impressionistic pictures recently exhibited were worthy of
Bedlam, the remainder being, to his subtle perception, but
evidence of shamming degeneration or malingering.

(Hyslop, 1911, p. 270.)

Impeccable logic, final truth: even a madman recognizes
Post-Impressionism for what it is. Hyslop's criticism is aimed
directly at the milieu to which Virginia Woolf belonged. All
of the Bloomsbury painters (including Vanessa Bell, Virginia's
sister), were influenced by the French movement; and
Leonard's first paid employment upon his return from
Ceylon and his marriage to Virginia was as secretary of the
Second Post-Impressionist Exhibition, held in 1912. The
exhibition was, on the whole, a failure, though it included
works by Cézanne, Matisse, Picasso, Bonnard, and Marchand.
Leonard explains in his autobiography that: 'The British
middle class — and, as far as that goes, the aristocracy and the
working class — are incorrigibly philistine, and their taste is
impeccably bad.'[16]

In Hyslop's opinion, the insane artist exhibiting at Bethlem
may not only be a better artist than the Post-Impressionist,
but is acting in a more authentic manner as well. The insane
artist is in earnest, and has no ulterior motive for his 'distor-
tion' of reality in his work — he simply can't help it, that's
the way he sees it. The Post-Impressionist, on the other hand,
wilfully perverts what he sees — 'faulty delineation, erroneous
perspective, and perverted colouring' are the hallmarks of
his work (Hyslop, 1911, p. 271). The artist confronted with
Hyslop as his critic is placed in a double bind: either he is
mad, or he is a Post-Impressionist, a poseur.

The Post-Impressionist is dangerous because he might
possibly gain a following, and thereby help to erect faulty
standards of taste. As a result, Hyslop feels obliged to insist
that not only is the artist mad, but that the critic who
appreciates his work is also mad: 'both the insane artist
and the borderland critic have certain characteristics which
are peculiar to them' (Hyslop, 1911, p. 271). Hyslop goes
on to explain more fully:

Degenerates   often   turn   their   unhealthy   impulses

toward art, and not only do they sometimes attain to an extraordinary degree of prominence but they may also be followed by enthusiastic admirers who herald them as creators of new eras in art. The insane depict in line and colour their interpretations of nature, and portray the reflections of their minds, as best they are able. Their efforts are usually not only genuine but there is also no wilful suppression of technique, which, were it otherwise, would brand them as impostors. They do not themselves pose as prophets of new eras, and, so long as they are in asylums and recognised as insane, both they and their works are harmless, inasmuch as they do not make any impression on the unprotected borderland dwellers from whose ranks they might otherwise enroll a large following.
(Hyslop, 1911, p. 271.)

It would follow that, for Hyslop, the business of criticism is a very important business indeed. And so it is, for the sane critic is the psychiatrist's counterpart in the aesthetic world, entrusted with a duty to see that standards are maintained, that deviation is singled out and discouraged:

The artistic works of lunatics, however, do not always bear evidence of degeneration. The ideas of the paranoiac (or deluded person) may be grotesque and fanciful, but the artistic merits shown in his works may be great. Except in conditions of progressive paralytic dementia and of gross cerebral degeneration the evidences of deterioration may be merely manifestations of disordered thought and imagination. All merit is neither obscured nor lost. When, however, no artistic merit is observable to the *fully qualified normal critic*, it usually means that there never has been any development of the artistic faculty, that the faculty has been lost through disease, or that there has been wilful imposture.
(Hyslop, 1911, pp. 271-2, my italics.)

There is no such animal as the 'fully qualified normal critic'. What Hyslop means is the man who respects tradition but is not prepared to concede that new schools of art, the significance of which may not be immediately apparent (i.e. the critic's intelligence is pushed to its limit), might possess some positive value. Terms such as 'qualified' and 'normal', when used to refer to the critic, are useless unless carefully defined. This Hyslop refuses to do (just as he will not attempt a definition of mind). As he is certain that the Church would 'fall in' with his schemes to control human reproduction, so he is certain that the majority of critics share his common-sense view of art, a view which needs no definition. As he is able to discuss undefined categories and concepts comfortably with his medical colleagues, so he can confidently speak of 'good taste', assuming that what he means by this is understood by all but the insane:

> In sculpture, as portrayed by the paralytic in his early stages of degeneration, the work may be sensuously charming and excellently executed, and the perfection of its form may cover even what may be suggestively pornographic or even immoral. It may be attractive or repellent according to the mental bent of the critic. When, however, the work is prompted by ideas which are repugnant to good taste, and depicted in all its ugliness as a technique devoid of all artistic merit, and stripped of all evidences of those finer co-ordinations and adjustments acquired through education and practice, then the predeliction in its favour of any critic is open to the charge of dishonesty or degeneracy.
>
> (Hyslop, 1911, p. 272.)

It is clear that the question of 'good taste' is an important one here: 'bad taste' is, for Hyslop, not only an aesthetic concept but a medical diagnosis with dramatic consequences for the victim. To put it simply: if Hyslop catches you working in an art form of which he does not approve, you may well end up in an asylum: 'The insane sometimes take glory in the attention they excite, and there appears to be no limit to their eccentricities. So long as they are confined in asylums, however, they do not rank as cranks or charlatans, but as degenerates' (Hyslop, 1911, pp. 272-3).

The criteria we may extract from Hyslop's comments make two things clear: plastic art, to remain within the bounds of sanity, must be representative ('their absurd crudities, stupid distortions of natural objects, and obscure

nebulous productions which, being merely reflections of their
own diseased brains, bear no resemblance to anything known
to the normal senses or intellect'); and it must be grounded in
technique rather than vision ('those finer co-ordinations and
adjustments acquired through education and practice').

As the 1911 essay progresses, the term 'post-illusionism'
ceases to be a play on words and acquires the status of a
medical category:

> The distorted representations of objects, or partial
> displacements of external facts, are known technically
> as 'illusions.' Their psycho-pathological significance is
> great and they may arise in consequence of the fallacy
> of expectant attention (whereby the image of the expected
> becomes superimposed on that of the real), though toxic
> affection of the brain cells (as in alcoholic post-prandial
> illusionism) or as the result of faulty memory (paramnesis,
> distorted memory, whereby post-illusionism becomes
> manifest). Post-maniacal illusionism is almost invariably
> distorted, and the faulty representations bear little signifi-
> cance except as manifestations of disease.
>
> (Hyslop, 1911, p. 273.)

Of course, Hyslop can take this pseudo-scientific jargon only
so far, and he soon reverts to his usual tack of talking in
confident generalities, and presents the following explanation
of what goes wrong when a picture in the Post-Impressionist
manner is painted: 'The trouble does not lie with the varied
aspects of nature, which feed the mind through the special
senses, but with the diseased mind which fails to digest the
sensory pabulum so derived'; there is 'a return to the primitive conditions of children' and 'an atavistic trend towards
barbarism' (Hyslop, 1911, p. 273). The artist 'reduces a
composite whole to its component parts . . . he becomes not
a synthesist, but an analyst. He leaves the reconstructive
process to the imagination of the critic' (Hyslop, 1911,
p. 274). Hyslop's aesthetic criteria are, like most aesthetic
criteria, an expression of a set of deeply-held general philosophical presuppositions. In this case, Hyslop demonstrates
his adherence to Locke's *tabula rasa* theory — the fundamental tenet of most behaviourist thinking. The human mind

is a passive receptor of sense-impressions from the natural world. To assert the opposite, that consciousness is actively intentional — that it ascribes meanings to the world — destroys the comfortable empirical ordering of the universe. The quality of things does not lie in the things themselves, but in the meaning ascribed to them, and the interrelationships perceived by the individual consciousness. We don't all see the same things. Perspective complicates all our attempts to deal with the natural world. We have to admit that things aren't always as clear, as ordered, as we might like them to be. For the Post-Impressionist to leave 'the reconstructive process to the imagination of the critic' is to violate the basic premise of a crudely empirical world view. While there is not sufficient space to consider this question in all its aspects here, one might reply to Hyslop that it is not only when looking at Post-Impressionist works that the critic's consciousness is obliged to play an active role in reconstruction; most forms of art require the addition of an active, perceiving consciousness to complete their meaning.[17]

This is certainly true of all good works of fiction. Who could read from beginning to end a novel which contained no ambiguities, which didn't require the reader to make connections based on hints given throughout the course of the story? Wolfgang Iser's *The Implied Reader* shows how any good work of fiction contains 'unwritten' parts — parts the reader must complete himself during the course of his reading.[18] (The examples Iser cites include 'classical' writers such as Fielding, who was not a Post-Impressionist, and is not a purveyor of degeneracy.)

Literature poses a more difficult problem than does painting, where the role of the actively reconstructive imagination is concerned, and Hyslop skirts the subject as much as he can. Symbolism in literature is dismissed in a brief paragraph:

> Symbolism is rife in the insane, who undoubtedly do perceive mysterious relations between colours and the sensations of the other senses. So-called secondary sensations, however, although occurring in great variety, are never theatrically displayed for the benefit of the public.

Sane critics would liken such efforts to those of the decadent Gautier, or of Baudelaire who died of general paralysis of the insane.

(Hyslop, 1911, p. 276.)

Yes; but what of the poetry?

It becomes clear that Hyslop is not speaking only of Symbolism, an isolated movement within French poetry at the turn of the century; he is referring to the universal human tendency to make symbols.[19] This universal human activity is, as far as Hyslop is concerned, pathological:

Many lunatics are mystics and imagine they perceive unusual relations amongst phenomena. They see signs of mysteries, and they regard ordinary external phenomena as but symbols of something beyond. Their earlier impressions become blurred and indistinct through disordered brain action. Faulty memory, and the superposition of distorted former meanings, give to present objective facts a sense of mystery. Thus, a blue colour will arouse associations of many things of blue, such as the sea, the sky, a flower, etc., which become merged into the primary concept of blueness and invest it with other meanings or associations. It is, of course, well-nigh impossible to follow the suggestions aroused in the insane mind by a primary expression. The consciousness is befooled and wrecked by will-o'-the-wisps and inexplicable relations between things. Things are seen as through a mist and without recognisable form, and both the insane artist and his degenerate critic forge chaotic meaningless jargon to express what is seen or felt. The pseudo-depth of the mystic is all obscurity. Outlines of objects become obliterated, and everything which has no meaning becomes profound. The step from mysticism to ecstasy is short, and, with failure to suppress the wanderings from the real to the imaginary, there are produced for the onlookers such manifestations of imbecility as can find adequate expression only in pseudo-art, pseudo-music, so-called literature, or in the ravings of the insane.

(Hyslop, 1911, p. 276.)

It would seem that not only is symbolism taken as evidence

of insanity, but that mere associationism — a fundamental part of human mental dynamics — is also to be seen as pathological. It is only too clear what Hyslop's reaction would be to reading *Mrs Dalloway*, *The Waves*, *To The Lighthouse* or *Between The Acts*.

One of the reasons, according to Hyslop, why movements such as Post-Impressionism are to be discouraged is that they are a 'swindle'. Honest citizens waste good money on objects which have no artistic value and which, in Hyslop's opinion, should have no monetary value either. These artists and critics 'follow the dictates of their pockets and easily prey upon a too gullible public'. In Bethlem, on the other hand, 'neither mysticism, symbolism, nor any other "ism" finds a foothold for advancement, and inasmuch as lunatics are free from sordid motives they are harmless in their ignorance and segregated in their snobbishness' (Hyslop, 1911, p. 279). Hyslop continues,

> To the borderland critic who is ignorant of disease and its symptoms the works of degenerates are sometimes more than mere sources of amusement; they may serve to provide inspiration for his own unbalanced judgement. They are seldom deliberate swindlers who play up as quacks for the ultimate gain of money. The truly insane critic is usually definite and significant in his language, and he seldom seeks to cover his ignorance by volubility in the use of obscure and purposeless words. Such being the case, there is no scope for the promotion of bubble-company swindles in asylums, and there is never any danger of leading the public by the nose.
>
> (Hyslop, 1911, p. 279.)

Hyslop's pointing up of the advantages of having the 'insane critic' confined to the asylum leads into the final section of his paper where he deals with the question of what is to be done with post-illusionists and their degenerate critics. Something must be done, Hyslop insists, because 'some creations which emanate from degenerates are revered by the borderland critic, blindly admired by the equally borderland public, and their real nature is not adequately dealt with by the correcting influence of the sane' (Hyslop, 1911, pp. 279-80). It is not only the degenerate artist and his critic who need to be dealt with, but the public too; for they are not clever enough to recognize a swindle when they see one. They must be re-educated, and persuaded not to part with their money. This correcting influence is to be brought to bear by the sane. (One wonders how many of them are left after the final diagnoses have been made.)

Hyslop sees himself as the protector of the future of the race. He maintains of Post-Impressionists and others that 'not only do they injure true art but they also tend to vitiate good taste among the majority of mankind' (Hyslop, 1911, p. 280). What is to be done? On the one hand, 'inasmuch as our asylums do not give shelter to all perpetrators of such mockeries or travesties of good taste and morality, it is difficult to suggest a remedy or means whereby they can be suppressed' (Hyslop, 1911, p. 281). On the other hand:

> The borderland critics, however, must ever run the risk of being classed with rogues or degenerates. How best to treat them is another matter. From motives of humanity we are prompted to aid in the survival of those who are biologically unfit; but, with regard to the encouragement, or even toleration, of degenerate art, there may be, with justice, quite another opinion.
>
> (Hyslop, 1911, p. 281.)

Hyslop's next paper on art and insanity comes in 1918. In 'Degeneration: The Medico-Psychological Aspects of Modern Art, Music, Literature, Science and Religion', Hyslop gives a quick summary of the 1911 paper, and proceeds to give his further thoughts on the subject.

It is relevant to this paper to note that, in 1925, Hyslop published a peculiar book entitled *The Great Abnormals*. It is a long collection of brief anecdotal case histories of famous historical personages whom Hyslop (and in some cases, other commentators) consider insane. However, there is no theoretical chapter, no comment on the significance of the particular symptoms which each subject displays — merely a straightforward collection of as many stories of human idiosyncrasy as Hyslop could gather. Hyslop's only motive

seems to have been to demonstrate just how many people
are — and have been and will be — insane. The 1918 paper on
degeneration gets under way with a similar catalogue of insanity among artists. Again, no connections are made, no
theoretical points offered or defended. It would seem as if
the purpose of the exercise is to demonstrate that nearly all
artists of repute are madmen:

> True insanity occured in Romney, Cosway, Haydon,
> and Landseer. Turner, with what Ruskin has set up as an
> example of a surpassing faculty for colour, has been
> accredited with a mental calibre little short of idiocy. It
> is true that his mother was confined in Bethlem, but there
> exists some doubt as to whether he himself was really
> profligate, and as to whether he might possibly have
> achieved greater things had he been better cared for.
> James Barry used to be afraid to go out by night lest the
> Academicians should murder him. William Blake had an
> uninterrupted succession of delusions, hallucinations and
> wild imaginings . . . . Many of the greatest painters, sculp-
> tors, and engravers, whose names live in their works, have
> their names inscribed in the case books of our asylums.
> The chronicles of Bedlam alone would provide enough
> material to form a substantial volume. For obvious
> reasons, however, such chronicles are sealed. Giorgione,
> Tintoretto, Paul Veronese, Botticelli, Leonardo da Vinci,
> Rubens, Raphael, Albert Durer, Claude Lorraine, Salvator
> Rosa, Benvenuto Cellini, Van dyck and Watteau, all
> suffered from some form of neurosis. Among artists we
> have only to mention Sir Joshua Reynolds, Flaxman,
> Morland, Fuseli, Lawrence, Liverseege, Wilkie, Mackie,
> Dore, and Meissonier, all of whom had distinct evidences
> of degeneracy.
> We are told Molière, Petrarch, Charles V, Handel, St.
> Paul, and Peter the Great were epileptics. Paganini, Mozart,
> Schiller, Alfieri, Pascal, Richelieu, Newton, and Swift
> were victims of diseases, epileptoid in character. Dr.
> Johnson, Napoleon, and Socrates suffered from spas-
> modic and choraeic movements. Zeno, Cleanthes, Lucan,
> Chatterton, Blount, Haydon, and Clive committed suicide.
> Coleridge, Sheridan, Steele, Addison, Hoffman, Chas.
> Lamb, Burns, Morland, Turner, Dussek, Handel, Gluck,
> and others abused the use of alcohol and other drugs.

Salhurst, Seneca, and Bacon were suspected felons. Rousseau, Byron and Caresa were grossly immoral. Dayner, Clement, Diderot, and Prayn were perverts, etc. Shelley, Bunyan, Swedenborg, and others had hallucinations.

(Hyslop, 1918, p. 275-6.)

Distinguished company; but not exclusive.

Music and painting are the arts about which Hyslop professes to know most, and his discussion of degenerate tendencies begins with the former. For Hyslop, the most pernicious example of degenerate music is the work of Schoenberg, whom he introduces and dismisses in one stroke:

A deaf and dumb personal friend of considerable mental power and ability expressed satisfaction at the performance of the Queen's Hall Orchestra, and said the music gave him pleasurable sensations in his thighs and glutei. Whether Schoenberg's music would have elicited the same symptoms I do not know. I am inclined to believe that the test would prove in this instance that there may be certain advantages to complete deafness.

(Hyslop, 1918, p. 278.)

As we see Hyslop wield this critical technique against opponents, a distinctly unpleasant side of his character begins to emerge. We see the sophisticated polymath, accompanied on one occasion by an inmate of Bethlem, on another by a deaf mute, hand outstretched in an appeal to reason and common sense, brows knitted in concentration — Frankenstein and his assistant.

While Hyslop dismisses the difficult as pathological, he finds the 'simple' even more so. He writes in haughty disgust:

When we return to the question of the music of the day we must first differentiate between the musical classes and the masses. By the latter I mean the devotees of western syncopated abominations, to the prandial absorbers and hummers of the fiddlings of ballads, and even the so-called lovers of music who judge the merits of the music solely by its physical effects on themselves.

(Hyslop, 1918, p. 279.)

In literature as well as art and music, Hyslop sees signs of degeneration and disease everywhere. He deplores the fact that 'authors use imperfect and disjointed sentences, trusting to their readers to comprehend their meaning. In these methods I see a somewhat close analogy to the incoherence of maniacs, whose ravings, though incoherent to others, are not so to themselves' (Hyslop, 1918, p. 285). He makes no attempt to suggest ways in which this degenerate tendency might be checked (nor does he name the practitioners of this degenerate literature). 'Literature of the classical type,' he concludes, 'seems to be on the wane' (Hyslop, 1918, p. 286).

Hyslop concludes with a virulent attack on German *Kultur*. He writes, 'Germany has never evolved to the higher plane of humanity. The indictment of posterity will be that, for centuries, it has been the fountain head of psychopathic epidemics' (Hyslop, 1918, p. 287). Hyslop puts this down to evolution: 'When the character of a nation is unmoral and lacking in honour, its inherent defectiveness is due to heredity and the influences of a pernicious ethical environment which is temporarily incapable of correction or regeneration' (Hyslop, 1918, p. 287). Finally,

Germany, by reason of its moral defects, is as yet incapable of evolving to the moral standard of modern civilization. I might also include 'mental' standard because of its faulty and unwarranted generalisations with regard to Science, its incompetent use of pure reason in metaphysics, and its travesties of justice in relationship to the individual rights of man.

(Hyslop, 1918, p. 290.)

These charges are not wholly without validity, especially in light of what was to come. What is striking about them, however, is their unwitting irony. Coming from the pen of a eugenist who is contemptuous of talk of 'liberty of the individual', who thinks the mission of eugenics a transcendental one, they appear singularly odd. They may be taken as an index of the state of Hyslop's mind at this point in his career, for he is totally oblivious of the irony of his remarks.

Hyslop's last statement on art and medicine occurs in a chapter of his book *The Borderland*, entitled 'Music, Literature, Science, Religion'. In it he restates (in many places, merely reprints) the views outlined in 'Degeneration'. However, it is worth pausing for a moment to consider a statement he makes prior to the chapter on the arts, for it calls into question the grounds for one of Hyslop's main complaints against new forms of 'degenerate' art. He writes,

> In health there is a standard of perception, i.e. there is an agreement amongst the greatest number as to the aspects of things seen. Beyond this we cannot go. We cannot define what shall appear as truly normal. Where the perceptive processes are not in agreement with the perceptive processes of others, it is outside or apart from normal, and it is to be noted that although that normal percept may be novel and even stimulative in its action, it may be simulated or copied by some, but it cannot by any mental or physiological process affect the perceptive processes of others, so as to gain for its particular type a majority. *This means that the abnormal is like a 'spontaneous variation' or 'sport', and that although its immediate effects may be manifest it does not alter or even modify the general trend of evolution.*
> (Hyslop, 1924, p. 140, my italics.)

This statement is of fundamental importance, for it virtually destroys what reasoning there is behind Hyslop's condemnation of the emancipation of women, the improvement of the workers' lot, and what he terms degenerate art. Hyslop's great fear was that the degenerate artist might attain a large following, and so pervert the standards of taste. Yet, if the abnormal is only a 'spontaneous variation' or 'sport' that 'does not alter or even modify the general trend of evolution', why campaign for its suppression? If the 'perceptive processes' have nothing to do with evolution — if there is no danger of one person's vision becoming genetic necessity — then why should it be assumed that an individual woman's exertion of her mental faculties should contribute to the dimming of the torch of intellect for the race as a whole?

In *The Borderland*, the chapter on art is immediately followed by one entitled 'Civilization'. Here are found Hyslop's final pronouncements on the general decline of the race, and the medical man's duty to put a halt to it. In my discussion of Hyslop's work, I have suggested that if Hyslop had his way — if his criteria for madness were to be universally applied — there would be fewer sane than insane persons to be found in Britain. In *The Borderland* Hyslop does not hesitate to say that this is indeed the case:

> Some fifteen years ago, when criticizing the Annual Statistical Returns of the Commissioners in Lunacy, I expressed the view that statistics were apt to lead to wrong conclusions if their fallacies were not sufficiently elucidated. I gave as an instance the statistics of the evidence of insanity in England, which seemed to indicate that unless some amelioration in its increase occurred, in about half a century the proportion of the sane to the insane would be such that there would be only just enough sane for the care and control of the insane.
>
> (Hyslop, 1924, p. 231.)

We recall from the 1905 paper on 'Occupation and Environment as Causative Factors of Insanity' that the current statistics (and it must be these to which he refers in 1924) did not give a full enough picture of who comprised the insane, and he had to supplement them with his own view that much larger sections of the population showed symptoms of insanity.

In taking the extreme positions which characterize his thought, Hyslop adopts an apocalyptic tone. He is no longer concerned to court the Church, the government or the press. He is in the grip of a certainty that England is on the brink of evolutionary (and, therefore, moral, political, social and economic) disaster. He writes, in a histrionic style, with bitter sarcasm and the frustration of a man occupying a solitary and untenable position.

When mankind has become universally civilized and universal harmony attained, shall we then have universal registration of the unfit? And shall we medical men, in our humanitarian enthusiasm, have served merely to aid the survival of the unfittest and in bringing about a regression towards mediocrity? Needless it is to point out how ably will our endeavours have been enhanced by the Church — as evidenced in the repeal of the Contagious Diseases Act, by its opposition to the eugenic problems involved in reform of the marriage laws, and by its methods of dealing with similar questions. It may be thought that my statements are unduly pessimistic. If so, the criticism is occasioned, not by failure to recognize the trend of evolution either as pre-determined and guided by an omnipotent control or evolved by natural causes, but rather as a criticism of the misinterpretations and misunderstandings of those who have administrative power in connection with the eugenics of mind and body.

(Hyslop, 1924, p. 234.)

Hyslop's medical and ethical view now combines with a large historical perspective which states clearly the nature of his fears:

Every race that has lived has sunk back into mediocrity through a process of terminal infection. The resistive mechanism against both the inroads of disease and all the factors which tend to diminish virility has always been at fault in the later periods of the lives of races, and are we warranted to assume that humanity when it is full and complete will depart from the rule and experience of all that pertained to its separate communities?

(Hyslop, 1924, p. 237.)

It is not easy to hang a label on Hyslop's diagnosis of the problem. However, when he begins to imply the cure, his political colours become clearly visible:

Great Britain is in an almost unique position as a dumping ground for the unfit. Ever since the late Sir H. Campbell-Bannerman said 'Shall we deny the alien the right of asylum?' aliens have flocked to our shores, and it is a strange irony that once a lunatic is on the sea his only landing-place appears to be England, which has thus become the asylum of the world.

(Hyslop, 1924, p. 240.)

Finally, Hyslop offers a rebuttal to those who have condemned him as a pessimist; these words testify to Hyslop's high earnestness, but also to the terribly misconceived nature of much of this thinking:

I repudiate any statement that my arguments are incompatible with the highest conceptions of life, mind, and the scheme of the universe in its entirety. All I seek to prove is that man, in his efforts to fashion nature, brings upon himself merely a more rapid return to the depths from which he came, and, when viewing the manifestations of humanity as but being in conformity with the universal laws of evolution and dissolution, it is but the feeblest of all criticisms to take refuge behind the statement that such remarks are merely instances of pessimism.

(Hyslop, 1924, pp. 239-40.)

8
The 'Discourse of Power': Burley and *Flush*

In a brilliant essay on Michel Foucault's work to date, Hayden White identifies Foucault's main theme as the 'discourse of power'.[1] White makes two points with regard to Foucault's studies of madness, medicine, the law, the penal system, sexuality and the human sciences. Firstly, 'what is at work in discourse — as in everything else — is always "desire and power", but in order for the aims of desire and power to be realized, discourse must ignore its basis in them'.[2] Secondly, White claims, 'Discourse wishes to "speak the truth", but in order to do this must mask from itself its service to desire and power, must indeed mask from itself the fact that it is in itself a manifestation of the operations of these two forces.'[3] These two points are vitally relevant to a study of Virginia Woolf and her doctors. They place the work of Savage, Craig and Hyslop firmly within the history of the discourse of power. The discourse of all three men claims to 'speak the truth', yet the service to power - political, social, economic, racial — always remains unstated. It masks from itself its true political character. Their discourse presents itself as 'medical', but uses the vehicle of social and professional position and the organs of medical writing, to conduct a political exercise. The identification of the work of the doctors as an example of the discourse of power gives us a means by which their enterprise can be located in an ontological and historical context. Having said what characterizes the discourse of power, White goes on to elaborate its role in society:

Like desire and power, discourse unfolds 'in every

242 All that Summer She was Mad

society' within the context of external restraints which appear as 'rules of exclusion', rules which determine what can be said and not said, who has the right to speak on a given subject, what will constitute reasonable and what 'foolish' actions, what will count as 'true' and what as 'false'. These rules limit the conditions of discourse's existence in different ways in different times and places. Whence the distinction, arbitrary but taken for granted in all societies, between 'proper', reasonable, responsible, sane, and truthful discourse, on the one side, and 'improper', unreasonable, irresponsible, insane, and erroneous discourse, on the other. Foucault himself vacillates between the impulse to justify the discourse of madness, criminality and sickness (whence his celebration of such writers as Sade, Hölderlin, Nietzsche, Artaud, Lautréamont, Roussel, and so on), on the one hand, and his constantly reaffirmed aim to probe beneath the distinction between proper and improper discourse, in order to explicate the ground on which the distinction itself arises, on the other. Despite this vacillation, his probings take the form of 'diagnoses' intended to reveal the 'pathology' of a mechanism of control which governs discursive and non-discursive activity alike.

As for the internal restraints placed on discourse, the 'rarefactions' noted above, all these are functions of the distinction, as false as it is insidious, between an order of words and an order of things, which makes discourse itself possible.[4]

What this anatomy of the discourse of power implies is a struggle between the representatives of power (the doctor, the politician) and the 'other' — the criminal, the sick, the non-conforming: those whose very existence contradicts the 'truth' which the discourse of power claims for itself. Paradoxically, the existence of the other serves further to define, by virtue of his difference, the discourse of power. The discourse of power is, in a sense, defined negatively in its attempt to suppress 'otherness'. This insight provides an opening by means of which we can begin to understand Virginia Woolf's position *vis à vis* her doctors (and in relation to the discourse of 'objectivity', of empiricism and rationality) and the nature of her own discourse.

It may be asked, how can Virginia Woolf be seen as a 'victim' of the discourse of power when she herself succeeded in creating a very powerful discourse of her own, one which was not silenced and was published and admired widely? The reply lies in a closer reading of her work in the light of the discourse of power. One has to locate her *oeuvre* biographically and ideologically; and, having done that, to consider the nature of the conflict between her position and that of her husband and other representatives of 'Cambridge rationality', her doctors and their perception of her, the trauma of her early sexual experiences at the hands of her half-brothers, and all of the images, symbols and situations which these realities charged with meaning in her writing.

Virginia's response to the discourse of power is characterized by two modalities: expression and repression. The former consists of what is written and what remains unwritten, but nevertheless implied, in her work. The latter is characterized by what is repressed in expression, and what is expressed in repression. A good example of these tactics may be found in a comparison of successive drafts of an important scene in *The Voyage Out*. Following Rachel and Terence's mutual profession of love, and her acceptance of his proposal, there occurs a strange scene in which Helen confronts the two lovers:

> Voices crying behind them never reached through the waters in which they were now sunk. The repetition of Hewet's name in short, dissevered syllables was to them the crack of a dry branch or the laughter of a bird. The grasses and breezes sounding and murmuring all round them, they never noticed that the swishing of the grasses grew louder and louder, and did not cease with the lapse of the breeze. A hand dropped abrupt as iron on Rachel's shoulder; it might have been a bolt from heaven. She fell beneath it, and the grass whipped across her eyes and filled her mouth and ears. Through the waving stems she saw a figure, large and shapeless against the sky. Helen was upon her. Rolled this way and that, now seeing only forests of green, and now the high blue heaven; she was speechless and almost without sense. At last she lay still, all the grasses shaken round her and before her by her panting.

Over her loomed two great heads, the heads of a man and woman, of Terence and Helen.

Both were flushed, both laughing, and the lips were moving; they came together and kissed in the air above her. Broken fragments of speech came down to her on the ground. She thought she heard them speak of love and then of marriage. Raising herself and sitting up, she too realized Helen's soft body, the strong and hospitable arms, and happiness swelling and breaking in one vast wave. When this fell away, and the grasses once more lay low, and the sky became horizontal, and the earth rolled out flat on each side, and the trees stood upright, she was the first to perceive a little row of human figures standing patiently in the distance. For the moment she could not remember who they were.

'Who are they?' she asked, and then recollected.

(*TVO*, pp. 287-8.)

This is, to say the least, a very curious and ambiguous passage. It would seem that Helen has (playfully?) pounced on Rachel and rolled her about, as playful children do one another. Yet the experience is upsetting for Rachel. In fact, she becomes totally disoriented for a few moments, and her situation seems quite alien to her.

But reading through the passage again, the ambiguity increases. We have ascertained what has happened, but the tone now seems strangely ominous. 'Helen was upon her' — we are reminded of the passage in *Mrs Dalloway* in which Septimus reflects, 'Once you fall, Septimus repeated to himself, human nature is on you. Holmes and Bradshaw are on you' (*MD*, p. 108). Grass whipping is certainly unpleasant. The action is violent, and not without sexual undertones. Bewildered, Rachel looks up to see Helen and Hewet kissing (is she congratulating him?); then, 'she too realized Helen's soft body'.

Before attempting to attach any particular significance to this passage we should consider two previous drafts which Mitchell Leaska has unearthed in an important article, 'Virginia Woolf's *The Voyage Out*: Character Deduction and the Function of Ambiguity'.[5] Leaska believes that 'everything in the published work is relevant in one way or another;

that *everything is not there by chance, but by choice*,[6] and the holograph and subsequent versions of *The Voyage Out* which he has studied show that the passage just quoted was re-written repeatedly, and that its violence is, if anything, toned down in the published version. This holograph version, dated 21 December 1912, emphasizes the violence of Helen's action:

> Before Mr Flushing could do more than protest, Helen was off, sweeping over the ground at a considerable pace. The figures continuing to retreat, she broke into a run, shouting Rachel's name in the midst of great panting. Rachel heard at last; looked round, saw the figure of her aunt a hundred yards away, and at once took to her heels. Terence stopped and waited for her. But she swept past . . . [Helen] pulling handfuls of grass and casting them at Rachel's back, *abusing her roundly* as she did so with the remnants of her breath. Rachel turned incautiously to look, caught her foot in a twist of grass and fell head-long. Helen was upon her. *Too breathless to scold, she spent her rage in rolling the helpless body hither and thither, holding both wrists in one firm grasp, and stuffing eyes, ears, nose, and mouth with the feathery seeds of the grass. Finally she laid her flat on the ground, her arms out on either side of her, her hat off, her hair down. 'Own yourself beaten!' she gasped. 'Beg my pardon!'* Lying thus flat, Rachel saw Helen's head pendant over her, very large against the sky. A second head loomed above it. 'Help! Terence!' she cried. 'No!' he exlaimed, when Helen was for driving him away. 'I've a right to protect her. We're going to be married.'
>
> For the next two seconds they rolled indiscriminately in a bundle, imparting handfuls of grass together with attempted kisses. Separating at last, and trying to tidy her hair, Helen managed to exclaim between her pants, 'Yesterday! I guessed it!'[7]

In addition to the physical violence (which, it seems, is less playful here), there is a psychological battle going on. Like a bullying child, Helen insists that Rachel 'give': 'Own yourself beaten! she gasped.' But Helen takes the childish tyranny further: 'Beg my pardon!' she demands. Beg pardon for what?

The whole thrust of the passage is toward Helen's learning of the engagement. Is this what she demands pardon for — or for the simple fact of Rachel's intimacy with Hewet, regardless of whether or not they are to be married? The demand for pardon here is crucial, for Helen's behaviour in this scene is untypical of her as we have seen her so far. Up until now, her attitude towards Rachel has been undemanding. Helen purports to help Rachel 'find herself'. A strange reversal (which may tie in with the reversal of the sexes of the figures in the tunnel during Rachel's hallucination) has occurred.

Is Helen motivated by jealousy? This earlier typescript version seems to suggest this:

> Suddenly Rachel stopped and opened her arms so that Helen rushed into them and tumbled her over on to the ground. 'Oh Helen, Helen!' she could hear Rachel gasping as she rolled her, 'Don't! For God sake! Stop! I'll tell you a secret! I'm going — to — be — married!' Helen paused with one hand upon Rachel's throat holding her head down among the grasses. 'You think I didn't know that!' she cried. For some seconds she did nothing but roll Rachel over and over, knocking her down when she tried to get up; stuffing grass into her mouth; finally laying her absolutely flat upon the ground, her arms out on either side of her, her hat off, her hair down.
> 'Own yourself beaten,' she panted. 'Beg my pardon, *and say that you worship me!*'
> Rachel saw Helen's head pendant over her, very large against the sky. 'I love Terence better!' she exclaimed.[8]

As Leaska points out, the versions become successively more obscure as they are rewritten; until, in the end, we are left with the baffling passage which is given in the published version. It would appear that earlier versions, in Virginia's view, gave too much away, that she rewrote them in order to play certain elements down. She did not succeed in hiding the fact that something very peculiar was afoot, and that it was of central importance. In the light of this earlier version, there can be little doubt that jealousy is this central factor; jealousy and, more than that, a conflict of affections: Rachel is forced to choose between Helen and Terence. Even if this is not clear from the published version of the scene we have just examined, there are nevertheless indications in the published version that this is the case. After Helen learns of the engagement, there is a scene in which Terence arrives at Helen's house with the news that the 'morally suspect' Evelyn Murgatroyd has been asked to leave the hotel. (The elderly Mr Thornbury saw her in the passage in her nightdress, and summoned the manager.) Hewet is going to the hotel to inquire into the affair, and wants to know if Rachel will come with him. This precipitates a small crisis, as Rachel usually spends her afternoons with Helen. Hewet asks Helen if she too would like to go, but Helen declines. Rachel decides to accompany Hewet, and the situation between her and Helen is oddly tense:

> 'So you're going, Rachel?' Helen asked. 'You won't stay with me?'
> She smiled, but she might have been sad.
> Was she sad, or was she really laughing? Rachel could not tell, and she felt for the moment very uncomfortable between Helen and Terence. Then she turned away, saying merely that she would go with Terence, on condition that he did all the talking.
>
> (*TVO*, p. 316.)

If we go back to the beginning of the novel, where Rachel takes a stroll round the deck with Clarissa Dalloway, we find further evidence of Helen's jealousy which, we must assume, has been latent from the start: 'Helen passed them, and seeing Rachel arm-in-arm with a comparative stranger, looking excited, was amused, but at the same time slightly irritated' (*TVO*, p. 58). Part of Helen's irritation may stem from the fact that she doesn't consider the Dalloways to be the kind of people with whom friendship would be profitably sought. But the passage makes it clear that it is seeing Rachel *arm-in-arm* with Clarissa which irritates Helen.

There is a great deal of sexual confusion here. Sexual love with a man has become an impossibility following Dalloway's kiss. Rachel's death is, to a large extent (as Roger Poole has pointed out)[9], a means of evading the consummation of her

relationship with Hewet. Whether or not there is an understated sexual element in Rachel's relationship with Helen,
Helen is certainly an attractive figure for Rachel. She has
given (or has seemed to give) Rachel freedom from her
father, and possesses many qualities which Rachel must
admire. After her dismissal by her father, Dalloway, and
St John Hirst as one to be taken seriously, Rachel longs for
sympathetic female company:

> 'There are trees,' she said aloud. Would the trees make
> up for St John Hirst? She would be a Persian princess far
> from civilization, riding her horse upon the mountains
> alone, and making her women sing to her in the evening,
> far from all this, from the strife and men and women. . .
> (*TVO*, p. 153.)

Here we find a parallel in Virginia's life. Possibly as a reaction
against her experience with the Duckworths, and her unfavourable opinion of masculine characteristics in general,
Virginia entertained, throughout her adolescence and young
adulthood, strong feelings for a few older women in whom
she found warmth and understanding. First among these
early passions was Violet Dickinson, and the romantic-
erotic tone of this relationship is documented in the first
volume of Virginia's correspondence, in the many letters
she wrote to her.[10] Vita Sackville-West was, of course,
Virginia's great passionate affair, the sexual nature of which
is substantially documented.[11] Ethel Smyth, whose relationship with Virginia is documented in the fourth volume of the
Letters, came into Virginia's life when Virginia was forty-
eight and she was seventy-two.

So the reversal in which the male dream-figures become
female suggests, in Rachel's case as well as in Virginia's, a
turning away from the male, and an embracing of more
sympathetic female qualities. There is a strong element of
sexuality involved in these feelings, and the deformity of
the figures may be suggestive of guilt.

While it is true, as Leaska points out, that 'everything in
the published work is relevant in one way or another — that
is, everything is not there by chance, but by choice', so is

the inverse: what is excluded from the published work is relevant in one way or another. That is, certain things are left out by choice, not by chance. This is the play of expression and repression.

In the remainder of this chapter I shall examine two texts (or groups of texts) in which repression is characteristically at work in the face of the discourse of power: the letters Virginia wrote from Burley, the Twickenham asylum where she was under the care of Jean Thomas and Sir George Henry Savage; and *Flush*, her 'biography' of Elizabeth Barrett Browning's dog, which most critics have relegated to last place among her works, but which is in fact one in which her response to the discourse of power is most sharply couched.

Jean Thomas and Burley

It is in 1910 that Virginia is first sent, by Savage, to Burley — 'a kind of polite madhouse for female lunatics' (Bell, 1, p. 164). Quentin Bell tells us,

> Here her letters, her reading, her visitors would all be severely rationed, she would be kept in bed in a darkened room, wholesome foods would be pressed upon her and she would be excluded from all the social enjoyments of London. Faced by the possibility of madness she accepted her fate; but she accepted it in a sullen and rebellious spirit.
>
> (Bell, 1, p. 164.)

The institution was run by Jean Thomas, who was on very good terms with Savage, who often referred his patients to her. Prior to considering the letters that Virginia wrote from Burley, it is useful to acquaint ourselves with the background information contained in Quentin Bell's biography and in the editorial notes to the *Letters* and *Diary* regarding Jean Thomas and her relationship with Virginia. Anne Olivier Bell, in a footnote to the first volume of Virginia's diary, writes that Virginia had known Jean Thomas 'not only in her professional capacity, but as a devoted friend' (*Diary*, 1,

p. 26n). This can be illustrated by very early letters in which Jean Thomas is mentioned; but as their relationship develops, Virginia comes to see her as intolerably oppressive. Upon leaving Burley in the autumn of 1910, Virginia writes to Clive Bell from Cornwall, where she is staying with Jean Thomas,

> With regard to happiness — what an interesting topic that is! Walking about here, with Jean (Thomas) for a companion, I feel a great mastery over the world. My conclusion upon marriage might interest you. So happy I am it seems a pity not to be happier; and yet when I imagine the man to whom I shall say certain things, it isn't my dear Lytton, or Hilton either. Its strange how much one is occupied in imagining the delights of sympathy. The future, as usual with these sanguine apes, seems full of wonder.
>
> (*Letters*, 1, p. 434.)

The essential thing to note in the letters and diary entries of the time is the remarkable good spirits and humour which Virginia expresses. Recalling the ordeal of Burley, Virginia writes to Violet Dickinson of the 'interesting' aspects of it:

> I went down to Twickenham, (Miss Thomas) last week, and had a most interesting time, trying to ignore the oddities of several not altogether like other people women. One of them leapt with fright when one looked at her, and shook her fork in one's face. The thing was to keep on talking.
>
> (*Letters*, 1, p. 438.)

It would indeed seem as though Virginia and Jean Thomas are on friendly terms. A fortnight later (27 November 1910) Virginia writes another letter to Violet Dickinson which shows that Virginia has current news of Miss Thomas and her affairs. She writes, 'One of Miss Thomas's most excitable lunatics — the one who leapt when she saw me — has been almost dying, but is now better again. Miss Thomas says that these excitements are the wine of life' (*Letters*, 1, p. 440). Within a month, however, the relationship changes. Miss

Thomas's Christianity assumes an evangelical form where Virginia is concerned, and this Virginia finds completely unacceptable:

> My only other letter was from Jean (Thomas), enclosing 'What I believe' by Tolstoy. She sent a long serious letter with it, exhorting me to Christianity, which will save me from insanity. How we are persecuted! The self conceit of Christians is really unendurable. But the poor woman has got into one of her phrases, which lasts a whole letter, about something lacking in your life, which alone will bring, etc. etc. Then it all comes over the other way round.
>
> (*Letters*, 1, p. 442.)

On 1 January 1911 Virginia writes a letter to Violet Dickinson which shows that relations between Jean Thomas and herself are cordial enough for the former to spend the night. On this occasion, Virginia's reference to Jean Thomas's Christianity is not mocking in tone; if it is ironical, it is only slightly so, and seems to be without malice:

> Miss Thomas came down for a night, in an interval between discharging a woman who wished to commit murder, and taking one, who wants to kill herself. Can you imagine living like that? — always watching the knives, and expecting to find bedroom doors locked, or a corpse in the bath? I said I thought it was too great a strain — but, upheld by Christianity, I believe she will do it.
>
> (*Letters*, 1, p. 447.)

A letter to Clive Bell in April 1911 shows that the relationship is still intact, but now the attitude towards Jean Thomas's Christianity is that of the laughing sceptic — though there is nothing malicious here:

> The succession of holidays, and the perfectly fine days, make one feel as though everything had gone to sleep. Jean (Thomas), indeed, comes knocking at the door. She had a river party yesterday with a very clever, but

not merely clever, cousin who is fellow of Trinity Dublin; She asked me to go. What will be the end of Jean I cant think. My letters are scattered about Europe, so you mayn't have heard of her determination to study French history. Suppose this ends in Atheism, and she gives up lunatic keeping: well, her blood will be on my head.

(*Letters*, 1, p. 461.)

Three months later, the relationship has declined, and Jean Thomas accuses Virginia of hard-heartedness and gross insensitivity:

I am also embroiled in one of my hottest broils with Jean (Thomas). It is about a dinner at Savages: she says I offered 'to go on Wednesday, knowing that she couldn't go that day; and thus showed callousness, brutality, immorality, lack of justice ("which one can see in your writings") and a "truly dreadful lack of consideration for the feelings and desires of your friends". To this I answered in sober fact; with one plain curse. I found a reply at Firle, which I read to Case [Janet Case, who taught Virginia classics]. It was a masterpiece. It seems likely that one will have to give her a sharp rap — the sort you give me; only she would die, while I manage to survive.

(*Letters*, 1, p. 472.)

The first sentence suggests that this is not the first 'broil' with Jean Thomas, but that the relationship has been declining steadily over the past few months, and that Virginia's refusal of Christianity is a central factor. It is clear that Jean Thomas accuses Virginia, both in her life and in her work, of a central lack of humanity which is the result of having no religion.[12] This is a view put forward by the critic D. S. Savage in one of the most unperceptive pieces on Virginia Woolf ever published.[13] It is clear from Virginia's work and from her autobiographical writings that she was always moving towards a clearer exposition of a view of the world which may be termed 'religious' in the sense that it put forward a philosophical view of the human spirit. This attempt is most apparent in *The Waves*.

It is almost certain that Jean Thomas was the model for the most unattractive character in the whole of Virginia's *oeuvre*: Doris Kilman in *Mrs Dalloway*. Like Jean Thomas, she is alternately referred to as 'Miss' and by her Christian name. She is a 'deeply religious' woman, but is consumed with hatred for those who possess what she lacks. 'She had seen the light two years and three months ago. Now she did not envy women like Clarissa Dalloway; she pitied them' (*MD*, p. 137). For Doris Kilman, religion is not a philosophy of love, but rather a means of harnessing hatred so that it is easier to endure. It is a means of combating envy, but the resulting position is a hollow and illusory superiority: 'So now, whenever the hot and painful feelings boiled within her, this hatred of Mrs Dalloway, this grudge against the world, she thought of God. She thought of Mr Whitaker [her converter]. Rage was succeeded by calm' (*MD*, p. 138). Love and conversion are the two forces operating in the novel, and they are, by nature, irreconcilable. The 'converters' include the doctors who treat Septimus Smith; Richard Dalloway, who wants to impose his vision of the ideal upon the world; Peter Walsh, whose love for Clarissa she finds stultifying; and Doris Kilman, who fails to respect the privacy and sanctity of the individual life. Clarissa thinks:

> Had she ever tried to convert anyone herself? Did she not wish everybody merely to be themselves? And she watched out of the window the old lady opposite climbing upstairs. Let her climb upstairs if she wanted to; let her stop; then let her, as Clarissa had often seen her, gain her bedroom, part her curtains, and disappear again into the background. Somehow one respected that — that old woman looking out of the window, quite unconscious that she was being watched. There was something solemn in it — but love and religion would destroy that whatever it was, the privacy of the soul. The odious Kilman would destroy it. Yet it was a sight that made her want to cry.
>
> (*MD*, p. 140.)

Clarissa Dalloway spells out her position in relation to the Kilmans and Walshes of this world, and the position is Virginia's:

the supreme mystery which Kilman might say she had solved, or Peter might say he had solved, but Clarissa didn't believe either of them had the ghost of an idea of solving, was simply this: here was one room; there another. Did religion solve that, or love?

(*MD*, p. 141.)

By the time Jean Thomas next appears in Virginia's correspondence, she and Leonard are married. In April 1913, Virginia writes to Vanessa,

To our horror, when we came down, two raw new Christmas trees, each with a note tied to it, were planted in front of the windows, the work of Jean and a lunatic, escaped from Eastbourne. The question is how to destroy them tactfully.

(*Letters*, 2, p. 24.)

From one point of view, Jean Thomas has done no more than commit an act of friendship. But, from another (and quite reasonable) point of view, the act is an imposition, and displays a fundamental lack of respect for the privacy of the individual. By this time, relations between Virginia and Jean Thomas have broken down altogether. She writes to Leonard in 1917, 'I travelled up from Richmond with Jean (Thomas)! She was in the next carriage, through a glass door, and didn't see me — at least we made no signs — She got out at Hammersmith' (*Letters*, 2, p. 194). By coincidence, a similar scene takes place in 1918, and there can be no mistaking Virginia's feelings:

in the carriage I saw Jean (Thomas), & remained hidden behind an officer. I dodged her successfully on getting out, & then, hurrying up the main road, distinctly heard myself called, 'O there's Virginia.' I hesitated, but judging such rudeness impossible, turned back, saw Jean! was received with the utmost surprise, for she had been talking about a cab, though thinking, so she said, of me — She introduced me to Ann, who used to figure so when I was in bed; the lady with the romance in India, which Jean prayed she might have strength to overcome. I could

only see a featureless shape, & strode on again, Jean
begging to come & see us, very cordially.

(*Diary*, 1, p. 154.)

The evidence presented in Virginia's *Letters* (curious that
there are none written to Jean Thomas herself) lead us to
qualify Anne Olivier Bell's statement that Virginia had
known Jean Thomas 'as a devoted friend'. Quentin Bell
gives a much fuller picture when he writes, 'according to
Leonard, one of the difficulties of the situation was that
Jean Thomas felt an unconscious but violent homosexual
passion for Virginia and was also devoted to George Savage'
(Bell, 2, p. 16n). The fact of this triangular fantasy relationship on Jean Thomas's part adds immeasurably to the complications of Virginia's position at Burley.

According to Quentin Bell's chronology, Virginia was
an 'inmate' of Burley on four occasions: 30 June to c. 10
August 1910; 16 to 26 February 1912; 25 July to 11 August
1913; and 25 March to 1 April 1915. Virginia's correspondence during these periods poses a multitude of questions.
Despite the fact that she is normally a prolific letter writer,
no correspondence survives from the second and fourth
stays at Burley. Indeed, the fourth stay occurs during an
unprecedented period during which there is a four month
gap in correspondence: from 2 March 1915 to 31 August
1915. It seems almost unthinkable that Virginia did not
write a single letter during these two periods.

Virginia's first letter from Burley is written to Vanessa
Bell on 28 July 1910, at the beginning of her first stay. This
is the full text of the letter:

I meant to write several days ago, although you do say
you dont care a damn. But in that too I was hoodwinked
by Miss Thomas. I gather that some great conspiracy is
going on behind my back. What a mercy we cant have
at each other! or we should quarrel till midnight, and
Clarissas (the coming 'niece') deformities, inherited from
generations of hard drinking Bells, would be laid at my
door. She — (Miss T.) wont read me or quote your letters.
But I gather that you want me to stay on here.

She is in a highly wrought state, as the lunatic upstairs

has somehow brought her case into court; and I cant make her speak calmly. Do write and explain. Having read your last letter at least 10 times — so that Miss Bradbury (nurse) is sure it is a love letter and looks very arch — I cant find a word about my future. I had agreed to come up on *Monday*; which would leave time for walking. Savage wanted me to stay in bed more or less this week. As I must see him again, I suppose I must wait over Monday. But I really dont think I can stand much more of this.

Miss T. is charming, and Miss Bradbury is a good woman, but you cant conceive how I want intelligent conversation — even yours. Religion seems to me to have ruined them all. Miss T. is always culminating in silent prayer. Miss Somerville (patient), the absent minded one with the deaf dog, wears two crucifixes. Miss B. says Church Bells are the sweetest sound on earth. She also says that the old Queen the Queen Mother and the present Queen represent the highest womanhood. They reverence my gifts, although God has left me in the dark. They are always wondering what God is up to. The religious mind is quite amazing.

However, what I mean is that I shall soon have to jump out of a window. The ugliness of the· house is almost inexplicable — having white, and mottled green and red. Then there is all the eating and drinking and being shut up in the dark.

My God! What a mercy to be done with it!

Now, my sweet Honey Bee, you know how you would feel if you had stayed in bed alone here for 4 weeks. But I wont argue, as I dont know what you have said. Anyhow, I will abide by Savage.

Miss T. and I have long conversations. She has a charming nature; rather whimsical, and even sensual. But there again, religion comes in; and she leads a spotless life. Apparently she is well off, and takes patients more or less as a spiritual work. She has harboured innumerable young women in love difficulties. They are always turning up to lunch, and I creep out of bed and look at them. At present there is one upstairs, and a barren wife across the passage. The utmost tact is shown with regard to our complaints; and I make Miss T. blush by asking if they're mad.

Miss Somerville has periods of excitement, when she pulls up all the roses, and goes to church. Then she is silent for weeks. She is now being silent; and is made very nervous by the sight of me. As I went out into the garden yesterday in a blanket with bare legs, she has some reason. Miss Bradbury is the woman you saw out of the window and said was homicidial (*sic*). I was very kind with her at dinner, but she then put me to bed, and is a trained nurse.

Miss T. talks about you with awe. How you smile, and say such quaint things — how your eyes fill with tears — how beautiful your soul is — and your hands. She also thinks you write such beautiful English! Your language is so apt and so expressive. Julian is the most remarkable child she ever saw. The worst of her is that she is a little too emotional.

I have been out in the garden for 2 hours; and feel quite normal. I feel my brains, like a pear, to see if its ripe; it will be exquisite by September.

Will you tell Duncan that I was told he had called, and that I am furious that they didn't let me see him. Miss T. thought him an extremely nice young man.

Do write, today. I long to see you. Its damned dull being here alone. Write sheets. Give Clive my love. His visits are my brightest spots. He must come again.

I will be very reasonable.

(*Letters*, 1, pp. 430-32.)

In this letter, the full extent of the oppressiveness of Burley is revealed. It appears, from the second sentence, that Virginia was occasionally prevented from writing to Vanessa. It is significant that she wanted to, for the first sentence tells us that Vanessa has made it clear to Virginia that she doesn't 'care a damn'. Virginia then claims (not unreasonably, given the circumstances), 'I gather that some great conspiracy is going on behind my back.' Quentin Bell's biography tells us that whenever Virginia showed signs of illness,

At that juncture, when most of the company sat in stupid amazement, two persons acted promptly: Leonard and Vanessa moved swiftly and decisively, with the efficiency of long training, to do what was necessary — to take Virginia away from the room to fresh air, to a bed, and to administer whatever medicines experience had shown to be useful.

(Bell, 2, p. 114.)

Bell is writing of a fainting fit in 1925, yet the passage shows
that Leonard and Vanessa *together* had the benefit of long
training in the matter. Given the fact that Virginia is not
allowed to write to her sister, and that, in turn, Jean Thomas
will not read or quote from Vanessa's letters, her feeling
regarding a conspiracy only seems further justified. It is
also clear that Vanessa is in charge of Virginia: 'I gather that
you want me to stay on here.'

Yet while Vanessa and Miss Thomas think Virginia too
unwell to be a party to their plans for her, she is lucid enough
to write of Burley in a controlled and witty fashion. Revers-
ing the agency of power, Virginia describes a scene in which
she is the paragon of rationality and Miss Thomas is seized
with agitation regarding 'the lunatic upstairs' who 'has somehow brought her case into court'. (It seems as if Virginia was
not the only dissatisfied patient at Burley.) Virginia writes
of Miss Thomas, 'I cant make her speak calmly.' This humour
is well-planned, as it precedes a desperate plea: 'I really dont
think I can stand much more of this.' Reading Vanessa's
last letter — at least ten times — 'I cant find a word about
my future.'

Discussing the religious atmosphere which prevails at
Burley, Virginia is critical but not uncharitable. She also
sees, almost immediately, what Jean Thomas's final opinion
of her is to be: 'They reverence my gifts, although God has
left me in the dark.' Here, a pattern begins to emerge. Having
written humorously, and with no little insight, about Burley,
Virginia offers another plea — this one desperate, faintly a
threat: 'However, what I mean is that I shall soon have to
jump out of a window . . . . there is all the eating and drinking and being shut up in the dark. My God! What a mercy to
have done with it!' This is followed by a plea for Vanessa to
try and see Virginia's situation from her point of view. She,
Vanessa, could not bear to be shut up in a 'home' (indeed,
we recall Vanessa's strenuous efforts, and Virginia's support
of her, to persuade Savage that she did not need a home
when she too was ill during Thoby's fatal illness): why should
Virginia like it any better?

Virginia shocks Jean Thomas by asking (of her patients),
'are they mad?' Finally, she is mocking of the 'empirical

method': 'I feel my brains, like a pear, to see if its ripe; it will be exquisite by September.' And then the final, humiliating promise: 'I will be very reasonable.'

It may be significant to recall that Virginia's 'flirtation' with Clive Bell began in 1908, with the birth of Vanessa's first child, Julian. Given the fact that Virginia regarded the entire episode as the one in her life which 'turned more of a knife in me than anything else', that Vanessa was about to have another child, and that Virginia writes to Vanessa that Clive's visits are her 'bright spots', it is certain that relations between the sisters were very strained, and that Virginia's stay at Burley was, from one point of view, not inconvenient. Within a few weeks, Virginia writes a pleading card to Clive: 'Can you possibly come down tomorrow (Wednesday) afternoon? Savage is ill and cant come. It would be a great joy to see you — Could you wire if you cant come.' Beneath her signature, Virginia includes the train time — '3.30 from Waterloo', and a postscript: '(as early as possible)' (*Letters*, 1, p. 432).

The only reference in Virginia's correspondence to her stay at Burley from 16 to 28 February 1912 is a note in a letter to Lytton Strachey, asking him to send the journals and correspondence of Mary Berry to Burley for her to read there (she was writing on 16 February from Brunswick Square) (*Letters*, 1, p. 490). It is highly probable that the main reason for Virginia's second stay at Burley was that she was severely anxious about the possibility of marriage to Leonard. After her return to Brunswick Square on this occasion, she wrote to Molly MacCarthy,

> I didn't mean to make you think that I was against marriage. Of course I'm not, though the extreme safeness and sobriety of young couples does apall me, but then so do the random melancholy old maids. I began life with a tremendous, absurd, ideal of marriage, then my bird's eye view of many marriages disgusted me, and I thought I must be asking what was not to be had. But that has passed too. Now I only ask for someone to make me vehement, and then I'll marry him! The fault of our society always seems to me to be timidity and self consciousness; and I feel oddly vehement, and very exacting,

and so difficult to live with and so very intemperate and changeable, now thinking one thing and now another. But in my heart I always expect to be floated over all crises, when the moment comes, and landed heaven knows where! I don't really worry about W(oolf): though I think I made out that I did. He is going to stay longer anyhow, and perhaps he will stay in England anyhow, so the responsibility is lifted off me.

(*Letters*, 1, p. 492.)

This letter suggests that Virginia's anxiety was increased by the fact that a man's career rested on her decision. If she would accept Leonard's proposal of marriage, he would resign his post in Ceylon. When Virginia refused his first proposal, Leonard extended his leave by four months, in the hope that Virginia would change her mind.

By the time Virginia enters Burley for the third time, on 25 July 1913, she has been married to Leonard for nine months. This stay is just prior to the disastrous return to the Plough Inn, Holford, in 1913, after which Virginia attempted suicide. What is significant in these letters is the radical change in her tone, from the strong, witty and pleading letters Virginia wrote to her sister from Burley in 1910, to a total acquiescence to the wishes of others. That is not to say that the intimacies and endearments they contain are to be the subject of criticism. The important point is that Virginia's belief in herself has been totally undermined, and that she grants (though, at the same time, her tone subverts this), Leonard the power of being absolutely right — and the power to be absolutely in charge of her. There are six letters written between 28 July and 5 August 1913. In the first, Virginia writes,

I got your two letters this morning. They made me very happy, but you shouldn't have gone out to the post again — poor tired little beast.

How are you, darling Mongoose? I'm very well, slept well, and they make me eat all day. But I think of you and want you. Keep well. We shall be together soon, I know. I get happiness from seeing you. I hope you've been out and not worked too much.

(*Letters*, 2, p. 32.)

'I'm very well, slept well, and they make me eat all day.'
Virginia is clearly the opposite of 'very well'. Her anxiety is
now approaching an unendurable limit which would culmin-
ate, in just over a month, with a suicide attempt which very
nearly achieved its aim. In this letter, she is telling Leonard
what he wants to hear: that she is sleeping and eating. Given
that the whole question of food and eating was bound up
with Virginia's rejection of Leonard, the emphasis placed
on food at Burley cannot have been beneficial for Virginia.

The next two letters, written on 1 and 2 August, are un-
characteristically short:

> I got up and dressed last night after you were gone,
> wanting to come back to you. You do represent all thats
> best, and I lie here thinking. I think of you in your white
> nightgown mongoose.
>
> (*Letters*, 2, p. 33.)

She adds in a postscript, 'I thought we were walking back
to Cliffords Inn together Darling.' In the next letter she
writes, 'You cant stay in London any more in this heat.
Do get away. Couldn't you go to Lytton until Thursday?
Jean (Thomas) says she will keep me till then. I want to
see you, but this is best' (*Letters*, 2, p. 33). These pathetic
letters are, in their way, a plea to Leonard to rescue Virginia
from the hell she is enduring. On 1 August she is clearly
expressing a plea to be with Leonard (is this fantasy too a
sign of madness?). On 2 August (we don't know what Leonard's reply was) she has sufficient strength to put aside her
own misery for the moment and advise Leonard that he
should leave London for a few days. Virginia *never* thought
Burley could be 'best' for her, but she writes to please
Leonard. On 3 August she writes again, and her tone is
totally subservient and obedient:

> I hope you got my wire this morning.
> Are you well, are you resting, are you out of doors?
> Do you do your little tricks? Here it is all the same . . .
> I've not been very good I'm afraid — but I do think it will
> be better when we're together. Here its all so unreal.

Have you written your review? How are you feeling? Is Asheham nice? I want you Mongoose, and I do love you, little beast, if only I weren't so appallingly stupid a mandril. Can you really love me — yes, I believe it, and we will make a happy life. You're so loveable. Tell me exactly *how you are*.

(*Letters*, 2, p. 33.)

The final two letters from this period, written on 4 and 5 August 1913, show that Virginia is trying even harder to make herself acceptable to Leonard. She is full of guilt over being 'disgraceful' — 'Its all my fault':

I did like your two letters this morning. They make all the difference.

But I wish you weren't working. I'm enormously fat, and well — very sleepy.

Have you ridden?

Nothing you have ever done since I knew you has been in any way beastly — how could it? You've been absolutely perfect to me. Its all my fault. But when we're together — and I go on thinking — it must be all right. And we shall be on Thursday — How are you? you dont say — I think about you and think of the things we've had together. Anyhow, you've given me the best things in my life.

Do try and get out, and rest, my honey mongoose. You did look so bad. When you say sleepy you mean tired, poor beast.

I have been trying to read American magazines which are lent to me by Miss Funk a tall American.

I do believe in you absolutely, and never for a second do I think you've told me a lie —

Goodbye, darling mongoose — I do want you and I believe in spite of my vile imaginations the other day that I love you and that you love me.

(*Letters*, 2, p. 34.)

and

This is only to say Goodnight — Dearest, I have been disgraceful — to you, I mean.

Savage was here today — says I may go on Thursday. Will you come tomorrow?

You've been working all day and I've been doing nothing. We went on the river.

Nothing has happened. I keep thinking of you and want to get to you.

(*Letters*, 2, p. 34.)

The other complicating factor in this episode is that Virginia had just completed *The Voyage Out*, which Leonard took to Gerald Duckworth on 9 March 1913. The novel was accepted by him on 13 March. Virginia had spent seven years working on this novel, and much of the material contained in it was highly painful for her to deal with. She had no confidence in its being accepted by the public, and now, more than at any other time, she needed confirmation and bolstering of her confidence by those closest to her, Leonard in particular. Virginia's feelings of anxiety about the public and critical reception of her novel (which was so bound up with her own life that 'self' may be substituted for 'novel') were not relieved by the fact that she was again bound over to the care of others. Also, Virginia was, at this time, still expecting to have children, and was not aware of Leonard's doubts on this subject.[14] Clearly, the idea of children is bound up with the 'birth' of her novel, at least in her mind. Indeed, Bell writes,

A book is so much a part of oneself that in delivering it to the public one feels as if one were pushing one's own child out into the traffic. If it be killed or hurt the injury is done to oneself, and if it be one's first-born, the product of seven years' gestation, if it be awkward and vulnerable and needing all the tenderness and all the understanding that no critic will ever give, anxiety for its fate becomes acute.

(Bell, 2, p. 11.)

It is clear from the Burley letters that Virginia's confidence in herself is shaken to the point where she is unable to function properly. These are the causes of her 'illness', and no amount of medical or pseudo-medical attention could do

anything to help. What she needed was the love and understanding of her husband, and those closest to her. When
Leonard had her sent to Burley at this juncture, it must
have seemed to Virginia as if she were being wholly rejected.
The letter written on 4 August speaks of 'lies', and 'vile
imaginations'. Clearly, Virginia feels as if she has been hoodwinked, and we may assume that she told Leonard so, and
that he reacted angrily, taking it as further evidence of her
insanity. This is the work of repression in the face of the
discourse of power.

Leonard sides with the doctors, whose theories cannot
accommodate the real and, it may be said, relatively easily
understood reasons for her anxiety. The result is a series of
letters which, in Quentin Bell's words, 'make one think of a
child sent away by its parents to some cruel school' (Bell,
2, p. 13). As Sir William Bradshaw says in *Mrs Dalloway*,
a place where 'we will teach you to rest'. After reading five
hundred pages of Virginia's correspondence in the first
volume of the *Letters*, all readers are familiar with the extravagant and delightful way in which Virginia weaves an
account of even the most humdrum event. Repression is
clearly at work when we read, instead of a detailed and
amusing account of a day out, the bare fact: 'We went on
the river.' If we look carefully at the Burley letters, we see
that Virginia feels guilty for imposing her madness and its
attendant worries on Leonard when he has so much work to
do. She feels guilty for adding to his burdens. Yet, on 5
August, she writes, 'You've been working all day and I've
been doing nothing.' This she clearly resents. Virginia, too,
has work to do.

Casting herself as the guilty one, the bad one in these
letters, Virginia sings Leonard's praises: 'Nothing you have
ever done since I knew you has been in any way beastly';
'I think about you and think of the things we've had together.
Anyhow, you've given me the best things in my life', and so
on. How are we to take these claims? They have been married
nine months. The honeymoon was a disaster. (More than anything, Virginia wants children, and these she is to be denied.)
At the moment when her first book is to be published, when
her first-born is to be delivered to the world, she is forcibly

separated from her husband. Clearly, she has not been happy. The first opportunity she gets, she tries to commit suicide. If we want to put these letters in perspective, we must refer to one of the last letters Virginia wrote — one of two suicide notes to Leonard:

> I feel certain I am going mad again. I feel we can't go through another of those terrible times. And I shan't recover this time. I begin to hear voices, and I can't concentrate. So I am doing what seems the best thing to do. *You have given me the greatest possible happiness.* You have been in every way all that anyone could be. I don't think two people could have been happier till this terrible disease came. I can't fight any longer. *I know that I am spoiling your life, that without me you could work.* And you will I know. You see I can't even write this properly. I can't read. What I want to say is *I owe all the happiness of my life to you.* You have been entirely patient with me and incredibly good. I want to say that — everybody knows it. If anybody could have saved me it would have been you. Everything has gone from me but the certainty of your goodness. *I can't go on spoiling your life any longer.*
> *I don't think two people could have been happier than we have been.*
>
> (Bell, 2, p. 226, my italics.)

Here, in the letter Bell dates 28 March 1941 (Nigel Nicolson dates this letter as 18? March in his final volume of the *Letters*), we find the same themes which dominate the Burley letters of 1913: 'You have given me the greatest possible happiness'; 'I know that I am spoiling your life, that without me you could work'; 'I owe all the happiness of my life to you'; 'I can't go on spoiling your life any longer'; 'I don't think two people could have been happier than we have been.'

Neither the woman of 1913, nor the one of 1941, was happy.

Flush

If we want to understand how these apparent contradictions operate, and how the mechanics of repression work, *Flush*, Virginia's 'biography' of Elizabeth Barrett Browning's dog, provides a unique opportunity. *Flush* is an imaginative incarnation of herself as a dog. While the book has never been considered very seriously (and it is, like *Orlando*, playful and entertaining in a way that her other books are not) by the critics, careful reading reveals a hitherto undiscussed significance.

Quentin Bell remarked that '*Flush* is not so much a book by a dog lover as a book by someone who would love to be a dog.' He continues, 'Her dog was the embodiment of her own spirit, not the pet of an owner. Flush in fact was one of the routes which Virginia used, or at least examined, in order to escape from her own human corporeal existence' (Bell, 2, pp. 175-6). This may be seen as a tantalizing clue, opening an unexplored line of inquiry. However, after suggesting the profound importance of the book for its author, Bell calls it a 'trifle': 'She prided herself on the care that she took in making this trifle fit for the Press' (Bell, 2, p. 172). Leonard dismissed both *Orlando* and *Flush* as wholly insignificant. For him, *Orlando* is 'a *jeu d'esprit*, and so is *Flush*, a work of even lighter weight; these two books again cannot seriously be compared with her major novels.'[15] But dogs played a central role in the lives of Leonard and Virginia (especially that of Leonard), and their appearance in Virginia's writings is always a significant detail. We recall, for instance, that Richard Dalloway's inability to tell his wife that he loves her is juxtaposed against a scene in which he lavishes great attention on the family dog, which has injured its paw. In *The Voyage Out*, as well as in *Flush*, we are told that Jane Carlyle's dog, Nero, attempted suicide: he 'had leapt from a top storey window with the intention of committing suicide. He had found the strain of life in Cheyne Row intolerable' (*F*, pp. 131-2). Dogs always appear against a background of unsatisfactory domestic relations.[16]

Leonard's autobiography shows that he was not a man

given to displays of affection. However, he reserved a special demonstrative feeling for dogs. The difference in Leonard's and Virginia's attitudes towards them underlines significant qualities in both of them. Bell considers this to be of sufficient importance to dwell on at some length. He gives this account of Leonard's attitude towards animals:

> Leonard had a feeling for animals which was, on the surface at all events, extremely unsentimental. He was gruff, abrupt, a systematic disciplinarian, extremely good at seeing that his dogs were obedient, healthy and happy. Whenever one met Leonard there would be a brief shouting match between him and whatever dog or dogs happened to be there, at the end of which the animals would subside into whining passivity and Leonard would be transformed from a brutal Sergeant Major into the most civilised of human beings.
>
> (Bell, 2, p. 175.)

Leonard himself discusses this in his autobiography, and the importance of his reflections is evident. He declares his disbelief in God, and takes a generally pessimistic view of the human race; but, he writes, 'I admit that every now and again I am amazed and profoundly moved by the beauty and affection of my cat and my dog.'[17] Also in the autobiography, Leonard expresses his affection (which was great) for his parlour maid in these terms: 'Lily was one of those persons for whom I feel *the same kind of affection* as I do for cats and dogs.'[18] One would hesitate to go so far as to say that Leonard was one of those people described by Sartre in *The Words*, who are unable to engage in authentic human relationships, and so transfer their affections to animals.[19] But he makes it clear that his attitude towards animals is to be considered alongside his attitude towards people. In the autobiography, it sometimes appears that the two become confused. For instance, he tells us that while supervising pearl divers in Ceylon, he wrote in a letter to Lytton Strachey that 'the Arabs will do anything if you hit them hard enough with a walking stick, an occupation in which I have been engaged for the most part of the last 3 days and

nights.'[20] Leonard justifies this by means of a strange logic:
'The Arabs . . . treated me as a fellow human being,' he
writes, and 'It was this attitude of human equality which
accounted for the fact, oddly enough, that I hit them with a
walking stick'.[21] This curious sense of equality also caused
him to remark that 'in the whole of my time in Ceylon I
never struck, or would have dared to strike, a Tamil or a
Sinhalese.'[22] Spater and Parsons write that Leonard was
'scrupulously fair, but (as he himself admits in his autobiography) outwardly truculent and often ruthless to the
natives to save them from themselves'.[23] If Leonard can treat
human being like animals, he can also treat animals as if they
were human. He recalls one of the pivotal experiences of
his childhood:

> My bitch had five puppies and it was decided that she
> should be left with two to bring up and so it was for me
> to destroy three. In such circumstances it was an age-old
> custom to drown the day-old puppies in a pail of water.
> This I proceeded to do. Looked at casually, three day-old
> puppies are little blind, squirming, undifferentiated objects
> or things. I put one of them in the bucket of water, and
> instantly an extraordinary, a terrible thing happened. This
> blind, amorphous thing began to fight desperately for its
> life, struggling, beating the water with its paws. I suddenly
> saw that it was an individual, that like me it was an 'I',
> that in its bucket of water it was experiencing what I
> would experience and fighting death, as I would fight
> death if I were drowning in the multitudinous seas. It
> was I felt and feel a horrible, an uncivilized thing to drown
> that 'I' in a bucket of water.[24]

Some may find this a touching and revealing passage, but a
story Leonard relates in *The Journey Not the Arrival Matters*
is only revealing, and ought to be juxtaposed against it, for
the parallels with Virginia's situation are alarmingly evident —
it is included in the chapter entitled 'Virginia's Death'. One
of the Woolf's neighbours had a mentally subnormal child.
The eldest son was due to leave for active service in France
(1940), and asked Leonard to help him persuade his mother
to have the child committed to an asylum before he left. The

mother had kept the child at home until this time, and wanted to continue looking after him in her own way. The story must be quoted at length, for it reveals Leonard's attitude toward a confrontation between the individual and the medical establishment, and also his attitude towards human, as opposed to animal, suffering:

I went to the Medical Officer, who already knew about the case, and asked him to get the boy into a home. He did so, and at first everything went well; but after about two weeks Mrs X came to me and said that the boy was being starved and ill-treated, was getting very ill, and must be given back to them. Then one morning Mr and Mrs X appeared in my garden dressed in their Sunday clothes. They had hired a taxi and asked me to accompany them to the Medical Officer and demand the child.

There followed some painful hours. I agreed to go to the M.O. provided that they left the business to me and did not start abusing him and the Home for starving the boy. They promised, but within five minutes of our being shown into the M.O.'s room Mrs X was making the wildest accusations against him, the Home, and the nurses. The M.O. behaved admirably; he rang up the Home and arranged that if we went there immediately, the boy would be handed over to us. I do not think that I have ever had a more unpleasant pilgrimage in my life than to that Home and back to Rodmell, sitting in the taxi with the unfortunate parents. The boy was delivered to us wrapped in blankets. He was obviously ill, and a week or ten days later he died. There was an inquest, at which Mrs X repeated her accusations against the nurses and everyone connected with the Home, but the verdict was death from natural causes.

This kind of tragedy, essentially terrible, but in detail often grotesque and even ridiculous, is not uncommon in village life. At the time its impact on me was strong and strange; somehow or other it seemed sardonically to fit into the pattern of a private and public world threatened with destruction. The passionate devotion of mothers to imbecile children, which was the pivot of this distressing incident, always seems to me a strange and even disturbing phenomenon. I can see and sympathize with the appeal of helplessness and vulnerability in a very young living creature — I have felt it myself in the case of an infant puppy, kitten, leopard, and even the much less attractive and more savage human baby. In all these cases, apart from the appeal of helplessness, there is the appeal of physical beauty; I always remember the extraordinary beauty of the little leopard cub which I had in Ceylon, so young that his legs wobbled a little under him as he began jerkily to gambol down the verandah and yet showing already under his lovely, shining coat the potential rippling strength of his muscles. But there is something horrible and repulsive in the slobbering imbecility of a human being.[25]

Leonard's unquestioning respect for the Medical Officer's opinion, as well as his acceptance of the hospital staff's insistance that the boy was given proper care, are a little peculiar in this context. What has this to do with 'Virginia's Death'?

Spater and Parsons, whose main purpose seems to be to reinforce the notion that Virginia was mad, and that Leonard was a man of unprecedented sanity, write that 'The mother figure dominated Virginia's thoughts for most of her life.'[26] They cite all of the instances of motherless girls in the novels, and make the point (which is not *wholly* a wrong one) that in her relationships with women, even with Vita Sackville-West, Virginia was essentially seeking a mother substitute. But they also imply that, in doing so, Virginia was unable to reciprocate the affection she received. And they write:

> Even when it came to animals, Virginia's affection followed a similar one-way pattern which Quentin Bell thought 'odd and remote'. She 'nearly always had a dog', but she was not a dog lover. Significantly, in her relations with many of her closest friends she viewed herself as an animal — an object to be loved and cared for.'[27]

All readers of the letters are aware of these pet names which Spater and Parsons call significant.[28] But what do they signify? Bell writes, 'These animal *personae*, safely removed from human carnality and yet cherished, the recipients indeed of hugs and kisses, were most important to her, but important as the totem figure is to the savage' (Bell, 2, p. 176). Bell is right to associate animal *personae* with human carnality. We recall the frightening nightmare faces which Rachel saw in her dreams in *The Voyage Out*, and Virginia's own reminiscences of this in *Moments of Being*. But while the Duckworths are portrayed by means of unpleasant animal images, this kind of portrayal can also have a positive side. The undistinguished but likable Jack Hills, who was to marry Stella Duckworth, is characterized over two pages by means of a pervasive 'dog metaphor': 'suggesting the figure of some tenacious wire-haired terrier, in whose obstinacy and strength of jaw there seemed, at a time when all the fates were against him, something honourable .... worrying his speech as a terrier a bone; but sticking doggedly to the word', and so on.[29] Indeed, the dog metaphor is a Virginia Woolf hallmark. A not untypical diary entry will read,

> Karin[30] came to give her lecture. She arrived at tea time. I can't help being reminded by her of one of our lost dogs — Tinker most of all. She fairly races round a room, snuffs the corners of the chairs & tables, wags her tail as hard as she can, & snatches at any scrap of talk as if she were sharp set; & she eats a great deal of food too, like a dog.
>
> (*Diary*, 1, pp. 118-19.)

And this applied to herself no less than to other people. Writing to Violet Dickinson, she would conclude, 'So, kiss your dog on its tender snout, and think him me' (*Letters*, 1, p. 309). There is a fairly substantial 'dog correspondence' to Vita Sackville-West. When Vita's dog dies in 1929, Virginia writes, 'Darling, we are so unhappy about Pippin. We both send our best love — Leonard is very sad' (*Letters*, 4, p. 74). A letter to Vita written during the same year shows that, while Virginia may not have been a 'dog lover' by Spater and Parsons' standards, she did care about people:

> Going to the garage yesterday the man said to me, 'I've been ill for a fortnight; my wife has been ill for a fortnight; our little boy died of double pneumonia last night; and *the dog has distemper*.' This he repeated three times,

always winding up solemnly, and *the dog has distemper* as if it were the most important of the lot. But there was the child dead in the cottage.

(*Letters*, 4, p. 109.)

When Virginia considered that Vita did not pay enough attention to her, she wrote the following letter, in which she characterizes herself as a dog:

I have to break a sad piece of news to you.

Potto [Virginia's name for her 'dog'-self when writing to Vita] is dead.

For about a month (you have not been for a month and I date his decline from your last visit) I have watched him failing. First his coat lost lustre; then he refused biscuits; finally, gravy. When I asked him what ailed him he sighed, but made no answer. The other day coming unexpectedly into the room, I found him wiping away a tear. He still maintained unbroken silence. Last night it was clear that the end was coming. I sat with him holding his paw in mine and felt the pulse grow feebler. At 7.45 he breathed deeply. I leant over him. I just caught and was able to distinguish the following words — 'Tell Mrs Nick that I love her . . . She has forgotten me. But I forgive her and . . . (here he cd. hardly speak) die . . . of . . . a . . . broken . . . heart!' He then expired.

And so shall I very soon.

(*Letters*, 4, p. 362.)

Even without Bell's hint that Flush is no ordinary dog, it is quite clear from Virginia's descriptions of his experiences that what is being presented is a human consciousness. Encountering the objects in Elizabeth Barrett's room for the first time, Flush's experience is likened to that of an archaeologist discovering a mausoleum:

only the sensations of such an explorer into the buried vaults of a ruined city can compare with the riot of emotions that flooded Flush's nerves as he stood for the first time in an invalid's bedroom, in Wimpole Street, and smelled eau-de-Cologne.

(*F*, p. 23.)

The manner in which Flush perceives is distinctly human. It is an actively intentional appropriation of the world around him:

> Very slowly, very dimly, with much sniffing and pawing, Flush by degrees distinguished the outlines of several articles of furniture. That huge object by the window was perhaps a wardrobe. Next to it stood, conceivably, a chest of drawers. In the middle of the room swam up to the surface what seemed to be a table with a ring round it; and then the vague amorphous shapes of armchair and table emerged. But everything was disguised. On top of the wardrobe stood three white busts; the chest of drawers was surmounted by a bookcase; the bookcase was pasted over with crimson merino; the washing-table had a coronal of shelves upon it; on top of the shelves that were on top of the washing-table stood two more busts. Nothing in the room was itself; everything was something else.
>
> (*F*, pp. 23-4.)

Flush is as capable of human emotions as he is of human visual perception. The objects which adorn Elizabeth Barrett's — Flush's — room, soon become friendly and sympathetic presences, fully of happy significance for Flush because they were chosen by Miss Barrett, whom he loves. But, when Robert Browning enters, threatening to cause Miss Barrett's affection to be diverted from Flush to himself, Flush's perception of the room and its furnishings changes. 'Upstairs came the dreaded, the inexorable footfall; upstairs, Flush knew, came the cowled and sinister figure of midnight — the hooded man' (*F*, p. 53). When Browning and Elizabeth Barrett immediately fall into conversation, and Flush is neglected, his pain and jealousy transform the once hospitable room into an ominous one:

> What was horrible to Flush, as they talked, was his loneliness. Once he had felt that he and Miss Barrett were together, in a firelit cave. Now the cave was no longer firelit; it was dark and damp; Miss Barrett was outside. He looked round him. Everything had changed. The bookcase, the five busts — they were no longer friendly deities presiding approvingly — they were hostile, severe. He

shifted his position at Miss Barrett's feet. She took no notice.

(F, p. 54.)

Similarly, after Flush has returned home from his ordeal in captivity ('dognapped', and kept in a cellar in Whitechapel),

> The old gods of the bedroom — the bookcase, the wardrobe, the busts — seemed to have lost their substance. This room was no longer the whole world; it was only a shelter. It was only a dell arched over by one trembling dock-leaf in a forest where wild beasts prowled and venomous snakes coiled; where behind every tree lurked a murderer ready to pounce.

(F, pp. 95-6.)

When Robert Browning takes his new bride (and Flush) to Italy, Flush is homesick, and we are told that 'All those draped objects of his cloistered and secluded days had vanished. The bed was a bed; the wash-stand was a wash-stand. Everything was itself, and not another thing' (F, pp. 112-13).

Bell maintains that Virginia's purpose in Flush is to 'escape from her own human corporeal existence'. Explain, deal with, or come to terms with might describe her purpose better. And this is two-fold: firstly, to describe in a light-hearted and literary way, using the Barrett-Browning story,[31] her experience of sickness and health, seclusion and freedom; and, secondly, to come to terms with some of the issues surrounding her 'flirtation' with Clive Bell, her brother-in-law. Quentin Bell writes:

> Biographically Flush is interesting, for in a way it is a work of self-revelation .... The narrator is Virginia herself but an attempt is made to describe Wimpole Street, Whitechapel and Italy from a dog's point of view, to create a world of canine smells, fidelities, and lusts.

(Bell, 2, p. 175.)

We might alter this judgement only by saying, more correctly, that an attempt is made to describe, from a dog's (who is human) point of view, the world of *human* smells, *in*fidelities, and lusts.

When Flush's previous owner, Miss Mitford, leaves Flush with his new mistress, there are a few awkward moments. But then an extraordinary thing happens:

> Each was surprised. Heavy curls hung down on either side of Miss Barrett's face; large bright eyes shone out; a large mouth smiled. Heavy ears hung down on either side of Flush's face; his eyes, too, were large and bright: his mouth was wide. There was a likeness between them. As they gazed at each other each felt: Here am I — and then each felt: But how different! Hers was the pale worn face of an invalid, cut off from air, light, freedom. His was the warm ruddy face of a young animal; instinct with health and energy. Broken asunder, yet made in the same mould, could it be that each completed what was dormant in the other?
>
> (*F*, pp. 26-7.)

It would appear that Flush and Elizabeth Barrett are opposite but complementary parts of a single personality, a point which is further stressed when Virginia tells us that Elizabeth Barrett (while pondering how to phrase a difficult and intimate point in a letter) drew a 'very neat and characteristic portrait of Flush, humorously made rather like myself' (*F*, p. 38). Flush is healthy, loves the sunshine and fields; Elizabeth Barrett is an invalid, and is forced to spend most of her time shut up in her room. Where one went, the other had to follow — a tragic compromise which Flush accepted with as much stoicism and fortitude as he could muster. Elizabeth Barrett 'was too just', Virginia tells us, 'not to realise that it was for her that he had sacrificed . . . the sun and the air' (*F*, p. 46). And Flush's reaction to being shut up at various times in his life coincides with Virginia's own hatred of the routine of bed, a darkened room, and warm milk, which was often imposed upon her. Flush's first summer with Elizabeth Barrett has strong parallels with Virginia's own experience during the summer following her mother's death, when she experienced her first mental breakdown.

The summer of 1842 was, historians tell us, not much different from other summers, yet to Flush it was so different that he must have doubted if the world itself were the same. It was a summer spent in a bedroom; . . .

(*F*. p. 28.)

Flush is plagued by the memory of unfettered romps through fields, the enjoyment of life, of sunshine and fresh air. Virginia wrote that, following her mother's death,

> That summer, after some hot months in London, we spent in Freshwater; and the heat there in the low bay, brimming as it seemed with soft vapours, and luxuriant with lush plants, mixes, like smoke, with other memories of hot rooms and silence, and an atmosphere all choked with too luxuriant feelings so that one had at times a physical need of ruthless barbarism and fresh air.[32]

Virginia declared that her mother's death was 'the greatest disaster that could happen'.[33] When Flush has to remain in his mistress's sickroom throughout an entire summer, 'to a dog of Flush's temperament, [it] was the most drastic [thing] that could have been invented' (*F*, p. 33). Bell writes that at the end of November 1931, '*Flush* was going well.' But, 'On 6 December she had agreed, no doubt at Leonard's request, to lead an invalid's life until Christmas — no writing, no parties' (Bell, 2, p. 163).

Flush's similarity to Virginia is documented down to such details as their mutual fear of being run down in the street. And when Flush is stolen and kept starving in a basement in Whitechapel, Virginia is recalling the horror of her confinement at Burley, at Dalingridge Place, and in her own home, attended by four nurses.

In *Flush*, Elizabeth Barrett's father is portrayed as a stern, unsympathetic authoritarian presence. She is not free to do as she pleases. *Flush*, at times, is written in the same tone that pervades *A Room of One's Own* and *Three Guineas*. In *A Room of One's Own*, Virginia describes the following experience:

I found myself walking with extreme rapidity across a

grass plot. Instantly a man's figure rose to intercept me. Nor did I at first understand that the gesticulations of a curious-looking object, in a cut-away coat and evening shirt, were aimed at me. His face expressed horror and indignation. Instinct rather than reason came to my help; he was a Beadle; I was a woman. This was the turf; there was the path. Only the Fellows and Scholars are allowed here; the gravel is the place for me.[34]

Flush has an identical experience, and arrives at the same conclusion by means of the same logic:

Men in shiny top-hats marched ominously up and down the paths. At the sight of them he shuddered. . . . Thus before many of these walks were over a new conception had entered his brain. Setting one thing beside another, he had arrived at a conclusion. Where there are flower-beds there are asphalt paths; where there are flower-beds and asphalt paths there are men in shiny top-hats; where there are flower-beds and asphalt paths and men in shiny top-hats, dogs must be led on chains. Without being able to decipher a word of the placard at the Gate, he had learnt his lesson — in Regent's Park dogs must be led on chains.

(*F*, p. 31.)

In the life of Elizabeth Barrett, Virginia found a story which, in many ways, closely paralleled her own; and at times, it seemed as if, for both of them, it was a 'dog's life'. The similarity between Virginia and Elizabeth Barrett is made clear in Virginia's essay on 'Aurora Leigh':

Again and again in the pages we have read, Aurora the fictitious seems to be throwing light upon Elizabeth the actual. The idea of the poem, we must remember, came to her in the early forties when the connexion between a woman's art and a woman's life was unnaturally close, so that it is impossible for the most austere of critics not sometimes to touch the flesh when his eyes should be fixed upon the page. And as everybody knows, the life of Elizabeth Barrett was of a nature to affect the most authentic and individual of gifts. Her mother had died when she was a child; she had read profusely and privately;

her favourite brother was drowned; her health broke down; she had been immured by the tyranny of her father in almost conventual seclusion in a bedroom in Wimpole Street.

(*Essays*, 1, p. 212.)

The similarities between the experiences of Virginia Woolf (down to losing the favourite brother) and Elizabeth Barrett are remarkable. But did Virginia never realize that, in *Flush*, she herself was 'guilty' of a 'close connexion between life and art'?

Clive Bell was at Cambridge with Thoby Stephen, Leonard Woolf, and most of the other male members of Bloomsbury. He did not have the intellectual capacities of Woolf or Strachey. His background was different from theirs: he was the son of a country squire, and he loved riding and shooting. But he did have a passionate love of art. He proposed to Vanessa Stephen in the summer of 1905 and was refused. But when Thoby died of typhoid on 20 November 1906, Clive proposed again, two days after the death. This time he was accepted.

The effect of the engagement upon Virginia was profound. Virginia had lost her mother, and then her father; Stella Duckworth had died soon after her marriage to Jack Hills; and now her brother, whom she loved and admired, died through medical incompetence. With the Duckworths and a gaggle of aunts her only remaining family (and she never felt close to her brother Adrian), she needed Vanessa for support and encouragement. She needed her confidence, and her affection. When Vanessa decided to marry Clive Bell, it seemed to Virginia as if her only ally had defected. She felt stranded in a hostile environment, with no one upon whom she could rely.

But as time went on, Virginia found that she could tolerate Clive. When he began to take an interest in her writing (she was then working on *Melymbrosia*, which became *The Voyage Out*), he became more and more acceptable. As his interest grew (and she found his criticism of her work useful), Virginia developed a positive affection for him. When the Bell's first child, Julian, was born in February 1908, their relationships grew into the 'flirtation' which Quentin Bell describes in his biography. Virginia herself described this episode in her life as 'having turned more of a knife in me than anything else has ever done' (*Letters*, 3, p. 172). The story is dealt with in *Flush* in the relations between Flush (Virginia), Robert Browning (Clive Bell) and Elizabeth Barrett (Vanessa).

With the arrival of the baby, Vanessa ceased to be the person Virginia had been used to. While Vanessa found her new baby every bit as interesting as the adults around her, Virginia and Clive did not. Bell writes that, from Virginia's point of view, 'all the comforts of sisterly intercourse were destroyed. She turned to Clive and found that his sentiments were nearly the same as hers. They were both, in a way, jealous of the child' (Bell, 1, p. 132). It is essential, when dealing with this delicate point, to quote Bell at length:

> Out of earshot of that dreadful caterwauling they could be comfortable again; they could talk about books and friends and they did so with a sense of comradeship, of confederacy, against the fearful tyrannies of family life. In such converse it was easier for Virginia to discover her brother-in-law's good qualities: the real good humour which lay beneath his urbanity, his tenderness for other people's feelings which could make him appear fussy, his almost invariable good temper, his quick sense of the absurd, his charm. He, for his part, had never doubted that she was a remarkable, an exhilarating, an enchanting companion; but perhaps it was now that he noticed, in certain lights and in certain phases of animation, that she was even more beautiful than Vanessa. Clive could never carry on more than five minutes' conversation with a personable woman and refrain from some slight display of gallantry; now perhaps he was a little warmer than mere homage required and — this was the crucial thing — she, who would ordinarily have repulsed all advances with the utmost severity, was now not entirely unkind. An ardent and sanguine temperament such as his was excited by resistance and fortified by the least hint of success. In a word, Clive, after fourteen months of marriage, entered into a violent and prolonged fliration with his sister-in-law.

I use the word flirtation, for if I called this attachment

an 'affair' it would suggest that Clive succeeded in his object, which was indeed no less, and I think not much more, than a delightful little infidelity ending up in bed. Many years later Virginia accused him of being a cuckoo that lays its eggs in other birds' nests. 'My dear Virginia,' was his cheerful reply, 'you would never let me lay an egg in your nest.' In fact I doubt whether the business would have lasted for so long or, for a time, have become so important to them both, if Virginia had given him what he wanted. But this she never did and, in a very crude sense, her conduct may be described as virtuous.

What then did she want? She was not in the least in love with Clive. In so far as she was in love with anyone she was in love with Vanessa.

(Bell, 1, pp. 132-3.)

While we cannot argue with Bell's ascription of dates and the external facts surrounding the flirtation (and some of his psychological interpretations are perfectly reasonable), we must pause and consider his judgement of Virginia's character. He seems to imply that Virginia ought to have 'given him what he wanted', and then to attribute a grudging moral significance to the fact that she chose not to commit adultery with her brother-in-law: 'in a very crude sense, her conduct may be described as virtuous.' So, in a very crude sense, Clive Bell's conduct may be described as virtuous. It is clear that Quentin Bell has failed to take very seriously the effects of the Duckworths' molestations. She found it nearly impossible to have sexual relations with her husband; why should she have found it any easier to conduct an affair with her brother-in-law?

Bell continues by saying that

Vanessa's situation, as Virginia must have understood, was in the highest degree painful and called for a remarkable exercise in prudence and in fortitude. An outright quarrel with high words and accusations never took place; it is probable that both sisters shrank from the notion of a 'scene'. In letters to Clive and to Virginia, Vanessa takes things lightly, easily, with a show of humour; inwardly she was both hurt and angry; she could, she said, have forgiven Virginia if Virginia had felt any passion, had been genuinely or indeed at all in love with Clive. But this clearly she was not; her conduct was therefore inspired by nothing save a delight in mischief. It made Clive irritable; it made her — Vanessa — very unhappy. What satisfaction did Virginia herself gain from it? None, it may be thought, save that which comes to him who teases an aching tooth with his tongue.

(Bell, 1, p. 134.)

During this time Virginia was confronted with declarations of love or proposals of marriage from Walter Lamb, Lytton Strachey, Sydney Waterlow, and Hilton Young. While Virginia initially accepted Strachey's proposal of marriage, they quickly (and mutually) saw the folly of this and backed out of the scheme. While Virginia felt little in the way of romantic attachment or passion towards these suitors, but most likely enjoyed the attention, she suffered little or no emotional upheaval as a result. However, Clive was jealous, and relations among male Bloomsbury were uneasy, and occasionally very awkward.

If pressed to make a judgement, we may say that while we may understand Virginia's position in relation to her sister's marriage, her behaviour was nonetheless selfish. As we shall see, Virginia herself came to realise this, and Flush's reconciliation with his mistress, her suitor, and his proper relation to them, tells this story.

But the truth is that the flirtation was more than a mere caprice, and it had profound emotional reverberations throughout Virginia's life. There is no doubt that, in its early stages, the affair was fairly passionate, if only in an emotional and cerebral way, on Virginia's side. She wrote to Clive in 1908,

Why do you torment me with half uttered and ambiguous sentences? my presence is 'vivid and strange and bewildering'. I read your letter again and again, and wonder whether you have found me out, or, more likely, determined that there is nothing but an incomprehensible and quite negligible femininity to find out. I was certainly of opinion, though we did not kiss — (I was willing and offered once — but let that be) — I think we 'achieved

the heights' as you put it. But did you realise how profoundly I was moved, and at the same time, restricted, by
the sight of your daily life. Ah — such beauty —grandeur —
and freedom — as of panthers treading in their wilds — I
never saw in any other pair. When Nessa is bumbling about
the world, and making each thorn blossom, what room is
there for me?

(*Letters*, 1, pp. 329-30.)

We may guess that letters to Clive have been omitted by the
editors, for there are no more passionate outbursts until
1910. Virginia writes to Clive (of their tea being interrupted):

Contrasting this with what might have been — its too
damnable. Next time (which I dont dare to suggest) I
will make the proper arrangements, but I'm certain that
I shall never have the courage to turn people out when
they're on the stairs — not if I'm in my lover's arms!

(*Letters*, 1, p. 439.)

A letter to Ethel Smyth in 1930 shows that Virginia did
experience some physical feeling for Clive, but that she
didn't/wouldn't/couldn't do anything about it:

when 2 or 3 times in all, I felt physically for a man, then
he was so obtuse, gallant, foxhunting and dull that I —
diverse as I am — could only wheel round and gallop the
other way. Perhaps this shows why Clive, who had his
reasons, always called me a fish. Vita also calls me fish.

(*Letters*, 4, p. 200.)

As late as 1922, Virginia could still write teasing, suggestive
letters to Clive:

Here am I, apparently the favourite breeding ground of the
influenza germ: but my head remains what is was; — and
my heart too.

In short, devote a morning to your poor sister in law,
and she will ever pray — for what?

Now what would you most like to happen?

(*Letters*, 2, p. 504.)

In 1911 the Bell marriage began to founder. Clive and Vanessa embarked on a trip to Constantinople with a party which included the painter and critic Roger Fry. During the journey, Vanessa became ill, and Fry took command when the other members of the party proved ineffectual. He organized doctors, servants, hotels, and so on, and when they returned to London, Vanessa and Roger realized that they were in love. Quentin Bell writes that:

> On the whole the break-up of the Bell marriage, that is to say its transformation into a union of friendship, which was slowly accomplished during the years 1911-1914, made for a relaxation of tension between the sisters and a slow dissolution (never quite complete) of Virginia's long troubled relationship with Clive.
>
> (Bell, 1, p. 169.)

Later, Virginia could write openly to Vanessa about the situation with Clive. But even in 1928, after Clive had allied himself with Mary Hutchinson, the snarls and tangles were still very much in evidence. Virginia wrote to Vanessa,

> I had a long rambling very indirect talk with Clive, who kept making allusions to my having told someone I saw too much of him, but wouldn't come to facts; and was rather apologetic; and also affectionate. But he says he cant help these outbursts, which date back to old horrors in the past; and as I am also scarred and riddled with complexes about you and him, and being derided and insulted and sacrificed and betrayed, I don't see how we can hope for a plain straightforward relationship. In fact, having kissed each other passionately, we met two days later and quarrelled — or rather he sneered and I became sarcastic — about my seeing Hugh Walpole. So it will go on till the daisies grow over us. But he told me he is much more settled and content; and talked of Mary as if she were under the earth for ever. I have had no dealings with her, nor shall, unless she makes the move.
>
> (*Letters*, 3, pp. 500-1.)

Further complicating the whole situation is Virginia's erotic feelings for her sister. There are many hints scattered through the letters, but this one, written in 1928, is typical:

> Now I'm off to Sibyl [Lady Colefax] to meet Noel
> Coward, with whom I am slightly in love — Why?
> But with you I am deeply passionately, unrequitedly
> in love—
>
> > B.

> and thank goodness your beauty is ruined, for my incest-
> uous feeling may then be cooled — yet it has survived a
> century of indifference.
>
> > (*Letters*, 3, pp. 546-7.)

While it is clear that Virginia's use of the word 'love' in the
first sentence is playful, the tone is somewhat more insistent
where Vanessa is concerned.

During the years 1917 to 1922, there are a number of
entries in Virginia's diary relating to Clive Bell. In 1917
she writes, 'Clive starts his topics — lavishing admiration &
notice upon Nessa, which doesn't make me jealous as once
it did, when the swing of that pendulum carried so much
of my fortune with it: at any rate of my comfort' (*Diary*, 1,
p. 86). In 1918 she records a scene which includes Clive,
Vanessa, Mary Hutchinson and herself, which illustrates
the kinds of difficulties which remain:

> Clive has never forgiven me — for what? I see that he is
> carefully following a plan in his relations with me — &
> resents any attempt to distract him from it. His personal
> remarks always seem to be founded on some reserve of
> grievance, which he has decided not to state openly.
> 'You've wrecked one of my best friendships' he re-
> marked; 'by your habit of describing facts from your own
> standpoint—'
> 'What you call God's Truth' said Nessa.
> 'One couldn't have an intimacy with you & anyone
> else at the same time — You describe people as I paint
> pots.'
> 'You put things in curl, & they come out afterwards'
> Mary murmured from the shadow of her sympathetic
> silence.
> Clive however had bitterness of some sort in what he

said. He meant me to see that somehow I had ended our
old relations — & now all is second best. It was clear also
that he lives in dread of some alliance between Mary &
me which shall threaten his position with her.

(*Diary*, 1, pp. 172-3.)

And an entry of 1922 shows how, despite the fact that the
affair had been so painful in many ways, Virginia still got a
kind of pleasure from seeing Clive:

Clive, via Mary, says he uses violet powder to make him
look cadaverous. Thus it appears that Mary is not on good
terms with Tom [T.S. Eliot]; & that I am seeing Clive
rather frequently. He comes on Wednesdays; jolly & rosy,
& squab: a man of the world; & enough of my old friend,
& enough of my old lover, to make the afternoons hum.

(*Diary*, 2, p. 171.)

That Vanessa figures centrally in *Flush* is apparent from a
comparison of Flush's consciousness and some of Virginia's
earliest recollections of her relationship with her sister.
When Flush first perceives the objects in Elizabeth Barrett's
room, this is likened to an archaeologist discovering the
human past. Various objects of perception (the first and most
important of which is the table) 'swam up to the surface',
as if emerging from a watery depth. The significance of
'underwater' imagery is spelled out in *The Voyage Out*,
when Rachel goes into a coma. Water connotes the past in
general, and has a strong connection with sexuality. Also,
Flush experiences the room as 'a firelit cave', a significant
image, the meaning of which becomes apparent when we
look at Virginia's reminiscences of her early relationship
with Vanessa. Just prior to Julian Bell's birth in 1908, during
the months preceding the beginning of her flirtation with
Clive, Virginia wrote an essay entitled 'Reminiscences'
which was to be a short biographical sketch about the
Stephen sisters and their life at 22 Hyde Park Gate, intended
for Julian Bell. One of Virginia's first recollections is of
Vanessa and herself playing under the nursery table. The
imagery which she uses to describe this experience is very

similar to that used to describe Flush's discovery of Elizabeth Barrett's room:

> I remember too the great extent and mystery of the dark land under the nursery table, where a continuous romance seemed to go forward, though the time spent there was really so short. Here I met your mother, *in a gloom happily encircled by the firelight*, and peopled with legs and skirts. We drifted together like ships in an immense ocean and she asked me whether black cats had tails. And I answered that they had not, after a pause in which her question seemed to drop echoing down vast abysses, hitherto silent. In future I suppose there was some consciousness between us that the other held possibilities.[35]

Virginia describes this early experience as a 'romance'. (The world under the table is resurrected at the end of *Flush* as he sits beneath the table while seances are held.) She met her sister 'in a gloom happily encircled by firelight'. In part, this enduring image of romance and happiness must have contributed to Virginia's unhappiness when her sister decided to marry Clive Bell. Flush's 'romance' with Elizabeth Barrett is described almost identically, and comes to an end with the arrival of Robert Browning:

> Flush, watching Miss Barrett, saw the colour rush into her face; saw her eyes brighten and her lips open.
> 'Mr. Browning!' she exlaimed.
> Twisting his yellow gloves in his hands, blinking his eyes, well groomed, masterly, abrupt, Mr. Browning strode across the room. He seized Miss Barrett's hand, and sank into the chair by the sofa at her side. Instantly they began to talk.
> What was horrible to Flush, as they talked, was his loneliness. Once he had felt that he and Miss Barrett were together, *in a firelit cave*. Now the cave was no longer firelit; it was dark and damp; Miss Barrett was outside.
> (*F*, pp. 53-4, my italics.)

The similarities between Virginia's experience with Vanessa and Flush's with Miss Barrett are obvious. Browning is characterized as a dandy (a note informs us that 'Mrs. Bridewell-Fox, meeting him in 1835-6, says, "he was then slim and dark, and very handsome, and — may I hint it — just a trifle of a dandy, addicted to lemon-coloured kid gloves and such things." ' (*F*, p. 154.) Clive Bell, too, had his affectations.

What is at work here — and the lesson may be applied to the Burley letters and the suicide note — are the Lacanian concepts of 'displacement' and 'overdetermination'. Displacement may be defined as:

> the fact that an idea's emphasis, interest or intensity is liable to be detached from it and to pass on to other ideas, which were originally of little intensity, but which are related to the first idea by a chain of associations.[36]

Building upon Hume's theory of association, Lacan provides a framework by means of which the association between Vanessa and the firelit cave of childhood, and the firelit cave of Flush and Elizabeth Barrett, may be put in perspective. Certainly, this is not a conscious act: in *Flush* we listen to Virginia's unconscious speak through her writing. Her writing here is overdetermined:

> If the unconscious is 'like poetry' in its overdetermined and polyphonic structures, then the writer who chooses to treat the unconscious, and wishes to obey its laws in his writing, must needs become more 'like a poet' the closer he gets to the quick of his subject. The overlapping and knotting together of signifiers with the written chain will show the reader what the unconscious is — and by enacting rather than describing it.[37]

From now on, Elizabeth Barrett's attitude towards Flush changes dramatically, at least from Flush's point of view. Now, 'She treated his advances more brusquely; she cut short his endearments laughingly; she made him feel that there was something petty, silly, affected in his old affectionate ways' (*F*, p. 60). (Here we may note that, for a moment, Virginia has forgotten that Flush is a mere dog. She never claims that he can speak, but she refers to his endearments.) We are told that Flush's 'jealousy was inflamed', and in a last-ditch effort to oust Browning and regain his mistress's affections, Flush attacks 'the hooded man', but the attack is a failure — the poet's leg is 'hard as iron'. What humiliates Flush most of all is that Browning takes no notice of the attempt. Flush welcomes the punishment meted out by his mistress (a slap on the ears) gladly (it is, after all, a kind of attention), but the next thing he cannot bear: 'she said in her sober, certain tones that she would never love him again. That shaft went to his heart. All these years they had lived together, shared everything together, and now, for one moment's failure, she would never love him again' (F, p. 61). Later, Miss Barrett forgives Flush, and so does Robert Browning — but Flush considers Browning's 'easy magnanimity' an insult. A few days later, Flush, while visiting Regent's Park, has the door of the four-wheeler shut on his paw. Elizabeth Barrett mocks his suffering, and writes to Browning, 'Flush always makes the most of his misfortunes — he is of the Byronic school — *il se pose en victime*' (F, p. 63). Miss Barrett's opinion of Flush in this instance is mistaken, as she fails to recognize the reality of his pride, and his point of view. Flush runs through the park despite his injured paw (as he would have done even if it were broken, we are told), and in spite of her mockery — 'I have done with you — that was the meaning he flashed at her as he ran' (F, p. 63). But Flush's defiance is to no avail, and when his mistress 'absent-mindedly slipped the chain over his neck, and led him home', Flush suffers an extreme humiliation of spirit (F, p. 64). He resolves to have final revenge on Browning, but is thwarted by Wilson, the maid. Exiled in the kitchen, Flush considers his situation, and his thoughts are Virginia's as she contemplates her flirtation with Clive Bell, behaviour which could yield no ultimate good, and much lasting regret for all involved:

And as he lay there, exiled, on the carpet, he went through one of those whirlpools of tumultuous emotion in which the soul is either dashed upon the rocks and splintered or, finding some tuft of foothold, slowly and painfully pulls itself up, regains dry land, and at last emerges on top of a ruined universe to survey a world created afresh on a different plan. Which was it to be —

destruction or reconstruction?

(F, pp. 66-7.)

Flush recognizes, along with the rightness of his position (at least from his own point of view), its extreme selfishness. In short, he begins to take the other into account. He is sensitive enough to be able to face his humiliation and recognize his own part in it — that he is not merely a victim, but is, to some extent, responsible for his predicament. It is from this recognition of responsibility that Flush's (or anyone else's) moral sense derives. 'Twice Flush had done his utmost to kill his enemy; twice he had failed. And why had he failed, he asked himself? Because he loved Miss Barrett' (F, p. 67). Virginia's love for her sister, though it suffered many injuries (from both parties) persisted throughout their lives in spite of the wrongs done. Flush too realizes that 'Things are not simple, but complex. If he bit Mr. Browning, he bit her too. Hatred is not hatred; hatred is also love' (F, p. 67). The moral truth consists in the simple complexity we find in the third of Blake's Four Zoas, Luvah, the Prince of Love, from whom we learn that love is the greatest of all emotions, and includes its contrary, hate.

But Flush's resolution, as fine as it is, can fully deliver him from selfishness only when it has somehow been demonstrated to the other person concerned. Here, Flush makes a symbolical gesture. Robert Browning, on the day of Flush's final attack, had brought some cakes to placate him. Flush, resolved not to accept the bribe, ignored them and proceeded directly to Browning's calf. But now, Flush eats the cakes, despite their being 'mouldy' and 'fly-blown':

> He had refused to eat the cakes when they were fresh, because they were offered by an enemy. He would eat them now that they were stale, because they were offered by an enemy turned to friend, because they were symbols of hatred turned to love. Yes, he signified, he would eat them now.

(F, p. 69.)

The correlation between Browning and Clive Bell is further

reinforced by these words from Virginia's diary of 1922: 'Clive came to tea yesterday, & offered me only the faded & fly blown remnants of his mind' (*Diary*, 2, p. 185). Furthermore, Flush 'was rewarded, spiritually . . . . He was with them, not against them, now; their hopes, their wishes, their desires were his' (*F*, p. 70). Flush's acceptance of Browning arises from a free choosing, not from coercion — and the violence, humiliation and suffering which preceded that choice make it authentic. Now, Flush thinks, 'We are all three conspirators in the most glorious of causes. We are joined in sympathy. We are joined in hatred. We are joined in defiance of black and beetling tyranny. We are joined in love' (*F*, pp. 70-1). However, Flush is not — nor will he ever be — completely 'cured' of his initial point of view. The tone of this final sentence, slightly exaggerated, slightly effusive, may conceal a trace of irony.

When Flush is abducted and held for ransom in a cellar in Whitechapel, Browning counsels Miss Barrett not to pay the ransom. He exhorts her twice daily to consider the wider political issue at stake: 'If she encouraged Taylor who stole dogs, she encouraged Mr. Barnard Gregory who stole characters' (*F*, p. 87). Browning does not want Flush's liberty or Elizabeth Barrett's personal happiness to set a dangerous precedent. Elizabeth Barrett, with the sort of reasoning that makes *Three Guineas* an exasperating book (but one we cannot dismiss),

read the letters. How easy it would have been to yield — how easy it would have been to say, 'Your good opinion is worth more to me than a hundred cocker spaniels'. How easy it would have been to sink back on her pillows and sigh, 'I am a weak woman; I know nothing of law and justice; decide for me'. She had only to refuse to pay the ransom; she had only to defy Taylor and his Society. And if Flush were killed, if the dreadful parcel came and she opened it and out dropped his head and paws, there was Robert Browning by her side to assure her that she had done right and earned his respect. But Miss Barrett was not to be intimidated. Miss Barrett took up her pen and refuted Robert Browning.

(*F*, p. 87.)

Browning's and Elizabeth Barrett's fundamental difference of opinion is one example of many underlined by situations in Virginia's novels. If Elizabeth Barrett were to go to Whitechapel and rescue her dog,

> she was siding against Robert Browning, and in favour of fathers, brothers, and domineerers in general. Still, she went on dressing. A dog howled in the mews. It was tied up, helpless in the power of cruel men. It seemed to her to cry as it howled: 'Think of Flush'. She put on her shoes, her cloak, her hat. She glanced at Mr. Browning's letter once more. 'I am about to marry you', she read. Still the dog howled. She left her room and went downstairs.
>
> (*F*, pp. 88-9.)

Elizabeth Barrett ignores Browning' political arguments, and rescues Flush. She demonstrates her essential love for Flush, and her refusal to let 'objective' considerations stand in the way of personal ones.

The language which tells the story of Flush's incarceration in Whitechapel is overdetermined to the extent that it barely conceals its ground in reality. Having established the nature of Flush's relation to those who wield power, Virginia has set the scene for the consequences which attend those who act in defiance of them:

> the only safe course for those who lived in Wimpole Street and its neighbourhood was to keep strictly within the respectable area and to lead your dog on a chain. If one forgot, as Miss Barrett forgot, one paid the penalty, as Miss Barrett was now to pay it.
>
> (*F*, p. 76.)

The penalty:

> As soon as a lady in Wimpole Street lost her dog she went to Mr. Taylor; he named his price, and it was paid; or if not, a brown paper parcel was delivered in Wimpole Street a few days later containing the head and paws of the dog.
>
> (*F*, p. 76.)

Virginia's description of Flush's experience in captivity is in direct contrast to Flush's experience of home, of the room he shares with Miss Barrett. The unity of the firelit cave is now destroyed. Terrifying, disparate objects exist in darkness and chaos:

> One moment he was in Vere Street, among ribbons and laces; the next *he was tumbled head over heels* into a bag; jolted rapidly across streets, and at length was *tumbled out* — here. *He found himself in complete darkness.* He found himself in chillness and dampness. As his giddiness left him he made out a few shapes in a low dark room — broken chairs, a *tumbled mattress*. Then he was seized and tied tightly by the leg to some obstacle. Something sprawled on the floor — whether beast or human being, he could not tell. Great boots and draggled skirts kept stumbling in and out. *Flies buzzed on scraps of old meat that were decaying on the floor. Children crawled out from dark corners and pinched his ears.* He whined, and a heavy hand beat him over the head. He cowered down on the few inches of damp brick against the wall. Now he could see that *the floor was crowded with animals of different kinds. Dogs tore and worried a festering bone that they had got between them. Their ribs stood out from their coats — they were half famished, dirty, diseased, uncombed, unbrushed; yet all of them, Flush could see, were dogs of the highest breeding, chained dogs, footmen's dogs, like himself.*
>
> (F, pp. 77-8, my italics.)

All of the italicized phrases refer to Virginia's experience of illness, and the 'empirical' treatment which she endured. Here, overdetermination and displacement are hard at work. Flush experiences his abduction as being 'tumbled head over heels'. He is 'tumbled out'. He makes out a 'tumbled mattress' in the room. Virginia describes Elinor Rendel's treatment of her in November 1925 in the following terms: 'Oh, what a blank! I tumbled into bed on coming back [to London from Sussex] — or rather Ellie tumbled me; & keeps me still prostrate half the day .... One visitor a day. Till 2 days ago, bed at 5' (*Diary*, 3, p. 46). The triple repetition of 'tumble' and its associations with the mattress make the

point. 'Darkness' is associated with empirical treatment of
a darkened room, warm milk, and enforced rest. It is also,
perhaps more importantly, the inverse of the light which is
experienced in the home — Wimpole Street/Hyde Park Gate —
with Miss Barrett and Vanessa. It is 'chillness and dampness'
as opposed to firelit warmth. These despairing images of
damp brick remind us too of the nightmare and hallucination scenes in *The Voyage Out*. Food is perhaps the most
important signifier here. We remember that during Virginia's
1913 stay at Burley she refused to eat, and that her refusal
of food was a refusal of Leonard, and his prohibitions against
childbirth — and evidence of the lack of sexual feeling. Here,
the two are combined in a powerfully juxtaposed pair of
images: 'Flies buzzed on scraps of old meat that were decay-
ing on the floor. Children crawled out from dark corners
and pinched his ears.' The circle of sexual love, childbirth
and nourishment — both literal and symbolic — has been
broken. None of it has meaning. There is an abundance of
food, but no nourishment is to be had; children become a
grotesque and mocking horror. We are told that 'Dogs tore and
worried a festering bone that they had got between them' —
yet, 'Their ribs stood out from their coats — they were half
famished'. When Flush recovers enough to look around him,
he sees that his fellow inmates are 'dogs of the highest
breeding ... like himself.' And so it must have seemed to
Virginia, an inmate of Jean Thomas's 'home' for genteel
lunatics; the home to which those whose purses were adequate were sent as an alternative to being committed to the
state asylum. 'Vexatious as it was, and especially annoying
at a moment when Miss Barrett needed all her money, such
were the inevitable consequences of forgetting in 1846 to
keep one's dog on a chain' (*F*, p. 77). For Miss Barrett is
about to be married, and she will need all the money she
can find to create a home of her own. The same held true
for Virginia. The process by which the dogs' freedom is
purchased is described thus: 'Then the women's bags were
opened, and out were tossed on to the table bracelets and
rings and brooches such as Flush had seen Miss Barrett
wear' (*F*, pp. 79-80). When Virginia mentions in a letter
to Ethel Smyth in 1931 that she is suffering from headaches,

her friend advises her to go to Harley Street. Virginia replies, 'As to seeing a doctor who will cure my headaches, no, Ethel No. And whats more you will seriously upset L, if you suggest it. We spent I daresay a hundred pounds when it meant selling my few rings and necklaces to pay (Sir G. Savage, Sir M. Craig, Sir M. Wright, T. Hyslop, etc. etc.)' (*Letters*, 4, pp. 325-6).

The final, and perhaps most significant association in this nightmare passage, describes 'a giant cockatoo that flustered and fluttered its way from corner to corner, shrieking "Pretty Poll", "Pretty Poll", with an accent that would have terrified its mistress, a widow in Maida Vale' (*F*, p. 79).

> The dogs barked. The children shrieked, and the splendid cockatoo — such a bird as Flush had often seen pendant in a Wimpole Street window — shrieked 'Pretty Poll! Pretty Poll!' faster and faster until a slipper was thrown at it and it flapped its great yellow-stained dove-grey wings in frenzy. Then the candle toppled over and fell. The room was dark. It grew steadily hotter and hotter; the smell, the heat, were unbearable, Flush's nose burnt; his coat twitched. And still Miss Barrett did not come.
>
> (*F*, p. 80.)

The cockatoo is Clive Bell. 'Cockatoo' is a word which Virginia used to describe him after their flirtation lost its passion. The appellation is derogatory (like calling him a bird which lays its eggs in other bird's nests), and refers to Bell's philandering and dandyish attitude which Virginia came to find absurd. She always referred, in her letters and diary, to Clive Bell and Mary Hutchinson, his mistress, as the 'parokeets'. When describing the area of Whitechapel in which Flush is held for ransom, Virginia writes,

> Aptly enough, where the poor conglomerated thus, the settlement was called a Rookery. For there human beings swarmed on top of each other as rooks swarm and blacken tree-tops . . . . at night there poured back again into the stream the thieves, beggars and prostitutes who had been plying their trade all day in the West End.
>
> (*F*, p. 75.)

In a letter of 1929 to Vanessa, Virginia wrote, '(. . . Whats Rooks to me, or me to Rookeries you say, quoting Shakespeare, as your way is) Clive, as I say, is under a cloud in London' (*Letters*, 4, p. 58).

As a result of his two experiences — his jealousy of Browning and his incarceration — Flush arrives at a maturity which banishes innocence forever. He is no longer able to trust anyone or anything at face value. Upon his return to Wimpole Street, Flush shrinks from Browning and his friend, Kenyon. 'He trusted them no longer. Behind those smiling, friendly faces was treachery and cruelty and deceit. Their caresses were hollow' (*F*, p. 96). Eliot wrote, in 'Gerontion', 'After such knowledge, what forgiveness?' In *The Family Reunion*, his statement of theme is a most apposite comment on Flush's experience, and the private experience with which Virginia attempted to come to terms:

What we have written is not a story of detection,
Of crime and punishment, but of sin and expiation.
It is possible that you have not known what sin
You shall expiate, or whose, or why. It is certain
That the knowledge of it must precede the expiation.
It is possible that sin may strain and struggle
In its dark instinctive birth, to come to consciousness
And so find expurgation.[38]

Conclusion

What I hope I have achieved in these pages is not so much the whole 'truth', but rather a corrective view of some popular and unexamined positions.

Roger Poole has said, in his work on Virginia Woolf, that 'In literary research of this kind, where one is dealing with hypothetical reconstructions at each point, there are no "facts".'[1] It is certainly true that irrefutable facts are hard to come by in this area of research. But it seems to me that the work of critics who do not accept the views put forward by Quentin Bell and other guardians of the Virginia Woolf legend has raised enough doubts about some of what passes for 'truth' in this area that it cannot be ignored.

There is, then, a crisis of truth. This is probably most evident when we consider the problem of Virginia's madness. Those critics who have assumed her madness have not been able to say what they mean by madness, or to prove that Virginia suffered from it. In a sense, this is understandable, as there has always been much confusion about this subject in what we might term the 'popular mind'. But it is the opposite of reassuring to discover, in the works of three of the doctors who treated Virginia, that they can present no useful or responsible definition of madness. In this area, scientific method has failed. The ideal of 'Objective Truth' is totally discredited in their works.

I think that it is right to view the question of Virginia's supposed madness as a conflict between two opposing points of view — that of the rationalism embodied by Leonard Woolf and others, and the more subjective world view held by Virginia. No critic has a right to formulate irresponsible and unfounded hypotheses where the personal life of his subject is concerned, but when certain conflicts within the personal life of the subject — familial and social conflicts — are at the heart of the subject's writing and of the unanswered questions which present themselves upon reflection, the critic's duty to confront these problems is clear. This problem is beginning to split Virginia Woolf scholars into factions between whom there is at present no dialogue.

In the summer of 1980, Oxford University Press republished the first two volumes of Leonard's autobiography in a paperback edition.[2] In his introduction to this volume, Quentin Bell writes, after reflecting on the importance of Leonard's book, *Quack, Quack!*,[3]

> Moreover I must note in passing that while rereading that book I have been struck by its strange topicality. In the very large volume of literature devoted to the study of Virginia Woolf there is a kind of lunatic fringe, and in this of late it has been possible to find authors who are ready to denounce Leonard, to find in his rationalism an unsympathetic and insensitive quality which, so the story goes, made him incapable of making his wife happy. There is a distinct air of quackery about such writers, a rejection of reason and indeed a sublime disregard of nearly all the available evidence. They too have their place in the records of intellectual dishonesty which Leonard so carefully examined.[4]

Thus the battle lines are drawn. Leonard and Professor Bell on one side, Bergson (a victim of *Quack, Quack!*) and such like on the other.

It is clear to anyone who reads Leonard's autobiography that there is evidence of a brand of rationalism which is marked by its overwhelming arrogance and its occasional blindness to individual human considerations which many would not hesitate to call 'insensitive'. A critic of universally acknowledged integrity, P. N. Furbank, tells, in his life of E. M. Forster, the following story which Leonard related to Forster:

He had been out riding with a man he disliked, and their

horses had bolted, making for a gap in the hedge only wide
enough for one man. It was clearly a problem in ethics;
one of them had to die, and it was up to him to choose
which. 'I'm more worth keeping alive than he,' had been
Woolf's conclusion, and, quite calmly, he had prepared
to murder his companion by charging at him. As it turned
out, the other man, in panic, had fallen off his horse, so no
murder was committed. And thereupon — the most
characteristic touch, thought Forster — Woolf had proceeded to tell the man exactly what his reasoning had
been. He wished, he told Forster, that the incident could
only happen again, this time with someone worth sacri-
ficing himself to.[5]

The sentence which concludes, 'he had prepared to murder
his companion by charging at him', has a footnote which
reads, 'A good instance of the influence of G. E. Moore's
ethical theories.'[6] Adding this to other revelations which
Leonard candidly offers in his autobiography, one can come
to the conclusion that this is, indeed, an admirably reasonable personality. But to take the view that this is reason
pushed to an extreme, that this is a character who, in many
ways, was capable of appearing unsympathetic, would not
make one guilty of 'sublime disregard of nearly all the evidence' as Quentin Bell suggests. It is judgements of this kind
which one has continually to make in this area, and the task
is not an easy one.

It is inevitable that battle lines have been drawn. But we
must not lose sight of the subject who is the occasion for
these critical investigations, and all who write have a responsibility to work towards a fuller elaboration of the truth,
even where this is painful to do, and where it is at odds with
comfortable assumptions.

Notes

Introduction

1 Woolf's autobiography is published in five volumes, all in London by the Hogarth Press: *Sowing: 1880-1904* (1960); *Growing: 1904-1911* (1961); *Beginning Again: 1911-1918* (1964); *Downhill All The Way: 1919-1939* (1967); *The Journey Not The Arrival Matters: 1939-1969* (1969).

2 Quentin Bell, *Virginia Woolf: A Biography*, Vol. 1: *Virginia Stephen 1882-1911*, Vol. 2: *Mrs Woolf 1912-1941*, St Albans, Herts: Triad/Paladin, 1976. Hereafter cited in the text as (Bell, 1), (Bell, 2).

3 Nigel Nicolson, ed., assisted by Joanne Trautmann, *The Letters of Virginia Woolf*. The *Letters* are published in six volumes, all in London by the Hogarth Press. Vol. 1: *The Flight of the Mind 1888-1912* (1975); Vol. 2: *The Question of Things Happening 1912-1922* (1976); Vol. 3: *A Change of Perspective 1923-1928* (1977); Vol. 4: *A Reflection of the Other Person 1929-1931* (1978); Vol. 5: *The Sickle Side of the Moon 1932-1935* (1979); Vol. 6: *Leave The Letters Till we're Dead 1936-1941* (1980). Hereafter cited in the text as (*Letters*, 1), etc. It must be noted that in their introduction to the final volume of the *Letters*, Nicolson and Trautmann argue that Virginia's suicide was a sane act, a matter of rational choice. Nevertheless, they retain the critical apparatus of 'insanity' which accompanies the five previous volumes.

4 Anne Olivier Bell, ed., assisted by Andrew McNeillie (from Vol. 2), *The Diary of Virginia Woolf*. Three volumes are published to date, all in London by the Hogarth Press. Vol. 1: *1915-1919* (1977); Vol. 2: *1920-1924* (1978); Vol. 3 *1925-1930* (1980). Hereafter cited in the text as (*Diary*, 1), etc.

5 See M. Jeanne Peterson, *The Medical Profession in Mid-Victorian London*, Berkeley and London: University of California Press, 1978. Peterson analyses the growth of professionalism, and the medical profession's emancipation from lay criticism. See also

my review, 'The Growth of a Cabal', *Bulletin of the Society For The Social History of Medicine*, 23, December 1978, pp. 44-7.

6   Roger Poole, *The Unknown Virginia Woolf*, Cambridge: Cambridge University Press, 1978, pp. 21-32.

7   Ibid., pp. 137-47.

8   See Virginia's essay, 'A Sketch of the Past' in Jeanne Schulkind, ed., *Moments of Being: Unpublished Autobiographical Writings of Virginia Woolf*, London: Sussex University Press, 1976, pp. 61-138. See Poole, p. 28.

9   *Moments of Being*, pp. 140-56.

10 In this work I consider her relation to Sir G. H. Savage, Sir Henry Head, Sir Maurice Craig and Dr. T. B. Hyslop. Virginia was also treated by D. J. Ferguson (1916-1923); Philip Hamill (1922); Harrington Sainsbury (1922); Herbert Vallance (1921-1922); Elinor Rendel (1926-1934); and, at the end of her life, by Octavia Wilberforce.

11 George Spater and Ian Parsons, *A Marriage of True Minds: An Intimate Portrait of Leonard and Virginia Woolf*, London: Jonathan Cape/Hogarth Press, 1977, passim.

12 R. D. Laing, *The Divided Self*, Harmondsworth: Penguin, 1965.

1   The Problem of Embodiment

1   *Sowing*, p. 29.

2   Virginia Woolf, *The Voyage Out*, Harmondsworth: Penguin (1970), p. 37. Hereafter cited in the text as (*TVO*).

3   See Jean O. Love, *Virginia Woolf: Sources of Madness and Art*, Berkeley and London: University of California Press, 1977, p. 77.

4   See the final chapter of this work.

5   *Moments of Being*, p. 58.

6   Ibid., p. 144, my italics.

7   Ibid., p. 155.

8   It is significant that images of facial deformity are employed where the Duckworths' attentions are concerned as well as on the occasions when the death of the mother is discussed. For an account of Virginia's reactions to kissing the face of her dead mother and its repercussions, see Love, p. 199. Catherine Oriel has suggested in conversation that the deformity of the inhabitants of the womb may suggest a fear on the part of Virginia that her own children might be deformed (because the doctors forbade childbirth). This restriction is discussed in Chapters 4 and 8 of this work.

9   *Moments of Being*, p. 135.

10 Ibid., p. 161.

11 Ibid., pp. 30-1.

12 Poole, p. 34.

13 Maurice Merleau-Ponty, *Phenomenology of Perception*, tr. Colin Smith, London and Henley: Routledge and Kegan Paul, 1962,

p. 158. My italics.
14 Ibid., pp. 168-9.
15 Ibid., p. 171.
16 Ibid., p. 291, my italics.
17 Ibid., p. 291.
18 Ibid., p. 291.
19 Laing, p. 67.
20 Ibid., p. 69.
21 Sylvia Plath describes a similar experience in *The Bell Jar*, London: Faber, 1966.
22 *Moments of Being*, p. 29, my italics.
23 Virginia Woolf, *The Years*, Harmondsworth: Penguin, 1968, p. 117. Hereafter cited in the text as (*TY*).
24 Merleau-Ponty, p. 134.
25 Ibid., p. 136.
26 Poole, pp. 7-20.
27 It may be significant that Virginia chose this particular image as her father was a great alpine climber.
28 The body as conceived by Merleau-Ponty. Also, Bruno Callieri, 'Perplexity — Psychopathological and Phenomenological Notes', in *Analecta Husserliana*, ed. A. Tymieniecka, Dordrecht: D. Reidel, 1978, pp. 51-64. 'My body is the place where I take possession of my world; it firmly attaches me to a kingdom of things, it ensures that I will have a solid base in the world, a station, a remaining in it, a *dwelling* in it' (pp. 59-60).
29 Virginia Woolf, 'On Not Knowing Greek', *Collected Essays Vol. 1*, ed. Leonard Woolf, London: Hogarth Press, 1966, p. 12.
30 Virginia Woolf, 'The Faery Queen', *Collected Essays Vol. 1*, p. 16.
31 Virginia Woolf, *Mrs Dalloway*, Harmondsworth: Penguin 1964, p. 13. Hereafter cited in the text as (*MD*).
32 Virginia Woolf, *Night and Day*, Harmondsworth, Penguin, 1969, pp. 46-7. Hereafter cited in the text as (*ND*).
33 Virginia Woolf, *The Waves*, Harmondsworth: Penguin, 1964, p. 53. Hereafter cited in the text as (*TW*).
34 'The most traumatic experience for Virginia occurred the evening after her mother died, when Stella took her and Vanessa to see and kiss their dead mother for the last time. Julia's face appeared to Virginia to be very stern in death, and kissing it was like pressing her lips against cold iron. Virginia said that forever afterward touching cold iron revived the emotions and reinstated the experience of that last visit to her mother's body' (Love, p. 199).
35 As Laing points out 'To the extent that he is thoroughly "in" his body, he is likely to have a sense of personal continuity in time' (p. 67). The section on 'Temporality' in Merleau-Ponty considers this question in depth. 'Time . . . arises from *my* relation to things' (p. 412); 'The passage of one present to the next is not a thing which I conceive nor do I see it as an onlooker, I effect it . . . I am myself time' (p. 421); 'We are saying that time *is*

someone, or that temporal dimensions in so far as they perpetually overlap, bear each other out and even confine themselves to making explicit what was implied in each being collectively expressive of that one single explosion or thrust which is subjectivity itself' (p. 422).

36 Virginia Woolf, *Jacob's Room*, Harmondsworth: Penguin, 1965. Hereafter cited in the text as (*JR*). 'It's not catastrophes, murders, deaths, diseases, that age and kill us; it's the way people look and laugh, and run up the steps of omnibuses' (*JR*, p. 78). Jacob thought at first that the lowly Florinda was the antithesis of poetry, but later discovered that she could be a source of it.

2   The Problem of Food

1 *Growing*, p. 28.

2 *Beginning Again*, pp. 79-80, my italics. It is curious that Leonard describes this symptom as 'troublesome' rather than 'troubling'. The *Concise OED* defines troublesome as '(of a person or thing) causing trouble, vexatious'. It seems that Leonard was not troubled by Virginia's refusal to eat, but that this refusal was vexatious to him. Leonard was nothing if not precise in his use of language.

3 'The empirical method, which consisted of rest, food, calm, and the avoidance of intellectual excitement' (Bell, 2, p. 19).

4 *Beginning Again*, p. 153.

5 Vita Sackville-West wrote to her husband in 1926, 'she has never lived with anyone except Leonard, which was a terrible failure, and was abandoned quite soon'. Quoted in Nigel Nicolson, *Portrait of a Marriage*, London: Futura, 1974, p. 212.

6 This becomes clearer in the light of the letters Virginia wrote from Burley, and from the tone of her suicide note to Leonard. See the final chapter of this work.

7 See *Letters*, 2, pp. 32-5.

8 *Beginning Again*, pp. 153-4.

9 Ibid., pp. 153-4.

10 This study was never completed. She did, however, publish a short preliminary paper entitled 'Virginia Woolf: An Outline of a Study on Her Personality, Illness, Work', *Confinia Psychiatrica* (Basel), 8, 1965, pp. 189-204.

11 Miyeko Kamiya to Leonard Woolf. Unpublished letter in the Monk's House Collection, University of Sussex Library, II D 9.

12 William A. R. Thomson, ed., *Black's Medical Dictionary*, 31st ed., London: A. and C. Black, 1978, p. 59. The best recent work on *anorexia* is A. H. Crisp's *Anorexia Nervosa: Let Me Be*, London: Academic Press, 1980.

13 Peter Lomas, *True and False Experience*, London: Allen Lane, 1973, p. 102.

14 Spater and Parsons, p. 69n.

15 Ibid., p. 69.
16 See Jeffrey Meyers, *Married To Genius*, London: London Magazine Editions, 1977, p. 101: 'She dislikes the possessiveness and love of domination in men. In fact, she dislikes the quality of masculinity.' Meyers is quoting Vita Sackville-West.
17 Lomas, p. 53.
18 Merleau-Ponty, pp. 160-1, my italics. Merleau-Ponty is reciting a case from Ludwig Binswanger's *Über Psychotherapie*, Nervenarts, 1935.
19 Ibid., p. 164, my italics.
20 Poole, p. 56.
21 Roland Barthes, *Roland Barthes by Roland Barthes*, tr. Richard Howard, London and Basingstoke: Macmillan, 1977, p. 30.
22 See Poole, p. 21. For Anne Olivier Bell's criticism of Poole's assertion, see her letter to *Virginia Woolf Miscellany*, 14, 1980, p. 7.
23 Virginia Woolf, *A Writer's Diary*, ed. Leonard Woolf, London: Hogarth Press, 1953, p. 365. Hereafter cited in the text as (*AWD*).
24 As Blanch Gelfant argues in 'Love and Conversion in *Mrs Dalloway*', *Criticism*, 8, 1966, pp. 229-45.
25 E. M. Forster wrote that Virginia's descriptions of food were marked by an 'enlightened greediness'. See Jane Russell Noble, ed., *Recollections of Virginia Woolf*, Harmondsworth: Penguin, 1975, p. 236.
26 See Roger Poole, 'Structuralism and Phenomenology: A Literary Approach', *Journal of the British Society For Phenomenology*, 1 (2), 1971, pp. 7-10.
27 Rhoda's problems with time and her face are Rachel-Virginia's pushed to an extreme.
28 The novels of Günter Grass, particularly *Flounder*, share this preoccupation.
29 Virginia Woolf, *Flush*, London: Hogarth Press, 1933. Hereafter cited in the text as (*F*). 'Hatred is not hatred; hatred is also love' (*F*, p. 67).

3   The Doctors: Real and Fictional

1 George Eliot, *Middlemarch*, Harmondsworth: Penguin, 1965, p. 212.
2 John Fowles, *The French Lieutenant's Woman*, St Albans: Triad/ Panther, 1977, p. 134.
3 Frederick W. Maitland, *The Life and Letters of Sir Leslie Stephen*, London: Duckworth, 1906, p. 28.
4 *c*. 1827-1917, MD Edin. 1856.
5 'Inflammation of the peritoneum or membrane investing the abdominal and pelvic cavities and their contained viscera. . . . The question of operation arises in every case of peritonitis. In cases due to perforation of the stomach or intestine which

are discovered early, operation is always advisable, because there is a good prospect of freeing the abdomen from the septic material which has entered it, and, if no operation is performed, the patient will almost certainly die' (*Black's Medical Dictionary*, 31st ed., pp. 660-1).

6   That is not to say that either physician is to blame, but that there was a lack of communication between them and the family which was regrettable.

7   *Moments of Being*, pp. 98-9.

8   This chronology follows that in Bell, 1, pp. 195ff.

9   Or very soon after. The questionable dates have been ascribed by Nicolson and Trautmann.

10   This is significant as there is evidence, as we shall see in the chapter devoted to Craig, that some of Virginia's doctors made judgements regarding her condition solely on the basis of reports submitted by Leonard, and without actually seeing Virginia themselves.

11   T. B. Hyslop, *Mental Handicaps in Golf*, London: Ballière and Co., 1927.

12   *British Medical Journal*, 12 January 1935, pp. 87-8.

13   Virginia also outlines Sir William Bradshaw's programme: 'You invoke proportion; order rest in bed; rest in solitude; rest without friends, without books, without messages; six months' rest; until a man who went in weighing seven stone six comes out weighing twelve' (*MD*, p. 110).

14   See final chapter of this work for a discussion of the doctors and their relation to the 'discourse of power'.

15   T. B. Hyslop, 'Post-Illusionism and Art in the Insane', *The Nineteenth Century*, 69, 1911, pp. 270-81. Hereafter cited in the text as (Hyslop, 1911). 'Symbolism is rife in the insane' (p. 276).

16   As we shall see in the work of Sir G. H. Savage, in Chapter 4 of this work.

17   Savage regularly sent his patients (those who could afford it) to Burley.

18   In Chapter 7 of this work we shall see how Hyslop attempted to gain the support of the Church in his efforts to suppress madness.

4   The Morality of Madness: Sir George Henry Savage

1   G. H. Savage, *Insanity and Allied Neuroses*, London: Cassell, 1884. Hereafter cited in the text as (Savage, 1884e).

2   Kathleen Jones, *Mental Health and Social Policy 1845-1959*, London and Henley: Routledge & Kegan Paul, 1960, p. 12. An excellent discussion of the reasons behind the medical profession's outrage at any form of lay intervention in what they considered to be purely medical affairs (but which others saw as political questions with individual human rights at stake) may be found in M. Jeanne Peterson's *The Medical Profession in Mid-Victorian*

London. The question of lay criticism becomes important later in this chapter, as Savage came under fire in the press for his treatment of patients at Bethlem in 1888.

3 G. H. Savage, 'Constant Watching of Suicide Cases', *Journal of Mental Science*, 30, 1884, pp. 17-19. Hereafter cited in the text as (Savage, 1884c).

4 This breakdown is described by Bell in the following terms: 'We do not know, although we may fairly guess, that there were headaches, sudden nervous leapings of the heart and a growing awareness that there was something very wrong with her mind . . . the symptoms of the previous months attained frantic intensity. Her mistrust of Vanessa, her grief for her father became maniacal, her nurses — she had three — became fiends. She heard voices urging her to acts of folly; she believed that they came from overeating and that she must starve herself' (Bell, 1, p. 89). It was during this breakdown of May 1904 that Virginia attempted suicide by jumping out of a low window at Violet Dickinson's house at Burnham Wood. 'It was here too that she lay in bed, listening to the birds singing in Greek and imagining that King Edward VII lurked in the azaleas using the foulest possible language' (Bell, 1, p. 90).

5 'When Virginia went mad in the summer of 1904 Vanessa told Savage of what had been happening and Savage, it seems, taxed George with his conduct' (Bell, 1, pp. 95-6).

6 Bell makes this point succinctly when he writes, 'the past was coming to live with them' (Bell, 1, p. 96).

7 Poole is quoting from Leonard Woolf's *Beginning Again*, p. 82.

8 Poole, p. 121.

9 It is equally hard to imagine Leonard as a father. Where in his writings do we find him expressing regret over not having had a child?

10 Bell neglects to dwell on Virginia's reasons for not wanting to return to Burley.

11 This is the term used by Anne Olivier Bell. See *Diary*, 1, p. 26n.

12 Fry had read Natural Science at Cambridge, and was familiar with Head's pioneering work in neurology. Head had also treated Fry's wife, who later died in an asylum.

13 In *Mrs Dalloway*, Dr Holmes becomes similarly annoyed; in *The Voyage Out*, Dr Rodriguez becomes incensed when a second opinion is sought.

14 G. H. Savage, 'Moral Insanity', *Journal of Mental Science*, 27, 1881, pp. 147-55. Hereafter cited in the text as (Savage, 1881c).

15 In 1891 Savage published an article entitled 'The Influence of Surroundings on the Production of Insanity', *Journal of Mental Science*, 37, 1891, pp. 529-35. Hereafter cited in the text as (Savage, 1891a). While he had previously held that insanity was due primarily to hereditary or physical factors, in this article Savage acknowledges that the patient's environment might be a contributing factor to behaviour classified as mad. The significance

of this change in Savage's thinking is discussed as the chapter proceeds.

16 Savage's concern with power here is very similar to the views expressed by Sir William Bradshaw in *Mrs Dalloway*.

17 This distinction allows Savage to attribute moral insanity to infants. See below and Savage, 1881c, p. 150.

18 Disease characterized by the presence of a fever.

19 Savage was very interested in the relation between influenza and the neuroses, and his thinking on this subject is presented in three articles: 'Influenza and Neurosis', *Journal of Mental Science*, 38, 1892, pp. 360-4. Hereafter cited in the text as (Savage, 1892b). 'Relationship Between Influenza and the Neuroses', *Transactions of the Medical Society of London*, 16, 1892, pp. 51-77. Hereafter cited in the text as (Savage, 1892c). 'Post-Influenzal Neuroses and Psychoses', *Medical Press and Circular*, 96, 1913, pp. 578-81. Hereafter cited in the text as (Savage, 1913a). These articles are of interest in that Virginia often suffered from influenza.

20 It will be noted that Quentin Bell is guilty of the same fault in his biography of Virginia, in those passages where he deals with sanity and madness. Nigel Nicolson, in his notes and commentaries on the *Letters*, does the same thing — confuses the medical or psychiatric with the moral.

21 In *The Divided Self*, Joan, one of Laing's patients, says that 'It's too awful if the doctor is going to be hurt by the sickness' (p. 168). This moralistic and defensive detachment from his patients often blinds Savage to the significance of their behaviour. This may be seen in many of the case histories which Savage relates throughout his work. It is also interesting to note how far removed Savage's view is from the one that Freud was on the verge of developing. Savage cannot be taken to task for his ignorance of Freud, though Craig, Wright and Hyslop, all contemporaries of Freud, either ignored or ridiculed his work.

22 G. H. Savage, 'Alternation of Neuroses', *Journal of Mental Science*, 32, 1887, p. 486. Hereafter cited in the text as (Savage, 1887a).

23 We remember Septimus's plight in *Mrs Dalloway*: 'Once you fall, Septimus repeated to himself, human nature is on you. Holmes and Bradshaw are on you. They scour the desert. They fly screaming into the wilderness. The rack and the thumbscrew are applied' (*MD*, p. 108).

24 Spater and Parsons, p. 146.

25 G. H. Savage, 'The Pathology of Insanity', *British Medical Journal*, 2, 1884, p. 239. Hereafter cited in the text as (Savage, 1884d).

26 G. H. Savage, 'On Some Modes of Treatment of Insanity as a Functional Disorder', *Guy's Hospital Reports*, 29, 1887, pp. 87-112. Hereafter cited in the text as (Savage, 1887b).

27 G. H. Savage, 'Insanity of Conduct', *Journal of Mental Science*, 42, 1896, pp. 1-17. Hereafter cited in the text as (Savage, 1896a). It is in the light of Savage's classifications of insanity ('moral',

'of conduct', etc.) that Virginia's comment to Violet Dickinson, 'I am dining with Savage tomorrow night, and I think I shall ask him what bee gets in my bonnet when I write to you. Sympathetic insanity, I expect it is,' has meaning (*Letters*, 1, p. 198).

28 G. H. Savage, 'Functional Mental Disorders', *The Lancet*, 1, 1905, pp. 409-11. Hereafter cited in the text as (Savage, 1905).

29 It must be noted that while Savage was unaware of some of the gross contradictions within his oeuvre, he nevertheless showed a lively critical intelligence where some problems of scientific epistemology were concerned. His best paper on this subject is 'The Definite in Medical Teaching', *The Medical Magazine*, 1, 1892, pp. 211-20.

30 Savage was much involved in the debate (which still continues) between law and psychiatry, not only where criminal cases are concerned, but with regard to the rights of the certified. Savage's papers on this subject are: 'The Case of Gouldstone', *Journal of Mental Science*, 29, 1884, pp. 534-9. 'Our Duties in Reference to the Signing of Lunacy-Certificates', *British Medical Journal*, 1, 1885, pp. 692-3. 'On Unsoundness of Mind and Insanity', *The Medical Magazine*, 22, pp. 14-24. Hereafter cited in the text as (Savage, 1903a). 'Uncertifiable Insanity and Certain Forms of Moral Defect', *Birmingham Medical Review*, 54, 1903, pp. 741-54. Hereafter cited in the text as (Savage, 1903b). 'The Feeble-Minded and Their Care', *The Medical Press and Circular*, 87, 1909, pp. 522-4.

31 'I wish to substantiate the distinction between simple medical unsoundness and lunacy from the certificate itself which says definitely that the person whom we have examined is a person of unsound mind, *and* a fit and proper person to be detained for treatment. Therefore a lunacy certificate implies two things to my mind: that the person is of unsound mind, and, in addition, that he is a person to be detained for treatment. Legal authorities of the Crown, as I have said, have contended that it means that the two are parallel; that being a person of unsound mind he therefore is a person who should be detained for treatment. But surely no one can for a moment, when considering the matter fully, admit that unsoundness of mind is necessarily insanity.' (Savage, 1903a, pp. 14-15.)

32 G. H. Savage, 'The Treatment of the Insane', *The Hospital*, 41, 1906-7, pp. 457-60. Hereafter cited in the text as (Savage, 1906-7).

33 G. H. Savage, 'The Factors of Insanity', *The Lancet*, 2, 1907, pp. 1137-40. Hereafter cited in the text as (Savage, 1907).

34 G. H. Savage, 'The Presidential Address, Delivered at the Opening Meeting of the Section of Psychiatry of the Royal Society of Medicine, on October 22nd, 1912', *Journal of Mental Science*, 59, 1913, pp. 14-27. Hereafter cited in the text as (Savage, 1913b).

35 This is not to say that morality has no place in medicine, that medicine should be amoral. Rather, it means that if a man is to be

judged as ill, then his conduct must not be seen, at the same time, as immoral. It must be the result of his illness. If a man's misconduct is to be judged by moral standards, then he must be seen as morally responsible for it. He cannot be seen as both 'mad' and 'bad'.

36 In *The Divided Self*, Laing notes three stages in the progress of an individual who is eventually labelled mad: '(1) The patient was a *good*, normal, healthy child; until she gradually began (2) To be *bad*, to do or say things that caused great distress, and which were on the whole "put down" to naughtiness or badness, until (3) This went beyond all tolerable limits so that she could only be regarded as completely mad' (Laing, p. 181).

37 Savage writes in the past tense as he is relating his thoughts while on a recent mountain-climbing expedition.

38 It should be noted that Savage, in this work, makes no effort to unite these disparate causes within some central theoretical framework — his choice of causes appears at first to be random. However, they appear less random when a pattern suggesting certain social and political assumptions begins to appear.

39 Again, these are the methods of Sir William Bradshaw.

40 Savage's use of the term 'gospel' serves to suggest further the nature of the medical mission where insanity is concerned.

41 T. S. Kuhn, *The Structure of Scientific Revolutions*, Chicago: University of Chicago Press, 1970.

42 It is interesting to note Savage's use of the term 'normal' here. A man's 'normal mind' seems to signify his individual *tabula rasa* prior to the time when his school, college and profession write on it.

43 I discuss Savage's role in relation to these forms of treatment at the end of this chapter, in the context of the controversy which arose during his last days at Bethlem.

44 G. H. Savage, 'Heredity in the Neuroses', *British Medical Journal*, 1, 1897, p. 128. Hereafter cited in the text as (Savage, 1897).

45 Charles Rycroft, *A Critical Dictionary of Psychoanalysis*, Harmondsworth: Penguin, 1977, p. 97.

46 G. H. Savage, 'The Mental Disorders of Childhood', *The Hospital*, 43, 1908, pp. 519-21. Hereafter cited in the text as (Savage, 1908b).

47 The passage continues, 'and I remember an interesting fact which came to light when talking to some medical men in the north of London just after a big epidemic of whooping cough in that district. One of them told me, and his experience was confirmed by others, that the disease was often found to disappear after successful vaccination, an example of how a real disease may cure a neurosis.'

48 After asserting that 'Every result has a cause', Savage concludes that 'Talking aloud and laughing causelessly are important symptoms of dissolution' (Savage, 1907, p. 1138).

49 G. H. Savage, 'Uses and Abuses of Chloral Hydrate', *Journal of*

Mental Science, 25, 1879, pp. 4-8. Hereafter cited in the text as (Savage, 1879c).

50 G. H. Savage, 'Hyoscyamine and its Uses', *Journal of Mental Science*, 25, 1879, pp. 177-84. Hereafter cited in the text as (Savage, 1879a).

51 G. H. Savage, 'Case of Mania Greatly Improved by the Use of Hyoscyamine', *Journal of Mental Science*, 27, 1881, pp. 60-2. Hereafter cited in the text as (Savage, 1881a).

52 Monk's House II D 9.

53 Again, these are the methods of Drs Holmes and Bradshaw in *Mrs Dalloway*.

54 Sir James Charles Bucknill was the son of the founding editor of the *Journal of Mental Science*, Sir John Charles Bucknill. He rebelled against his father's attitudes, and became a reformer of asylum practices. See Kathleen Jones, *Mental Health and Social Policy 1845-1959*.

55 Editorial, *The Lancet*, 2, 1888, p. 680.

56 This letter was entitled 'The Mechanical Restraint of the Insane', *The Lancet*, 2, 1888, pp. 738-9. Hereafter cited in the text as (Savage, 1888a).

57 *The Lancet*, 2, 1888, p. 946.

58 Lady Bradshaw is a case in point. This is the manner in which Bradshaw deals with Septimus in *Mrs Dalloway*.

59 Virginia Woolf, *Three Guineas*, London: Hogarth Press, 1938, p. 33. Hereafter cited in the text as (*TG*).

60 G. H. Savage, 'On Insanity and Marriage', *Journal of Mental Science*, 57, 1911, pp. 97-112. Hereafter cited in the text as (Savage, 1911b).

61 She neglects to say precisely what she means by this term; one criterion, as we shall see, is to be unemployed.

5   A Sympathetic Empiricist: Sir Henry Head

1 Henry Head, 'On Disturbances of Sensation, With Especial Reference to the Pain of Visceral Disease', *Brain*, 16, 1893, pp. 1-33; On Disturbances of Sensation, With Especial Reference to the Pain of Visceral Disease. Part II: Head and Neck', *Brain*, 17, 1894, pp. 339-480; 'On Disturbances etc. Pain in Diseases of the Heart and Lungs', *Brain*, 19, 1896, pp. 153-276.

2 J. D. Rolleston, 'Sir Henry Head', *Dictionary of National Biography 1931-1940*, pp. 410-12. Rolleston's article is long and informative, and gives a good, concise explanation of Head's achievements in non-technical terms.

3 Henry Head et al., *Studies in Neurology*, 2 vols., London: H. Froude, 1920. Hereafter cited in the text as (Head, 1920c).

4 Henry Head, *Aphasia and Kindred Disorders*, 2 vols., Cambridge: Cambridge University Press, 1926.

5 'They were talking about this Bill. Some case Sir William was mentioning, lowering his voice. It had its bearing upon what he was saying about the deferred effects of shell shock' (*MD*, p. 202).
6 Rolleston, p. 411.
7 Jonathan Miller, *The Body in Question*, London: Jonathan Cape, 1979. See my review, 'Human Bodies?' in *Books & Issues*, 1 (1), 1979, pp. 21-5.
8 Gordon Rattray Taylor, *Natural History of the Mind*, London: Secker and Warburg, 1979, pp. 173-5.
9 I. A. Richards, *Principles of Literary Criticism*, 2nd ed., London: Kegan, Paul, Trench, Trubner and Co., 1926.
10 A good explanation of Head's 'body scheme' may be found in E. Clarke and K. Dewhurst, *An Illustrated History of Brain Function*, Berkeley: University of California Press, 1972, p. 132.
11 Kurt Koffka, *Principles of Gestalt Psychology*, London: Routledge & Kegan Paul, 1935, pp. 15, 100-2, 117, 173, 424n, 438, 514-20.
12 Seymour Fisher and Sidney E. Cleveland, *Body Image and Personality*, Princeton: Van Nostrand, 1968, p. 206. Quoted in Ted Polhemus, ed., *Social Aspects of the Human Body*, Harmondsworth: Penguin, 1978, p. 114.
13 Henry Head, *Destroyers and Other Verses*, Oxford: Humphrey Milford/Oxford University Press, 1919, p. 80.
14 G. Riddoch, 'Personal Appreciation' in Head's obituary, *British Medical Journal*, 2, 1940, p. 541.
15 Rolleston, p. 411.
16 Quentin Bell tells us that from 20 August Leonard began to keep a secret diary in a code composed of Sinhalese and Tamil characters, in which he recorded the vicissitudes of his wife's health. See Bell, 2, p. 14.
17 Bell, 2, Appendix A, pp. 227-52.
18 *Beginning Again*, p. 155.
19 Ibid., p. 156.
20 In final chapter of this work.
21 See R. D. Laing and Aaron Esterson, *Sanity, Madness and the Family*, Harmondsworth: Penguin, 1970, pp. 93, 96.
22 Henry Head, 'Some Mental States Associated With Visceral Disease in the Sane', *British Medical Journal*, 2, 1895, pp. 768-9. Hereafter cited in the text as (Head, 1895).
23 *Black's Medical Dictionary*, 31st ed. defines viscera as 'the general name given to the large organs lying within the cavities of the chest and abdomen' (p. 904).
24 Henry Head, 'Some Principles of Neurology', *The Lancet*, 2, 1918, p. 659. Hereafter cited in the text as (Head, 1918).
25 'Ah yes (those general practitioners!) thought Sir William. It took half his time to undo their blunders. Some were irreparable' (*MD*, p. 106).
26 Henry Head, 'Disease and Diagnosis', *British Medical Journal*, 1, 1919, p. 365. Hereafter cited in the text as (Head, 1919). My italics.

27 Henry Head, 'Observations on the Elements of the Psycho-Neuroses', *British Medical Journal*, 1, 1920, pp. 389-92. Hereafter cited in the text as (Head, 1920a).

28 Unfortunately, Head does not give a definition of the term 'psycho-neurosis'. However, since he displays a good knowledge of Freud in his later articles, and a good deal of agreement with him over certain issues, it is reasonable to assume that Head's definition may be similar to Freud's. Charles Rycroft gives the following definition of psycho-neurosis in his *A Critical Dictionary of Psychoanalysis*: 'Technical psychoanalytical term for one group of the neuroses, viz. those in which the symptoms are interpretable as manifestations of conflict between ego and id. Psychoneurosis differs from psychosis in that reality-testing is unimpaired, i.e., the patient has insight into the fact that he is ill and that his symptoms are valid; from the perversions in that symptoms are in themselves distressing and that the ego is intact; from character neurosis in that the conflict has produced symptoms and not character traits; and from actual neurosis in that the conflict dates from the past. The three subdivisions of psychoneurosis are *conversion hysteria*, *anxiety hysteria* (phobia), and *obsessional neurosis*. They have in common not only the characteristics cited above but also that they are accessible to psychoanalytical treatment' (p. 131).

29 Henry Head, 'Discussion on Early Symptoms and Signs of Nervous Disease and Their Interpretation', *British Medical Journal*, 2, 1920, p. 692. Hereafter cited in the text as (Head, 1920b).

30 Henry Head, 'The Diagnosis of Hysteria', *British Medical Journal*, 1, 1922, p. 827. Hereafter cited in the text as (Head, 1922).

31 However, on p. 768, at the beginning of the article, Head writes of attacks of melancholia, 'These attacks are completely cause-less and may occur with such suddenness as to interrupt a conversation.'

32 ' "Try to think as little about yourself as possible," said Sir William kindly' (*MD*, p. 109).

33 Phyllis Rose, *Woman of Letters: A Life of Virginia Woolf*, London and Henley: Routledge and Kegan Paul, 1978, p. 86.

6   Enforcing Conformity: Sir Maurice Craig

1 Obituary, *British Medical Journal*, 1, 1935, pp. 87-8.
2 Ibid., p. 87.
3 Ibid., p. 87.
4 See *MD*, p. 202.
5 Maurice Craig, *Psychological Medicine*, London: J. and A. Churchill, 1905. Hereafter cited in the text as (Craig, 1905).
6 Maurice Craig, *Nerve Exhaustion*, London: J. and A. Churchill, 1922.

7   Although Leonard says (*Beginning Again*, p. 178) that it was
    Dr Maurice Wright who gave him the certificate, Virginia wrote
    on 14 May 1916 to Vanessa, 'Leonard went to Craig who said that
    he would give him a certificate of unfitness on his own account,
    as well as mine. He had written a very strong letter, saying that L.
    is highly nervous, suffers from permanent tremor, & would prob-
    ably break down if in the army. Also that I am still in a very shaky
    state, & would very likely have a bad mental breakdown if they
    took him' (Bell, 2, p. 30n). Spater and Parsons give this account:
    'The passage of the Military Service Act in 1916, with its pro-
    visions for conscription, had brought new anxieties. Although
    Leonard was 35, he was in danger of being called up. Two Harley
    Street Doctors (Craig and Hyslop) who had been treating Leonard
    for years certified that he was unfit for service because of "an
    inherited Nervous Tremor which is quite uncontrollable" and
    headaches that "easily come on with fatigue". Dr. Craig, who
    had been consulted about Virginia's health, mentioned that
    Leonard had personally nursed Virginia through her mental break-
    downs and stated that it would be highly detrimental to her health
    if Leonard's care were removed. Happily, the decision of the
    Military Service Act Tribunal granted him exemption from military
    service on medical grounds, which removed another question mark
    from their lives. Virginia wrote to her friend Ka Cox: "Leonard has
    been completely exempted from serving the Country in any
    capacity. He went before the military doctors trembling like an
    aspen leaf, with certificates to say he would tremble and has
    trembled and would never cease from trembling. It's a great mercy
    for us" ' (Spater and Parsons, pp. 84-90).
8   *Beginning Again*, pp. 159-60.
9   Spater and Parsons, p. 73. Leonard received similar treatment.
    Virginia writes to Janet Case on 20? March 1914, 'Leonard is
    better, according to him, and to me too. In fact I think if only I
    can behave now, he will soon be quite right. (Dr Maurice) Craig
    gave him a new medicine, and said he would get well if he was
    sensible. He's now fixed his mind on weighing eleven stones, and
    so he certainly will' (*Letters*, 2, p. 45). 'a man who went in weigh-
    ing seven stone six comes out weighing twelve' (*MD*, p. 110).
10 'a book said to want doing by Ponsonby'. The editors include the
    following note: 'Probably Arthur Ponsonby (later Lord Ponsonby
    of Shulbrede) the pacifist politician and author)' (*Diary*, 2, p. 77n).
11 Sidney and Beatrice Webb, the Fabian campaigners.
12 A fuller portrait of Norton may be found in David Garnett, ed.,
    Carrington: Letters and Extracts From Her Diaries, Oxford:
    Oxford University Press, 1979, pp. 83, 96, 110, 29n, 32, 250.
    See especially Michael Holroyd, *Lytton Strachey: A Biography*,
    Harmondsworth: Penguin, 1979, pp. 365-6.
13 The use of legalistic jargon may be significant here.
14 See Kathleen Nott, *The Good Want Power: An Essay on the*

Psychological Possibilities of Liberalism, London: Jonathan Cape, 1977. Nott shows how unclear and ambiguous language bedevils the philosophy of liberalism.

15 Maurice Craig, 'What Is Meant By Insanity', *The Hospital*, 49, 1911, pp. 603-5. Hereafter cited in the text as (Craig, 1911).

16 Maurice Craig, 'Some Aspects of Education and Training in Relation to Mental Disorder' (The Third Maudsely Lecture, delivered at the Quarterly Meeting of the Medico-Psychological Association of Great Britain and Ireland, 25 May 1922), *Journal of Mental Science*, 68, 1922, pp. 209-28. Hereafter cited in the text as (Craig, 1922b).

17 Maurice Craig, 'The Importance of Mental Hygiene in Other Departments of Medical Practice', *Mental Hygiene*, 14, 1930, pp. 565-79. Hereafter cited in the text as (Craig, 1930).

18 An autotoxin is a poisonous substance produced by changes within the organism.

19 Joseph Berke, *I Haven't Had to Go Mad Here: The Psychotic's Journey From Dependence to Autonomy*, Harmondsworth: Penguin, 1979, p. 42.

20 Craig's estate was valued at £41,357 at his death.

21 Maurice Craig, 'The Treatment of Insomnia', *The Practitioner*, 115, 1925, pp. 98-9. Hereafter cited in the text as (Craig, 1925b).

22 The prohibitions of Savage and Craig against hard work and advancement for certain parts of the public form a curious footnote to the history of incarceration as told by Michel Foucault in *Madness and Civilization*. After the seclusion of the lepers, incarceration of the indigent (those who violated the work ethic) and the insane followed. One could at least follow the reasoning of the authorities who built and populated the workhouses (spurious as it was), but the justification for Craig's and Savage's criteria is much more difficult to construct.

7   The Madness of Art: T. B. Hyslop

1 T. B. Hyslop, 'Post-Illusionism and Art in the Insane', *The Nineteenth Century*, 69, 1911, p. 276. Hereafter cited in the text as (Hyslop, 1911).

2 T. B. Hyslop, *The Borderland*, London: P. Allan, 1924, pp. 132-3. Hereafter cited in the text as (Hyslop, 1924).

3 Michel Foucault, *Madness and Civilization: A History of Insanity in the Age of Reason*, London: Tavistock, 1977, pp. 241-78.

4 Ibid., p. 257.

5 Ibid., p. 261. This, in a nutshell, is what Flush experiences.

6 Ibid., p. 276.

7 T. B. Hyslop, *Mental Physiology*, London: J. and A. Churchill, 1895. Hereafter cited in the text as (Hyslop, 1895).

8 T. B. Hyslop, *The Great Abnormals*, London: P. Allan, 1925.

Hereafter cited in the text as (Hyslop, 1925).

9   T. B. Hyslop, *Mental Handicaps in Art*, London: Ballière, Tindall & Cox, 1927.

10 W. H. B. Stoddart, Obituary, *British Medical Journal*, 1, 1933, p. 347. My italics.

11 T. B. Hyslop, 'Degeneration: The Medico-Psychological Aspects of Modern Art, Music, Literature, Science and Religion', *Transactions of the Medical Society of London*, 41, 1918, pp. 271-95. Hereafter cited in the text as (Hyslop, 1918).

12 T. B. Hyslop, 'A Discussion of Occupation and Environment as Causative Factors of Insanity', *British Medical Journal*, 2, 1905, p. 941. Hereafter cited in the text as (Hyslop, 1905).

13 T. B. Hyslop, 'Address on Clinical Psychiatry', *The Medical Magazine*, 22, 193, p. 708. Hereafter cited in the text as (Hyslop, 1913).

14 T. B. Hyslop, 'Faith and Mental Instability', in *Medicine and the Church*, ed. Geoffrey Rhodes, London, 1910, pp. 103-13. Hereafter cited in the text as (Hyslop, 1910).

15 T. B. Hyslop, 'The Mental Deficiency Bill, 1912', *Journal of Mental Science*, 57, 1912, pp. 548-97. Hereafter cited in the text as (Hyslop, 1912).

16 *Beginning Again*, p. 94.

17 See my review of Susan Dean's *Hardy's Poetic Vision in 'The Dynasts'*, *Notes & Queries*, 26 (3), 1979, pp. 365-6. This is not to say that one simply makes *any* meaning of the text; but that, following the basic structures and guides laid down in the text, variant readings are possible; there is no one correct reading which sums up the work once and for all. The ultimate meaning of the text always eludes our grasp.

18 Wolfgang Iser, *The Implied Reader*, Baltimore and London: Johns Hopkins University Press, 1974.

19 See David Bleich's *Subjective Criticism*, Baltimore and London: Johns Hopkins University Press, 1978.

8   The 'Discourse of Power': Burley and *Flush*

1   Hayden White, 'Michel Foucault' in *Structuralism and Since: From Lévi-Strauss to Derrida*, ed. John Sturrock, Oxford: Oxford University Press, 1979, pp. 81-115.

2   Ibid., p. 89.

3   Ibid., p. 90.

4   Ibid., pp. 89-90, my italics.

5   Mitchell Leaska, 'Virginia Woolf's *The Voyage Out*: Character Deduction and the Function of Ambiguity', *Virginia Woolf Quarterly*, 1 (2), 1973, pp. 18-41.

6   Ibid., p. 36, Leaska's italics.

7   Ibid., pp. 36-7, my italics.

8   Ibid., p. 37, my italics.

9 Poole, p. 40.
10 See, for example, *Letters*, 1, pp. 62, 70-1, 73, 76, 82-4, 97, 176.
11 See *Letters*, 3; Nigel Nicolson's *Portrait of a Marriage*; and, of course, *Orlando*.
12 See Bell, 2, pp. 26-7.
13 D. S. Savage, 'The Mind of Virginia Woolf', *South-Atlantic Quarterly*, 46, 1947, pp. 556-73.
14 'At this time, Virginia was still cheerfully expecting to have children. Leonard already had misgivings but I do not think that Virginia became aware of them until the beginning of 1913' (Bell, 2, p. 7).
15 *Downhill All The Way*, p. 146.
16 See Geffrey Meyers, *Married To Genius*, London: London Magazine Editions, 1977. Meyers writes of Leonard, 'his fanatical capacity for work was clearly a sublimation of his sexual drive just as his passionate attachment to dogs was a compensation for his lack of children' (p. 101).
17 *Sowing*, p. 12.
18 *Beginning Again*, p. 173, my italics.
19 See Jean-Paul Sartre, *The Words*, Greenwich, CT: Fawcett Premier, 1964, pp. 18-19. 'Last year at the dog's cemetery, I recognized my grandfather's maxims in the trembling discourse that ran from grave to grave: dogs know how to love; they are gentler than human beings, more faithful; they have tact, a flawless instinct that enables them to recognize Good, to distinguish the good from the wicked. "Polonius," said one unconsoled mistress, "you are better than I. You would not have survived me. I survive you." An American friend was with me. With a burst of indignation he kicked a cement dog and broke its ear. He was right; when one loves children and animals *too* much, one loves them against human beings.'
20 *Growing*, p. 91.
21 Ibid., pp. 94-5.
22 Ibid., p. 95.
23 Spater and Parsons, p. 52.
24 *The Journey Not the Arrival Matters*, pp. 20-1.
25 Ibid., pp. 50-1.
26 Spater and Parsons, p. 60.
27 Ibid., p. 60.
28 A long list of them may be found in the Appendix to *Letters*, 1, p. 509.
29 *Moments of Being*, p. 47.
30 Karin Stephen, wife of Virginia's brother Adrian.
31 In 1930 Virginia went to see a play entitled *The Barretts of Wimpole Street*. See *Letters*, 4, p. 224.
32 *Moments of Being*, p. 45.
33 Ibid., p. 40.
34 Virginia Woolf, *A Room of One's Own*, Harmondsworth: Penguin, 1975, pp. 7-8.

35 *Moments of Being*, pp. 28-9, my italics.
36 J. Laplanche and J.-B. Pontalis, *The Language of Psychoanalysis*, London, 1973. Cited in Malcolm Bowie, 'Jacques Lacan', in *Structuralism and Since*, ed. John Sturrock, p. 119n.
37 Ibid., p. 143.
38 T. S. Eliot, *The Complete Poems and Plays of T. S. Eliot*, London: Faber, 1975, p. 333. *The Family Reunion*, I:3.

Conclusion

1 Poole, p. 5.
2 Leonard Woolf, *An Autobiography 1: 1880-1911*, Oxford: Oxford University Press, 1980.
3 Leonard Woolf, *Quack, Quack!* London: Hogarth Press, 1935.
4 Quentin Bell, 'Introduction' to Leonard Woolf, *An Autobiography 1: 1880-1911*, pp. xii-xiii.
5 P. N. Furbank, *E. M. Forster: A Life, Vol. 1*, London: Secker and Warburg, 1977, p. 217.
6 Ibid., p. 217.

Bibliography of Literary, Philosophical and Critical Works

This bibliography includes, in addition to works cited in the text, works which have exerted a significant influence on my reading of Virginia Woolf.

Alexander, Ian W., 'The Phenomenological Philosophy in France', in *Currents of Thought in French Literature*, eds. T. V. Benn et al., Oxford: Basil Blackwell, 1966

Alvarez, A., *The Savage God*, Harmondsworth: Penguin, 1974

Armitage, Doris May, *A Challenge to Neurasthenia*, London: Williams & Norgate, 1930

Bachelard, Gaston, *The Poetics of Reverie*, Boston: Beacon Press, 1971

—, *The Poetics of Space*, Boston: Beacon Press, 1969

—, *The Psychoanalysis of Fire*, Boston: Beacon Press, 1964

Bannan, John F., *The Philosophy of Merleau-Ponty*, New York: Harcourt, Brace & World, 1967

Barnes, Hazel L., *Sartre*, London: Quartet, 1974

Barthes, Roland, *A Lover's Discourse*, tr. Richard Howard, London: Jonathan Cape, 1979

—, *The Pleasure of the Text*, tr. Richard Howard, London: Jonathan Cape, 1975

—, *Roland Barthes by Roland Barthes*, tr. Richard Howard, London and Basingstoke: Macmillan, 1977

—, *S/Z*, tr. Richard Howard, London: Jonathan Cape, 1975

Bazin, Nancy Topping, *Virginia Woolf and the Androgynous Vision*, New York: Rutgers University Press, 1973

Bell, Anne Olivier, Letter, *Virginia Woolf Miscellany*, 14, 1980, p. 7

Bell, Quentin, *Virginia Woolf: A Biography*, 2 vols., St Albans, Herts: Triad/Paladin, 1976

Bennett, Joan, *Virginia Woolf: Her Art As A Novelist*, Cambridge: Cambridge University Press, 1945

Benthall, Jonathan and Polhemus, Ted, eds. *The Body As a Medium of Expression*, London: Allen Lane, 1975

Berke, Joseph, *I Haven't Had To Go Mad Here: The Psychotic's Journey From Dependence to Autonomy*, Harmondsworth: Penguin, 1979

Black's Medical Dictionary, 31st ed., ed. William A. R. Thomson, London: A. & C. Black, 1978

Blackstone, Bernard, *Virginia Woolf: A Commentary*, London: Hogarth Press, 1972

Bleich, David, *Readings and Feelings*, Urbana, IL: National Council of Teachers of English, 1975

—, *Subjective Criticism*, Baltimore and London: Johns Hopkins University Press, 1978

—, 'The Subjective Paradigm in Science, Psychology, and Criticism', *New Literary History*, Winter, 1976, pp. 313-34

Bowen, Elizabeth, 'The Principle of Her Art Was Joy', *New York Times Book Review*, 21 February 1954

Bozarth-Campbell, Alla, *The World's Body: An Incarnational Aesthetic of Interpretation*, University, AL and London: University of Alabama Press, 1979

Brenan, Gerald, *Personal Record 1920-1972*, Cambridge: Cambridge University Press, 1979

Breuer, Josef and Freud, Sigmund, *Studies on Hysteria*, Harmondsworth: Penguin, 1974

Callieri, Bruno, 'Perplexity -- Psychopathological and Phenomenological Notes' in *Analecta Husserliana Vol. VII*, ed. A. Tymieniecka, Dordrecht: D. Reidel, 1978, pp. 51-64

Carrington, Dora, *Letters and Extracts From Her Diary*, ed. David Garnett, Oxford: Oxford University Press, 1979

Caruso, Igor, A., *Existential Psychology*, London: Darton, Longman and Todd, 1964

Clarke, E. and Dewhurst, K., *An Illustrated History of Brain Function*, Berkeley: University of California Press, 1972

Crisp, A. H., *Anorexia Nervosa: Let Me Be*, London: Academic Press, 1980

Culler, Jonathan, *Structuralist Poetics*, London: Routledge, Kegan and Paul, 1975

Daiches, David, *Virginia Woolf*, New York: New Directions, 1963

Doubrovsky, Serge, *The New Criticism in France*, Chicago: University of Chicago Press, 1973

Edel, Leon, *Bloomsbury: A House of Lions*, London: Hogarth Press, 1979

ver Eecke, Wilfried, 'Freedom, Self-Reflection and Intersubjectivity or Psychoanalysis and the Limits of Phenomenological Method', *Analecta Husserliana Vol. III*, ed. A. Tymieniecka, Dordrecht: D. Reidel, 1974, pp. 252-70

Eliot, George, *Middlemarch*, Harmondsworth: Penguin, 1965

Eliot, T. S., *The Complete Poems and Plays of T. S. Eliot*, London: Faber, 1975

Eng, Erling, 'Constitution and Intentionality in Psychosis' in *Analecta Husserliana Vol. III*, ed. A. Tymieniecka, Dordrecht: D. Reidel, 1974, pp. 279-89

Esterson, Aaron, *The Leaves of Spring*, Harmondsworth: Penguin, 1972

Ey, Henri, 'the Subject of Action — Phenomenology and Psychotherapy' in *Analecta Husserliana Vol. VII*, ed. A. Tymieniecka,
Dordrecht: D. Reidel, 1978, pp. 99-106

Fedida, Pierre, 'Depressive Doing and Acting — A Phenomenological
Contribution to the Psychoanalytical Theory of Depression' in
Analecta Husserliana Vol. VII, ed. A. Tymieniecka, Dordrecht:
D. Reidel, 1978, pp. 81-92

Fisher, S. and Cleveland, S. E., *Body Image and Personality*, Princeton,
NJ: Van Nostrand, 1968

Fleishman, Avrom, *Virginia Woolf: A Critical Reading*, Baltimore and
London: Johns Hopkins University Press, 1977

Forster, E. M., *Abinger Harvest*, Harmondsworth: Penguin, 1974

——, *Howard's End*, Harmondsworth: Penguin, 1975

——, *Two Cheers For Democracy*, Harmondsworth: Penguin, 1965

Forster, Robert and Ranum, Orest, eds., *Food and Drink in History*,
Baltimore and London: Johns Hopkins University Press, 1979

Foucault, Michel, *The Birth of the Clinic*, London: Tavistock, 1976

——, *Discipline and Punish*, Harmondsworth: Penguin, 1979

——, *Madness and Civilization: A History of Insanity in the Age of
Reason*, London: Tavistock, 1977

Fowles, John, *The French Lieutenant's Woman*, St Albans: Triad/
Panther, 1977

Frankl, Viktor, *The Doctor and The Soul*, Harmondsworth: Penguin,
1973

——, *Psychotherapy and Existentialism*, Harmondsworth: Penguin, 1978

Freedman, Ralph, *The Lyrical Novel*, Princeton, NJ: Princeton University Press, 1963

Fry, Roger, *The Letters of Roger Fry*, 2 vols., ed. Denys Sutton, Chatto
& Windus, 1972

Frye, Northrup, *The Anatomy of Criticism*, Princeton, NJ: Princeton
University Press, 1957

Garnett, David, *The Familiar Faces*, London: Chatto & Windus, 1962

Gelfant, Blanch, 'Love and Conversion in *Mrs Dalloway*', *Criticism*, 8,
1966, pp. 229-45

Goldstein, Jan Ellen, 'The Woolfs' Response to Freud', *Psychoanalytic
Quarterly*, 43, 1974, pp. 438-76

Guiget, Jean, *Virginia Woolf and Her Works*, tr. Jean Stewart, London:
Hogarth Press, 1969

Halliburton, David, *Edgar Allan Poe: A Phenomenological View*,
Princeton, NJ: Princeton University Press, 1973

Hawkes, Terrence, *Structuralism and Semiotics*, London: Methuen,
1977

Heidegger, Martin, *Being and Time*, London: SCM Press, 1962

Holbrook, David, *Sylvia Plath: Poetry and Existence*, London: Athlone
Press, 1976

Holland, Norman, *Poems in Persons: An Introduction to The Psychoanalysis of Literature*, New York: Norton, 1973

——, *5 Readers Reading*, New Haven, CT: Yale University Press, 1975

——, 'The New Paradigm: Subjective or Transactive?', *New Literary History*, Winter, 1976, pp. 335-46

Holroyd, Michael, *Lytton Strachey: A Biography*, Harmondsworth, Penguin, 1979

Hungerford, A., 'Mrs Woolf, Freud, and J. D. Beresford', *Literature and Psychology*, 5, 1955, pp. 49-51

Husserl, Edmund, *Cartesian Meditations*, The Hague: Martinus Nijhoff, 1973

——, *Phenomenology and the Crisis of Philosophy*, New York: Harper and Row, 1965

Ingarden, Roman, 'Psychologism and Psychology in Literary Research', *New Literary History*, 5 (2), 1974, pp. 213-23

Iser, Wolfgang, *The Act of Reading*, Baltimore and London: Johns Hopkins University Press, 1978

——, *The Implied Reader*, Baltimore and London: Johns Hopkins University Press, 1974

——, 'The Reading Process: A Phenomenological Approach', *New Literary History*, 3, 1972, pp. 279-99

Jones, Kathleen, *A History of the Mental Health Services*, London and Henley: Routledge & Kegan Paul, 1960

Kaelin, Eugene, *An Existentialist Aesthetic*, Madison, WI: University of Wisconsin Press, 1966

Kamiya, Miyeko, 'Virginia Woolf: An Outline of a Study on Her Personality, Illness, Work', *Confinia Psychiatrica* (Basel), 8, 1965, pp. 189-204

Kelley, Alice van Buren, *The Novels of Virginia Woolf: Fact and Vision*, Chicago and London: University of Chicago Press, 1973

Keynes, J. M., *Essays in Biography, Collected Writings Vol. X*, London: Macmillan, 1972

Koffka, Kurt, *Principles of Gestalt Psychology*, London: Routledge & Kegan Paul, 1935

Kuhn, T. S., *The Structure of Scientific Revolutions*, Chicago: University of Chicago Press, 1970

Kupfermann, Jeannette, *The MsTaken Body*, London: Robson, 1979

Laing, R. D., *The Divided Self*, Harmondsworth: Penguin, 1965

——, *The Politics of Experience and the Bird of Paradise*, Harmondsworth: Penguin, 1967

——, *The Politics of the Family*, Harmondsworth: Penguin, 1976

——, *Self and Others*, Harmondsworth: Penguin, 1971

—— and Esterson, Aaron, *Sanity, Madness and the Family*, Harmondsworth: Penguin, 1970

Leaska, Mitchell A., *The Novels of Virginia Woolf: From Beginning to End*, London: Weidenfeld and Nicolson, 1977

——, 'Virginia Woolf's *The Voyage Out*: Character Deduction and the Function of Ambiguity', *Virginia Woolf Quarterly*, 1 (2), 1973, pp. 18-41

Lomas, Peter, *True and False Experience*, London: Allen Lane, 1973

Love, Jean O., *Virginia Woolf: Sources of Madness and Art*, Berkeley and London: University of California Press, 1977

Lund, M. G., 'The Androgynous Moment: Woolf and Eliot', *Renascence*, 12 (2), 1960, pp. 74-8

McConnell, Frank D., 'Death Among the Apple Trees: *The Waves* and the World of Things', *Bucknell Review*, 16, 1968, pp. 23-39

Maitland, F. W., *The Life and Letters of Leslie Stephen*, London: Duckworth, 1906

Mansfield, Katherine, *Letters and Journals*, ed. C. K. Stead, Harmondsworth: Penguin, 1977

May, Rollo, et al., eds., *Existence: A New Dimension in Psychiatry and Psychology*, New York: Basic Books, 1958

Merleau-Ponty, Maurice, *The Essential Writings of Merleau-Ponty*, ed. A. Fisher, New York: Harcourt, Brace & World, 1969

—, *Phenomenology of Perception*, tr. Colin Smith, London and Henley: Routledge, Kegan & Paul, 1962

—, *The Primacy of Perception and Other Essays*, ed. J. M. Edie, Evanston, IL: Northwestern University Press, 1964

—, *The Prose of the World*, tr. John O'Neill, London: Heinemann Educational Books, 1974

—, *The Structure of Behaviour*, Boston: Beacon Press, 1973

Meyers, Geffrey, *Married to Genius*, London: London Magazine Editions, 1977

Miller, Jean Baker, *Psychoanalysis and Women*, Harmondsworth: Penguin, 1973

Miller, Jonathan, *The Body in Question*, London: Jonathan Cape, 1979

Moloney, Michael F., 'The Enigma of Time: Proust, Virginia Woolf and Faulkner', *Thought*, 37, 1957, pp. 69-85

Moore, G. E., *Principia Ethica*, Cambridge: Cambridge University Press, 1959

Naremore, J., *The World Without a Self: Virginia Woolf and the Novel*, New Haven, CT: Yale University Press, 1973

Natanson, Maurice, 'Solipsism and Sociality', *New Literary History*, 5 (1), 1973, pp. 237-44

Nelson, James B., *Embodiment*, London: SPCK, 1978

Nelson, John O., 'G. E. Moore' in *The Encyclopedia of Philosophy*, ed. Paul Edwards, New York: Macmillan/Free Press, 1967

Nicolson, Nigel, *Portrait of a Marriage*, London: Futura, 1974

Noble, Jane Russell, ed., *Recollections of Virginia Woolf*, Harmondsworth: Penguin, 1975

Nott, Kathleen, *The Good Want Power*, London: Jonathan Cape, 1977

Owens, Thomas J., *Phenomenology and Intersubjectivity*, The Hague: Martinus Nijhoff, 1970

Peterson, M. Jeanne, *The Medical Profession in Mid-Victorian London*, Berkeley and London: University of California Press, 1978

Plath, Sylvia, *The Bell Jar*, London: Faber, 1966

Polhemus, Ted, ed., *Social Aspects of the Human Body*, Harmondsworth: Penguin, 1978

Poltawski, Andrzej, 'Ethical Action and Consciousness — Philosophical and Psychiatric Perspectives' in *Analecta Husserliana Vol. VII*, ed. A. Tymieniecka, Dordrecht: D. Reidel, 1978, pp. 115-50

Poole, Roger, 'From Phenomenology to Subjective Method', *New Universities Quarterly*, 29 (4), 1975, pp. 412-40

—, 'Structuralism and Phenomenology: A Literary Approach', *Journal of the British Society for Phenomenology*, 1 (2), 1971, pp. 3-16

—, *Towards Deep Subjectivity*, London: Allen Lane, 1972

—, *The Unknown Virginia Woolf*, Cambridge: Cambridge University Press, 1978

Poulet, Georges, *The Interior Distance*, Anne Arbor, MI: University of Michigan Press, 1964

—, *The Metamorphoses of the Circle*, Baltimore and London: Johns Hopkins University Press, 1966

—, *Proustian Space*, Baltimore and London: John Hopkins University Press, 1977

—, *Studies in Human Time*, Baltimore: Johns Hopkins University Press, 1956

Pound, Ezra, *Selected Poems 1908-1959*, London: Faber, 1975

Presas, Mario A., 'Bodilyness (Leibhaftigkeit) and History in Husserl' in *Analecta Husserliana Vol. VII*, ed. A. Tymieniecka, Dordrecht: D. Reidel, 1978, pp. 37-42

Richards, I. A., *Principles of Literary Criticism*, 2nd ed., London: Kegan, Paul, Trench, Trubner & Co., 1926

Richter, Harvena, *The Inward Voyage*, Princeton, NJ: Princeton University Press, 1970

Rolleston, J. D., 'Sir Henry Head' in *Dictionary of National Biography, 1931-1940*, Oxford: Oxford University Press, 1949, pp. 410-12

Rose, Phyllis, *Woman of Letters: A Life of Virginia Woolf*, London and Henley: Routledge & Kegan Paul, 1978

Rosenbaum, S. P., 'The Philosophical Realism of Virginia Woolf' in *English Literature and British Philosophy*, ed. Rosenbaum, Chicago: University of Chicago Press, 1971

Rosenthall, Michael, *Virginia Woolf*, London: Routledge & Kegan Paul, 1979

Rudnick, Hans S., 'Roman Ingarden's Literary Theory', *Analecta Husserliana Vol. IV*, ed. A. Tymieniecka, Dordrecht: D. Reidel, 1976, pp. 105-19

Rycroft, Charles, *A Critical Dictionary of Psychoanalysis*, Harmondsworth: Penguin, 1977

Said, Edward, *Beginnings*, Baltimore and London: Johns Hopkins University Press, 1978

Sartre, Jean-Paul, *The Words*, Greenwich, CT: Fawcett, Premier, 1964

Savage, D. S., 'The Mind of Virginia Woolf', *South Atlantic Quarterly*, 46, 1947, pp. 556-73

Schlack, Beverly Ann, *Continuing Presences: Virginia Woolf's Use of Literary Allusion*, University Park, PA: Penn State University Press, 1979

Schlipp, Paul Arthur, ed., *The Philosophy of G. E. Moore*, Evanston and Chicago: Northwestern University Press, 1942

Simon, J. K., ed., *Modern French Criticism*, Chicago: University of Chicago Press, 1972

Smith, Colin, *Contemporary French Philosophy*, London: Methuen, 1964

Sontag, Susan, *Illness as Metaphor*, New York: Vintage, 1978

Spater, George and Parsons, Ian, *A Marriage of True Minds: An Intimate Portrait of Leonard and Virginia Woolf*, London: Jonathan Cape/Hogarth Press, 1977

Spender, Stephen, *World Within World*, London: Hamish Hamilton, 1950

Spiegelberg, H., ed., *The Phenomenological Movement*, 2 vols., The Hague: Martinus Nijhoff, 1969

Stephen, Karin, *Psychoanalysis and Medicine: A Study of the Wish to Fall Ill*, Cambridge: Cambridge University Press, 1933

Stephen, Mrs. Leslie (Julia), *Notes From Sick Rooms*, London: Smith Elder and Co., 1883

Strauss, Erwin W., *Phenomenological Psychology*, London: Tavistock, 1966

Sturrock, John A., ed. *Structuralism and Since: From Lévi-Strauss to Derrida*, Oxford: Oxford University Press, 1979

Taylor, Gordon Rattray, *Natural History of the Mind*, London: Secker and Warburg, 1979

Thomson, William A. R., ed., *Black's Medical Dictionary*, 31st ed., London: A. & C. Black, 1978

Trombley, Stephen, 'The Growth of a Cabal', *Bulletin of the Society For the Social History of Medicine*, 23, 1978, pp. 44-7

—, 'Human Bodies?', *Books & Issues*, 1 (1), 1979, pp. 21-5

—, 'Kierkegaard's Contradictions', *Books & Issues*, 1 (2), 1979, pp. 8-9, 28-9

—, 'Review of Susan Dean's *Hardy's Poetic Vision in "The Dynasts"* ', *Notes & Queries*, 23 (3), 1979, pp. 365-6

—, 'Review of Sylvia Plath's *Letters Home* and David Holbrook's *Sylvia Plath: Poetry and Existence*', *Critical Quarterly*, 19 (2), 1977, pp. 93-5

—, 'Virginia Woolf', *Literary Review*, 16, 1980, pp. 21-2

Watkins, Renée, 'Survival In Discontinuity — Virginia Woolf's *Between The Acts*', *Massachusetts Review*, 10, 1969, pp. 356-76

Wellek, Renée and Warren, Austin, *Theory of Literature*, London: Jonathan Cape, 1966

Wilson, J. S., 'Time and Virginia Woolf', *Virginia Quarterly Review*, 18, 1942, pp. 267-76

Wojtyla, Karol, *The Acting Person*, tr. Andrzej Potocki, Dordrecht: D. Reidel, 1979

Woolf, Leonard, *Sowing: An Autobiography of the Years 1880-1904*, London, Hogarth Press, 1960

—, *Growing: An Autobiography of the Years 1904-1911*, London:

Hogarth Press, 1961
—, *Beginning Again: An Autobiography of the Years 1911-1918*, London, Hogarth Press, 1964
—, *Downhill All the Way: An Autobiography of the Years 1919-1939*, London, Hogarth Press, 1967
—, *The Journey Not the Arrival Matters: An Autobiography of the Years 1939-1969*, London: Hogarth Press, 1969
—, *An Autobiography 1: 1880-1911*, Oxford: Oxford University Press, 1980
—, *Quack, Quack!*, London: Hogarth Press, 1935
Woolf, Virginia, *Between The Acts*, Harmondsworth: Penguin 1953
—, *Collected Essays Vol. 1*, ed. Leonard Woolf, London: Hogarth Press, 1966
—, *Collected Essays Vol. 2*, ed. Leonard Woolf, London: Hogarth Press, 1966
—, *Collected Essays Vol. 3*, ed. Leonard Woolf, London: Hogarth Press, 1967
—, *Collected Essays Vol. 4*, ed. Leonard Woolf, London: Hogarth Press, 1967
—, *Diary Vol. 1, 1915-1919*, ed. Anne Olivier Bell, London: Hogarth Press, 1977
—, *Diary Vol. 2, 1920-1924*, ed. Anne Olivier Bell, London: Hogarth Press, 1978
—, *Diary Vol. 3, 1925-1930*, ed. Anne Olivier Bell, London: Hogarth Press, 1980
—, *Flush*, London: Hogarth Press, 1933
—, *A Haunted House and Other Short Stories*, Harmondsworth: Penguin, 1973
—, *Jacob's Room*, Harmondsworth: Penguin, 1965
—, *Letters Vol. 1: The Flight of the Mind 1888-1912*, ed. Nigel Nicolson and Joanne Trautmann, London: Hogarth Press, 1975
—, *Letters Vol. 2: The Question of Things Happening 1912-1922*, ed. Nigel Nicolson and Joanne Trautmann, London: Hogarth Press, 1976
—, *Letters Vol. 3: A Change of Perspective 1923-1928*, ed. Nigel Nicolson and Joanne Trautmann, London: Hogarth Press, 1977
—, *Letters Vol. 4: A Reflection of the Other Person 1929-1931*, ed. Nigel Nicolson and Joanne Trautmann, London: Hogarth Press, 1978
—, *Letters Vol. 5: The Sickle Side of the Moon 1932-1935*, ed. Nigel Nicolson and Joanne Trautmann, London: Hogarth Press, 1979
—, *Letters Vol. 6: Leave the Letters Till We're Dead 1936-1941*, ed. Nigel Nicolson and Joanne Trautmann, London: Hogarth Press, 1980
—, *Moments of Being: Unpublished Autobiographical Writings*, ed. Jeanne Schulkind, London: Sussex University Press, 1976
—, *Mrs Dalloway*, Harmondsworth: Penguin 1964
—, *Night and Day*, Harmondsworth: Penguin, 1969
—, *Orlando: A Biography*, Harmondsworth: Penguin, 1942
—, *Roger Fry: A Biography*, Harmondsworth: Penguin, 1979

——, *A Room of One's Own*, Harmondsworth: Penguin, 1945

——, *Three Guineas*, London: Hogarth Press, 1938

——, *To The Lighthouse*, Harmondsworth: Penguin, 1964

——, *The Voyage Out*, Harmondsworth: Penguin 1970

——, *The Waves*, Harmondsworth: Penguin, 1964

——, *A Writer's Diary*, ed. Leonard Woolf, London: Hogarth Press, 1953

——, *The Years*, Harmondsworth: Penguin, 1968

Zaner, Richard M., *The Problem of Embodiment*, The Hague: Martinus Nijhoff, 1964

Select Bibliography of Works by Virginia Woolf's Doctors

Craig, Maurice, (1905) *Psychological Medicine*, London: J. and A. Churchill

—, (1911) 'What is Meant By Insanity', *The Hospital*, 49, pp. 603-5

—, (1922a) 'Mental Symptoms in Physical Disease', *The Lancet*, 2, pp. 945-9

—, (1922b) 'Some Aspects of Education and Training in Relation to Mental Disorder', *Journal of Mental Science*, 67, pp. 209-28

—, (1922c) *Nerve Exhaustion*, London: J. & A. Churchill

—, (1925a) 'Early Treatment of Mental Disorders', *The Lancet*, 2, pp. 967-9

—, (1925b) ' The Treatment of Insomnia', *The Practitioner*, 115, pp. 97-101

—, (1930) 'The Importance of Mental Hygiene in Other Departments of Medical Practice', *Mental Hygiene*, 14, pp. 565-79

—, 'Obituary', *British Medical Journal*, 1, 1935, pp. 87-8

Head, Henry, (1893) 'On Disturbances of Sensation, With Especial Reference to the Pain of Visceral Disease', *Brain*, 16, pp. 1-133

—, (1894) 'On Disturbances of Sensation, With Especial Reference to the Pain of Visceral Disease, Part II: Head and Neck', *Brain*, 17, pp. 339-480

—, (1895) 'Some Mental States Associated With Visceral Disease in the Sane', *British Medical Journal*, 2, pp. 768-9

—, (1896) 'On Disturbances of Sensation, With Especial Reference to the Pain of Visceral Disease, Part III: Pain in Diseases of the Heart and Lungs', *Brain*, 19, pp. 153-276

—, (1918) 'Some Principles of Neurology', *The Lancet*, 2, pp. 657-60

—, (1919) 'Disease and Diagnosis', *British Medical Journal*, 1, pp. 365-6

—, (1919) *Destroyers and Other Verses*, Oxford: Humphrey Milford/ Oxford University Press

—, (1920a) 'Observations on the Elements of the Psycho-Neuroses', *British Medical Journal*, 1, pp. 389-92

—, (1920b) 'Discussion on Early Symptoms and Signs of Nervous Disease and Their Interpretation', *British Medical Journal*, 2, pp. 691-3

329

——, *Studies in Neurology*, 2 vols., London: H. Froude

——, (1922) 'The Diagnosis of Hysteria', *British Medical Journal*, 1, pp. 827-9

——, (1923-4) 'The Conception of Nervous and Mental Energy', *British Journal of Psychology*, 14, pp. 126-47

——, (1926), *Aphasia and Kindred Disorders*, 2 vols., Cambridge: Cambridge University Press

——, 'Obituary', *British Medical Journal*, 2, 1940, pp. 539-41

——, 'Obituary', *Nature*, 2 November 1940, pp. 583-4

Hyslop, T. B., (1890) 'Parotitis in the Insane', *Journal of Mental Science*, 36, pp. 522-4

——, (1895) *Mental Physiology*, London: J. and A. Churchill

——, (1905) 'A Discussion of Occupation and Environment as Causative Factors of Insanity', *British Medical Journal*, 2, pp. 941-5

——, (1910) 'Faith and Mental Instability' in *Medicine and The Church*, ed. Geoffrey Rhodes, London

——, (1911) 'Post-Illusionism and Art in the Insane', *The Nineteenth Century*, 69, pp. 270-81

——, (1912) 'The Mental Deficiency Bill, 1912', *Journal of Mental Science*, 57, pp. 548-97

——, (1913) 'Address on Clinical Psychiatry', *The Medical Magazine*, 22, pp. 704-12

——, (1915a) 'Anger', *Journal of Mental Science*, 61, pp. 371-91

——, (1915b) 'Internal Secretions and the Psychoses', *The Practitioner*, 94, pp. 310-16

——, (1918) 'Degeneration: The Medico-Psychological Aspects of Modern Art, Music, Literature, Science and Religion', *Transactions of the Medical Society of London*, 41, pp. 271-95

——, (1924) *The Borderland*, London: P. Allan

——, (1925) *The Great Abnormals*, London: P. Allan

——, (1927a) *Mental Handicaps in Art*, London: Ballière, Tindall & Cox

——, (1927b) *Mental Handicaps in Golf*, London: Ballière, Tindall & Cox

——, 'Obituary', *British Medical Journal*, 1, 1933, p. 347

Rolleston, J. D., 'Sir Henry Head', *DNB 1931-1940*, pp. 410-12

Savage, G. H., (1878) 'Case of Malformation of Genitalia With Insanity', *Journal of Mental Science*, 24, pp. 459-61

——, (1879a) 'Hyoscyamine and its Uses', *Journal of Mental Science*, 25, pp. 177-84

——, (1879b) 'Two Cases of Recovery From Insanity After Many Years in an Asylum', *Journal of Mental Science*, 25, pp. 57-9

——, (1879c) 'Uses and Abuses of Chloral Hydrate', *Journal of Mental Science*, 25, pp. 4-8

——, (1881a) 'Case of Mania Greatly Improved By the Use of Hyoscyamine', *Journal of Mental Science*, 27, pp. 60-2

——, (1881b) 'Cases of Contagiousness of Delusions', *Journal of Mental Science*, 26, pp. 563-7

——, (1881c) 'Moral Insanity', *Journal of Mental Science*, 27, pp. 147-55

——, (1883a) 'Case of Acute Loss of Memory', *Journal of Mental Science*, 29, pp. 85-90

——, (1883b) 'Mental Symptoms, Precursors of an Attack of Apoplexy', *Journal of Mental Science*, 27, pp. 90-1

——, (1884a) 'The Case of Gouldstone', *Journal of Mental Science*, 29, pp. 534-9

——, (1884b) 'Case of Sexual Perversion in a Man', *Journal of Mental Science*, 30, pp. 390-1

——, (1884c) 'Constant Watching of Suicide Cases', *Journal of Mental Science*, 30, pp. 17-19

——, (1884d) 'The Pathology of Insanity', *British Medical Journal*, 2, pp. 239-43

——, (1884e) *Insanity and Allied Neuroses*, London: Cassell

——, (1885) 'Our Duties in Reference to the Signing of Lunacy-Certificates', *British Medical Journal*, 1, pp. 692-3

——, (1887a) 'Alternation of Neuroses', *Journal of Mental Science*, 32, pp. 485-91

——, (1887b) 'Some Modes of Treatment of Insanity As a Functional Disorder', *Guy's Hospital Reports*, 24, pp. 87-112

——, (1888a) 'The Mechanical Restraint of the Insane' (letter), *The Lancet*, 2, p. 738

——, (1888b) 'Mental Disorders Associated With Marriage Engagements', *Journal of Mental Science*, 34, pp. 394-9

——, (1888c) 'Quietening Medicines' (letter), *The Lancet*, 2, p. 889

——, (1891a) 'The Influence of Surroundings on the Production of Insanity', *Journal of Mental Science*, 37, pp. 529-35

——, (1891b) 'The Plea of Insanity', *Journal of Mental Science*, 37, pp. 238-45

——, (1892a) 'The Definite in Medical Teaching', *The Medical Magazine*, 1, pp. 211-20

——, (1892b) 'Influenza and Neurosis', *Journal of Mental Science*, 38, pp. 360-4

——, (1892c) 'Relationship Between Influenza and the Neuroses', *Transactions of the Medical Society of London*, 16, pp. 51-77

——, (1893) 'Some Mental Disorders Associated With the Menopause', *The Lancet*, 2, pp. 1128-9

——, (1896a) 'Insanity of Conduct', *Journal of Mental Science*, 41, pp. 1-17

——, (1896b) 'Prevention and Treatment of Insanity of Pregnancy and the Puerpal Period', *The Lancet*, 1, pp. 164-5

——, (1897) 'Heredity in the Neuroses', *British Medical Journal*, 1, p. 128

——, (1903a) 'On Unsoundness of Mind and Insanity', *The Medical Magazine*, 22, pp. 14-24

——, (1903b) 'Uncertifiable Insanity and Certain Forms of Moral Defect', *Birmingham Medical Review*, 54, pp. 741-54

——, (1905) 'Functional Mental Disorders', *The Lancet*, 1, pp. 409-11

——, (1906-7) 'The Treatment of the Insane', *The Hospital*, 41, pp. 457-60

——, (1907) 'The Factors of Insanity', *The Lancet*, 2, pp. 1137-40

——, (1908a) 'Dreams: Normal and Morbid', *St. Thomas's Hospital Gazette*, 18, pp. 24-35

——, (1908b) 'The Mental Disorders of Childhood', *The Hospital*, 43, pp. 519-21

——, (1909a) 'Experimental Psychology and Hypnotism', *British Medical Journal*, 2, pp. 1205-12

——, (1909b) 'The Feeble-Minded and Their Care', *The Medical Press*, 87, pp. 522-4

——, (1910), 'Discussion on Insanity and Marriage', *British Medical Journal*, 2, pp. 1242-4

——, (1911a) 'Mental Disorders and Suicide', *The Lancet*, 1, pp. 1334-5

——, (1911b) 'On Insanity and Marriage', *Journal of Mental Science*, 57, pp. 97-112

——, (1912) 'Some Dreams and Their Significance', *Journal of Mental Science*, 58, pp. 407-10

——, (1913a) 'Post-Influenzal Neuroses and Psychoses', *Medical Press and Circular*, 96, pp. 578-81

——, (1913b) 'The Presidential Address, Delivered at the Opening Meeting of the Section of Psychiatry of the Royal Society of Medicine, on October 22nd, 1912', *Journal of Mental Science*, 59, pp. 14-27

——, (1916) 'Mental Disabilities For War Service', *Journal of Mental Science*, 62, pp. 653-7

Index